Playing It Dangerously

ACKNOWLEDGMENTS

I would like to thank the many people who assisted in the research and preparation of this book and without whose support it could not have come about. First, I am indebted to Suzanna Tamminen and the staff at Wesleyan University Press for their belief in and dedication to presenting this text in its best scholarly and material form. I am also grateful to the Music/Culture Series editors and to the two anonymous readers who provided insightful feedback on my monograph. In addition, I extend my thanks to Don Dyer, editor of *Balkanistica*, for permitting the reprinting of substantial portions of an article (MacMillen 2014) in this book's introduction and chapter 1, and to him, the anonymous reviewers of that publication, and the editors of an earlier conference proceedings version (MacMillen 2011b) for their comments. I thank Jerry Grcevich as well for permission to publish the notated melody and arrangement of "Moja Juliška."

I received generous support for researching this book from the American Council of Learned Societies in the form of a dissertation research fellowship in East European studies. The University of Pennsylvania funded much of my doctoral research on this topic through Benjamin Franklin doctoral fellowships and summer travel research funding, and I am grateful as well for the scholarly support and guidance of my dissertation committee: Dr. Timothy Rommen, adviser; Dr. Carol Muller, reader; and Dr. Jane Sugarman of the City University of New York, reader. Liliana Milkova, Gavin Steingo, Anna Casas Aguilar, Alvaro Santana-Acuña, Svanibor Pettan, Denise Gill, Carol Silverman, Jakša Primorac, Stiliana Milkova, Naila Ceribašić, Alan Zemel, Anna Stirr, Katie Graber, Ana Hofman, Luis-Manuel Garcia, Matthew Sumera, Srđan Atanasovski, Ana Petrov, and Dragana Stojanović offered critical feedback and suggestions at various stages of this project's completion. The University of Pittsburgh's ACLS and Foreign Language and Area Studies scholarships assisted greatly in my study of Bosnian/

Croatian/Serbian and Bulgarian languages. I wish also to thank Pitt's faculty and Center for Russian, East European, and Eurasian Studies for welcoming me as a research associate, as well as Zagreb's Institut za Etnologiju i Folkloristiku for hosting me as a foreign researcher. The Association for Recorded Sound Collections funded additional research, and as a faculty member at Oberlin College & Conservatory I received three Powers Travel Grants that contributed to my ongoing fieldwork on Southeast European tambura music.

I am particularly indebted to the multitude of tambura players and enthusiasts in Europe and North America who granted me time, insights, car rides, beds, and other forms of generosity. Too many to name here in entirety, they include Jerry Grcevich; Rankin's Junior Tamburitzans and Tamburaški Zbor Svete Marije; Dave Urban; the Zoretich family; the Brooks/Mann family; the directors and members of the Duquesne University Tamburitzans, especially Mrs. Susan Stafura; members of the Pennsylvania and Ohio bands Barabe (especially Dario Barišić), Gipsy Stringz (especially George Batyi), Šarena, Junaci (especially Justin Greenwald), Otrov (especially Peter Kosovec), Radost, Trubaduri, Sviraj (especially Danilo Yanich), Trzalica, and Zabava; Antun and Gordana; Darko, Vesna, and the other directors and leaders at STD "Pajo Kolarić"; Duško Topić and the members and other directors of HKUD "Osijek 1862"; Maestro Mirko Delibašić and the rest of Prosvjeta/Vučedolski Zvuci in Vukovar; Zvonko Bogdan; Zoran and Mira; Andrija Franić; Miroslav Škoro; Ljiljana and Antun (and family); Damir "Budo" Butković; the rest of the Caffe Bar Kaktus crew (Bernard, Mladen, and Bruno); tambura pedagogues Mihael Ferić, Jelena Kovačić, Franjo Batorek, Julije Njikoš, Marko Benić, and Mark Forry; members of the Croatian and Serbian bands Hrvatski Sokol (especially Filip Pešut), Berde Band, Biće Skoro Propast Sveta, Dule Bend, Garavuše, Graničari, Slavonske Lole, Slavonski Bećari, Šokci, Ravnica, Zora, and numerous others; and the members of Sto Tamburaša.

Most of all, I give my thanks, love, and appreciation to my family for their support in this project. My parents, Barbara and Richard MacMillen, have been unwavering in their encouragement; it is to them that I owe my love for meanderings, serendipity, and the field (from the department to the bush). My wife, Liliana, has been a constant source of intellectual inspiration and challenge, of warmth and understanding, and of perspective. Our daughter, Malvina, has brought new energy and curiosity to our music making, travels, work, and intellectual endeavors. As companions, friends, dancers, and fellow thinkers and enthusiasts of Southeast European traditions, they have shared with me so many marvels in the world.

INTRODUCTION

Dangerous Playing and Affective Block

May 2010: "Even as a child he played dangerously," Damir told me, referring to the Croatian American *tambura* virtuoso Peter Kosovec, whose recordings we were discussing as we drove through the Croatian city of Slavonski Brod. Damir was himself a well-respected performer of the *berda* (or *bas tambura*, the lowest member of a family of plucked, fretted tambura chordophones that had reemerged as Croatia's national instruments in the 1990s during Yugoslavia's wars of dissolution); he knew Peter from North American tours that he (Damir) had made with his Slavonski Brod tambura band. Damir also knew Peter from the tambura compositions that the latter had been writing and recording since 1994 (when the Michigan-born *tamburaš*[1] was thirteen years old) and premiering since 1997 at the Golden Strings of Slavonia festival in the nearby city of Požega. There, Kosovec's speed and deftness in improvising solos of great technical complexity, wide pitch range, and daring interchange between chromatic and diatonic scales had earned him an even wider reputation as someone who could play as "dangerously" (*opasno*) as any contemporary tamburaš.

Numerous well-respected tambura players in Croatia, as well as in Croatian communities in Austria, Bosnia and Herzegovina, and Hungary, made similar comments about Jerry Grcevich's abilities. The famous tambura player, composer, and NEA National Heritage fellow, then in his fifties, had involved Kosovec in several Pittsburgh-area projects, including the band Gipsy Stringz, and was still largely regarded as one of the tambura world's finest bandleaders, composers, and virtuosi. The attribution to these two Croatian American men of "playing dangerously" was an implicitly gendered appraisal of musical bravado and the highest form of praise a Croatian musician could bestow on a fellow male tamburaš. It evinced the intimate familiarity and respect with which musicians across a transnational Croatian tambura performance network regarded one another's fast and progressive techniques on this popular, traditional, and nationally charged instrument.

Yet as the term itself suggests, playing dangerously, if ideally *progressive* and thereby stimulating in its virtuosic technical execution, also threatens with a *transgressive* power, a sonic capacity for an affective mix of excitement and fear. This is due in no small part to the common recognition across the former Yugoslavia of dangerous playing, less in Croatian or Serbian than in Romani performance, with its associations of racial, geographic, cultural, and sometimes religious Otherness.[2] Take, for example, "Lijepe Ciganke" (Beautiful Gypsy women), a recording by Bosnian singer Halid Bešlić, who with this and other popular newly composed folk music hits has dominated Croatian music markets and venues since its release in 2003.[3] The text sets the song's nighttime scene of "crazily" performing tamburas and Romani dancers with an evocative opening line describing older Cigani "playing dangerously" as the scent of "wine and smoke" wafts in on the breeze.[4] For a Croatian, Serbian, or other non-Rom tamburaš, playing dangerously warrants praise from that musician's peers but also risks transgressing into the often revered yet (allegedly) socially and corporally deleterious practice of the Cigan: the crazed "Gypsy" nightlife and unrestrained affect attributed to Roma musicians and their clientele (and associated especially with Croatia's religiously distinct [Orthodox] neighbor Serbia). Thus another Croatian musician told me in somewhat halting English at a gathering of Croatia's finest tamburaši that Jerry, who played most dangerously of all, "is Gypsy *faah*-cker." He noted that this was a joke but claimed that "all" of Grcevich's Croatian peers referred to him in this way.[5] This appellation attests to the social, cultural, and (perhaps sexually) embodied transgression that musicians risk by playing in a style (and in groups such as Gipsy Stringz) that can earn them distinction on Croatia's "national" instrument but also possibly inscribe them in the sonic and affective realm of racialized Others and the reverence and suspicion accorded to their style.

NATIONAL INTIMACY, RACIAL DANGER

This book is about performing dangerously and the intimacies that such affective transgressions jeopardize but may also engender. While tracing these intimacies' development in precarious contexts of war and postwar states, it argues avoiding (though not ignoring). This avoidance is just as central to differentiating boundaries: between oneself and an other who is perceived to embody that feeling, between oneself and an Otherness that *is* embodied feeling.

Sara Ahmed has more recently turned from the "I" to the collective "we" to consider diversity work and connections across such boundaries. She frames their challenges as a *wall* against diversity ("the feeling of coming up against something that does not move") and a *will* that either "allows [diversity] to accumulate positive affective value" and "encourages people to do something" or else "is made out of sediment: what has settled and accumulated over time" (2012, 26, 67, 129). In the latter case, institutionalized resistance to including Others (racialized, affective, etc.) does not require individual actors to make the wall "into an object of will. No individual has to block an action that is not continuous with what has already been [collectively, institutionally] willed" (129). The feelings and intentionality undergirding a collective will for the status quo form a habit of continuation that needs no utterance or deliberate *willing* until "a decision is made that is discontinuous with the institutional will"; the "gap between the signs of will (the [discursive] yes or will to diversity) and institutional will (the no or the wall [internalized, affective block] to diversity) is noticeable only when one attempts to cross a limit" (129). Thus race-thinking also has a basis in feeling that is not coterminous with its ideological underpinnings.

This incongruence of feeling and thinking comes to a head at the crossing of a threshold. The "racial contract" regarding the social place of whiteness and diversity reveals itself most clearly in contestations of values and "the corresponding crystallization of feelings of vastly differential outrage" (and other emotions) with respect to the disparate societal lots of racially differentiated groups (Mills 1997, 101). It is the tension between the collective, social will (particularly its affective dimensions) and individual agency of crossing limits that this book examines, emphasizing the boundaries of appropriate musical feeling, comportment, and technique—and how musicians (especially musical Others) expose these limits by crossing them.

Thus *Playing It Dangerously* examines musical affect as a cultural resource rather than essence—as an important but often overlooked instrument that individuals cultivate (block in aggregation) or stave off (block in delimitation) in order to jar larger social assemblages out of affective habitus that they perceive to be dangerous (in either a positive or a deleterious sense). Affect plays a critical role within what sociologist Ann Swidler, in retheorizing culture from the standpoint of strategy rather than values, called a "'tool kit' of symbols, stories, rituals, and world-views, which people may use in varying configurations to solve different kinds of problems" (1986, 273). Like discourse, affect as a cultural "tool" is subject to constraint and strategy as well as to excess and abandon. Approaching music's relationship to race, nation, danger, and intimacy in diverse contexts within postwar Croatia and its neighboring and diasporic enclaves, this book argues that musical affect's power and primacy lie in its flexibility: its alternate mobilization and denial in the conflicts, reconciliations, and becomings through which musical selves and societies emerge.

POSITIONALITIES AND THE ALTERITY OF REPRESENTATION

I myself felt and witnessed such conflicts, reconciliations, and becomings as I researched tambura music's social and geographical movement between 2007 and 2015. My longest periods of intensive research were during the 2008/2009 and 2009/2010 academic years, which I spent, respectively, in Pittsburgh, Pennsylvania, among the Steel City's Croatian, Romani, and Serbian enclaves, and in the Croatian cities of Osijek and Slavonski Brod (I completed additional fieldwork in subsequent years and in nearby countries, including Austria, Bosnia and Herzegovina, Hungary, and Serbia). The physical dangers of the 1990s conflicts, except for landmines remaining untriggered in a few rural areas, had largely faded by 2007 and were not directly a part of what I experienced in any of these countries, whose communities were exceedingly warm and generous in their hospitality. Simultaneously, I was continually impressed by two matters relating to my own racialized and ethnicized profile: (1) the territorializing effects of my presence in Croatia and elsewhere when I failed to confirm my interlocutors' expressed assumptions that I was one of "theirs" from the diaspora who had come to study "our" music; and (2) the lasting effects of the years of war (1991–1995) on the diverse ways in which my interlocutors figured and felt me as a territorialized and racialized, or race-thought, being—as white, as a Scot, as an American, as an Australian, and so forth.

That I was born in Australia and that I had grown up largely in the United States, countries where large Southeast European communities maintain what literary scholar Svetlana Boym calls "diasporic intimacy" (2001, 253), informed in constantly shifting ways a number of important research modalities. These ranged from my reception into the tutelage of Jerry Grcevich and my mobility as his student and friend within musical circles in Europe, to my being invited to serve as the beginning tambura instructor for the Slavonian Tambura Society "Pajo Kolarić" in 2009 and 2010, to the coaching I received from Damir and musicians of various backgrounds on how to appreciate and feel the dangerous playing of Grcevich and Kosovec as well as "my own" musical heritage and the tambura styles of other specific peoples and territories. My surprising lack of familial connection to tambura music and Southeast Europe, as well as the fact that I had connections to both the Catholic and Orthodox Churches while being a practitioner of neither, facilitated to a certain extent my movement between different groups.

At times this cultural and religious distance seemed even to amplify the status that I held as a researcher funded by American institutions, for I was perceived as having come from a country of great economic wealth, musical variety, and global ignorance, and all rather improbably "because of the sound of the tamburica," as one Osijek newspaper put it (Sekol 2010; my translation). That appreciation for tambura music's sonic dimensions and an interest in its embeddedness in contemporary urban geography had attracted me against all odds seemed constantly to intrigue my tamburaši interlocutors. To an extent this was due to differing connotations of my professed field of ethnomusicology; many of my interlocutors expected that, as an ethnomusicologist, I had come to learn local folkloric knowledge that Croatian scholars had written up and/ or that folklore ensembles had preserved in their arrangements (both written and performed), but the project that I outlined instead was, in the words of one tamburaš, "closer to sociology." This pointed to another difference in my scholarly interest from that of many of my interlocutors, however: my expressed aim was to trace tambura music's role and the instrument's usage in particular in the geography of my research and in relations among diverse populations. I took interest in individual and group claims to the instrument and to particular music traditions as belonging to and representative of specific ethnic groups, but also strove to identify and offer an ethnographic platform for diverse perspectives within our lived local realities (which individual narratives of tradition sometimes left out). This work intensified as I came to recognize the importance of affect and other nondiscursive tambura relations. I have usually framed my study as examining the tambura's role in the local area ("here," as I would tell my interlocutors). Both in the research and in this ethnography I am ethically committed to representing the passions, generosity, desires, and challenges of people occupying distinct (and sometimes opposed) ethnic/racialized, gendered, religious, and socioeconomic positionalities.

Responding to this ethical challenge has required not just a careful representation of alterity but also a deliberate *alterity of representation*. My relationships with musicians and audiences were diverse and invariably affected by our "reciprocal witnessing" (MacMillen 2015) of differing degrees and dimensions of commonality and otherness. The landscape of the music that is "here" (in Osijek, in Pittsburgh, etc.), as my research bore out and as minority perspectives in particular demanded be recognized, sometimes conflicted with the narratives that other interlocutors asked me to communicate from my perceived position as an outsider who was gaining both the authority and the access needed to represent my field sites in print (see chapter 3). I have worked extensively with Croat, Rom, and Serb musicians in each of my main field sites, and also to a more limited extent with people of other ethnoreligious (typically Muslim Bosniak or Catholic Hungarian) communities. In postwar Croatia, tambura music is an arena in which these three ethnic groups rarely perform together, and while my moving among different circles has been possible and ethnographically fruitful, it has not universally been encouraged or well received.

In this ethnography, I prioritize a balance between representing tambura discourses narrated from different ethnic positionalities and mediating data gleaned from alternative sites as I examine the broader material geography (affective, sonic, and spatial) that connects musicians and audiences of diverse backgrounds. Such an analytical move, though by no means unilateral or permanent, aims at making overt representations Other, *alter*, even subaltern to the material realities that so often channel them in lived experience (but that so often evade the representation-oriented, hegemonic hermeneutics of both musicians and scholars). While the interest of many Croatian Serb and Roma minorities in representing tambura music's role singularly within their own bounded ethnic traditions paralleled that of numerous Croat counterparts, many minorities also demonstrated a vested interest in a project that would focus ethnographic attention on their contributions to the *diversity* of tambura music in Croatia. My research engaged with some individuals whose politics of identifying as Croats could not support this vision of Croatia's tambura landscape, but I was encouraged by the number who did support it. This book examines the discursive tropes in which ethnic (typically racialized) positionalities have become entrenched, as well as the potential of affective strategies and counterdiscourses to block them and advance the alternative, progressive postwar politics of reconciliation that many of my interlocutors have been promoting.

Beyond race and ethnicity, however, it was the dimensions of me as an individual that were *unsurprising*—and perhaps least challenging—that were often most important to my integration into tambura scenes. Like most tamburaši, I was a white, male musician with enough time and economic resources (albeit paid in advance as research funding rather than received as compensation for performance) to dedicate ample amounts of my attention to the trade and to the jovial, often reckless carryings-on of the *bećar* ("bachelor" or "rake") lifestyle associated with playing dangerously and with tamburanje more generally. However salient, these aspects of my selfhood often went unspoken and registered most prominently in the affective exchanges and bonds in which musicians included me. These constituted some of the most important field experiences of my project.

HISTORY, MATERIALITY, AND SPACE

If, as I argue, it is necessary to consider the limits to the autonomy of such affect and to the saturation of musical feeling, it also became clear through my interactions and communications with musicians that a study of this nature could too easily veer dangerously in the opposite direction, examining solely the roles of ideology and discourse, as though these, too, were autonomous. Studies of music's role in the structures and physical events of Croatian nationalism in the nineteenth and twentieth centuries (Blažeković 1998; Majer-Bobetko 1998; March 2013), particularly during and since the war following Croatia's 1991 secession from Yugoslavia (Bonifačić 1998; Pettan 1998; Ceribašić 2000; Baker 2010), have largely focused on the power of songs and musicians to articulate specific nationalist ideas, narratives, discourses, rhetorics, and systems of thinking. In this they engage a large body of ethnomusicological literature concerned with the ideological constitution and discursive construction of nations around the globe (Turino 2000; Wade 2000; Askew 2002; Radano 2003; Bohlman 2004; Largey 2006; Brinner 2009; Kotnik 2010; McDonald 2013). This book similarly takes discourse and ideology seriously, analyzing how expressed conceptualizations of race, danger, and intimacy have guided performance practices undertaken in the name of nations and states.

Within such integral elements of immaterial nationalist culture, however, loom very concrete, material consequences for citizens. They must constantly negotiate ideology as they confront the repression of state apparatuses (Althusser 1971, 142) and also deal with the procedures by which "the production of discourse is at once controlled, selected, organized and canalized [in order] to subdue the powers and dangers of discourse, to evade its heavy and threatening materiality" (Foucault 1984, 10–11). To acknowledge that such materiality nonetheless undergirds ideologies and discourses requires, first and foremost, a recognition of their constitution in affective, embodied perception. As Tim Ingold has argued, "any attempt to separate out the discourse surrounding vision" or "any other sensory modality" from "the actual practices of looking, watching, and seeing is unsustainable. [. . .] For what is discourse, if not a narrative interweaving of experience born of practical, perceptual activity?" (2000, 286).

This acknowledgment requires, second, an appreciation for ideologies' and discourses' mutually constitutive relationship with physical space. Rather than taking national territory as a given material dimension whose assumedly limited and static nature implicitly justifies focusing on the deconstruction of dynamic nationalist discourses and ideologies, this book follows musicians' (and my own ethnographic) mobility across bounded territories. It examines how physical movement in space and within/between musical bodies variously produces, shapes, delimits, and subverts material experiences and discursive understandings of the nation in flux. Interrogating a priori assumptions by both academics and nationalists about immaterial culture's rule over physical action, it situates narratives of musical nation-building, discourses on dangerous racial aesthetics, and ideologies of gendered and religious power in the material bases of sonic affect and intimate musical spatialization (Krims 2007). The latter are in turn shaped by narratives, discourses, and ideologies, but significantly, they operate also at the level of desire, motivating the transnationalisms, transracialisms, and other transgressions that characterize the paradoxically centripetal pull of playing it dangerously. Thus the analyses that follow comprise a study of intimacy—of national intimates—rather than an examination of the machinations of musical nationalism in the context of a particular folk and its state.

The book's chapters focus primarily on the transnational engendering of and threats to such intimacy since the outbreak of war in 1991, a period that I examine ethnographically and through histories of the recent past researched through interviews and in archives. Tambura music is not the only medium of these intimacies, and the book also considers how competing genres have eclipsed tambura music in Croatia over the past two decades. These genres reveal what anthropologist Michael Herzfeld has called "cultural intimacy" within the tambura's persistent yet ambivalent mobilization as a national instrument but also a source of "external embarrassment" (1997, 3). Nor is tambura music alone within such complex webs of signification and feeling; since Yugoslavia's dissolution and the less violent but politically and economically turbulent changes of late socialism and postsocialism elsewhere in Southeast Europe, musical performance practices ranging from Bulgarian folk orchestras (Buchanan 2006) to Serbian turbo-folk (Rasmussen 2007) to Croatian rock bands (Baker 2010) have emerged as important sites of ambivalent engagement with state nationalism and majority identity politics. In focusing on affect within and beyond the ubiquitous yet ambiguous role that music has played in this region's politics (as in others'), I offer new perspectives on the conflicting attachments to nation, state, and bureaucracy that are particularly common during regime change.

MUSIC AND DANGER

Ethnomusicologists have often celebrated music for opposing danger and for its ability to comfort during periods of uncertainty. Alan Lomax claimed that "the primary effect of music is to give the listener a feeling of security, for it symbolizes the place where he was born, his earliest childhood satisfactions, his religious experience, his pleasure in community doings, his courtship and his work" (1959, 29). When scholars have, conversely, considered "the danger of music" (Taruskin 2008, 168), they have typically situated it within the reactionary ideologies of oppressive regimes. They highlight musicians' resistance to authoritative measures, ranging from "suspicion" and "control" among Western Christian powers (168), to censorship of popular styles in countries such as the Soviet Union (Cushman 1995; Yurchak 2005) and Iran (Hemmasi 2011), to outright bans on anything considered "music" under regimes such as the Taliban (Baily [2001] 2003). Even scholars who illuminate music's role in physical violence typically read this as misappropriation and extreme manipulation of an otherwise potentially soothing art (Cusick 2013).

This book also calls for serious attention to music's capacities for an affect of danger that is coded positively within its artistic aesthetic. I argue that feelings of risk and excitement are also primary effects of music and that these may in fact register most intensely during times of relative comfort and security. This is so in part because the aesthetic and affective dimensions of danger often work *beyond* the sort of territorializing representation of the home that Lomax cites;

they constitute part of what Deleuze and Guattari indeed identify as music's "power of deterritorialization" ([1980] 1987, 309). This power, which Gary Tomlinson glosses as distinguishing musicking from the "refrain" (e.g., birdsong, a national anthem, "a frozen territoriality"; 2016, 167), lies in the fact that "the indexicality of the refrain, its alliance with territoriality, is seen to be subject [. . .] to the transformations of the assemblage"; thus in deterritorialization "the effect of the refrain-as-actual [. . .] is unmade by musicking-as-virtual" (168).

Yet the affect and aesthetic of musical danger may also enter in *before* territoriality. Their power is not restricted to unmaking the territorial claims of song; rather, musical deterritorialization links forward to the reterritorialization of the refrain ("voices may be reterritorialized on the distribution of the two sexes" or on other coordinates: racial, national, etc.; Deleuze and Guattari [1980] 1987, 308). Deleuze and Guattari state that music, in comparison to flags, "seems to have a much stronger deterritorializing force, at once more intense and much more collective, [which] explains the collective fascination exerted by music, and even the potentiality of the 'fascist' danger [. . .]: music (drums, trumpets) draws people and armies into a race that can go all the way to the abyss" (333). The abyss itself is dangerous, but music's initial danger lies in its draw, in deterritorializing drives and desires before they are reterritorialized on a land as the object of military strategy.

This danger is simply the promise of change, of becoming. In tambura music, it is the allure of improvisatory freedom, the potential to push beyond the strictures of known refrains and traditional ways of performing; the abyss (both aesthetic and social) into which dangerous players risk falling is complete melodic and rhythmic chaos, "riding the brink of chaos," in Grcevich's words. Or, in Tomlinson's words, musicking "affirms the becoming and change immanent in all repetition and signification" (2016, 168). Importantly, danger and affirmation require meta-affective and meta-significatory levels of awareness: systems of feeling and signifying on affects and significations. It is at these levels that affective block operates by affording a strategic ordering of stimuli and initial processing. While eliminating neither affective nor representational understandings (these are often dynamically dialectic, and the experienced salience of one is part of the internalization of the other), it variously privileges one or the other in ways that allow musickers (musicians, audience members, performance facilitators, etc.; see Small 1998) to make sense of and respond to forms of danger coded as positive or negative and often felt to be both simultaneously.

RACE, NATION, AND AFFECTIVE BLOCK

This book focuses on questions of danger and intimacy in experiences of nation and territory. It thereby traces the varying emergence, solidification, or weakening of social relations through actual sentiments (not just symbols) of closeness and the racialized desires and fears that often accompany them. In examining less the politics of identity than the affect of becoming, the book builds on recent scholarship that criticizes the reifying (Waterman 2002) and racializing (Gelbart 2010) effects of studying a *people* from the perspective of an assumed authenticity of identity (Jackson 2005) articulated in music. It joins other music studies (Yurchak 2005; Cimini 2010; Kielian-Gilbert 2010; Atanasovski 2015) in eschewing interpreting race and ethnicity as dualistic (subject-object) representations, performances, or imitations of identities by an agent and focuses instead on minoritarian *becoming*. Such a pursuit, while recognizing national imaginaries, nonetheless moves beyond them to situate racialized desires and anxieties in the intimate materialities of spatial and affective relations that music enables.

Philip Bohlman and Ronald Radano have written that music, "as a key signifier of difference [. . .] — in its wonder, in its transcendence, in its affective danger — historically conjures racial meaning" (2000, 1). Yet its "danger," I argue, lies in its very capacity, through the speed and slowness of becoming, to unmoor its signifiers from ossified, representational narratives and ideologies. Thus, as Bohlman and Radano also suggest, "'race' defines not a fixity, but a signification saturated with profound cultural meaning and whose discursive instability heightens its affective power" (5). Within such instability "heavy and threatening materiality" (Foucault 1984, 11) weighs upon its moorings to signification, meaning, and rationality and opens them to the influence of feeling.

Lila Ellen Gray hints at affect's relationship to discourse in a footnote to her study of *fado*'s affective politics: "Theorists of affect differ in [. . .] the degree to which they mark affect as non-discursive, as 'embodied,' as an 'intensity,'" but musical studies can perhaps most effectively "use affect here in co-constitutive relation to the discursive" (2014, 245n16). Drawing on the diverse theoretical work on affect of scholars such as Deleuze and Guattari ([1980] 1987), Michael Hardt and Antonio Negri (2004), Kathleen Stewart (2007), Lauren Berlant (2008), and Brian Massumi (2010), I argue for a similar relationship between the discursive and the affective as co-delimiting. I demonstrate affect's partial assimilability to signification, particularly as the latter operates in discourse and other linguistic processes (and thus against affect's complete autonomy). Yet I also argue for affect's partial inassimilability, for its blocking (in aggregation) outside of the planes of conscious thought and of referential qualifications of emotion, for a remainder in which dangerous playing registers in a less-than-coded block of scary-exciting feeling. Eschewing affect theorists' attraction to music "because they think it accommodates their vague ideas of intensities unfettered by sign, meaning, or agency" (Tomlinson 2016, 166), I examine the very fettering that mutually transpires between musical and linguistic signs and the affects that attach to them. Simultaneously, I consider the limits of this mooring and an agency for a resilience of feeling beyond representation.

Tomlinson criticizes Brian Massumi's early and influential essay on the "autonomy of affect" (1996) for pointing to affect's separation from systems of representation by "substituting a local precinct of signification for the whole of it; for his idea of conventionalized difference pertains only to the Peircean symbol, not to semiosis in general" (Tomlinson 2016, 151). Massumi, too, has more recently called for "a logic of mutual inclusion" that could situate affect theory alongside other paradigms on a continuum of logics, albeit with important cuts in its continuity (2015). I present a similar logic of mutual inclusion, locating an ethnomusicological approach to affect between discursive work and participatory embodiment. It draws inspiration here from the "intricate interplay between discourse and practice within the sphere of performance" that Jane Sugarman locates in Prespa Albanian singing and from her theorization of the dialectical relationship between discursive objectification and experiential understandings of music, self, and gendered difference (Sugarman 1997, 30). In bringing attention to affect and its negation as forces bridging these two poles, I show that such processes not only are dialectical but also reveal a specific dynamic within the dialectic: an intensification of thought and feeling that manifests not so much a binary as a differential in their mutual continuation, a blocking of affect in the sense of both aggregation and delimitation. This blocking retains a residual, resilient intensity that aggregates beyond, and delimits, systems of representation of race and nation, but an intensity whose power lies in its secondary yet persistent interaction with other systems of signification. Put simply, even when one's thoughts overpower a conflicting feeling, something of that feeling may remain as an attraction or aversion to danger and Otherness.

Thus *affective block* accounts for both aspects of this partial assimilability to conscious signification: (1) the capacity for affective responses to certain styles of tambura performance to circumvent or supersede cultural representations (e.g., these styles' indexing to Cigani or "Croatian tradition"); and (2) the capacity for these responses to amount to something of significance (in secondary sense making, manifesting for example as a recognition of "danger") through their distancing from overcoded meanings. Such is the duality intended in invoking the two senses of the word "block": affect blocks, or aggregates as a block of intensity, in the sense in which Deleuze and Guattari use the French noun *bloc* (as in "a block of becoming"; [1980] 1987, 293), and it also blocks, or keeps at a remove (the related French term would be the verb *bloquer*).

The corollary to the dual attention to the blocking and blocking of affect called for here is the recognition of how this limits the autonomy of signification and discourse. This requires accounting for musicians' practices, intentional or otherwise, of constraining their affective investments (e.g., in the shared intensities of racialized Others) through discursive gambits yet also of retaining a resilience (e.g., for a feeling of Otherness) that aggregates as a remainder, a strangeness that is still part of their becoming. This feeling of strangeness is an affective relation to an Other, to what Deleuze and Guattari term the "something else" with which you "make your organism enter into composition" in becoming ([1980] 1987, 274). Thus this is not a neatly symmetrical corollary; at stake here is the blocking of discourse in the sense of *bloquer* (how it blocks/is blocked by affect) but not the additional blocking of discourse in the sense of *bloc* (see figure I.1, upper right cell). That is, the additional block (the aggregation) is not of discourse but again of affect—hence the term *affective block*.

In other words, *affective block* is a notion of how intensities aggregate in the processes of becoming, one that also accounts for the dialectic dynamics between affect and discourse when musicians' feelings conflict with their thoughts. In their contradictory differences, affects and discourses can be excessive rather than purely oppositional, generating feelings of Otherness to varying intensities when affect blocks or is blocked by discourse. This is my primary premise: that blocking in aggregation is simultaneous and complementary to blocking in delimitation, and thus that people can be affected residually even when their discursive strategies effectively flatten or forestall undesirably intense reactions to musical performance. Such discursive blocks to affect (lower left cell of figure I.1) and residual accumulation (upper left cell) occur, for example, when musicians use humor to prevent socially dangerous indulgences in racially improper depths of musical enjoyment. Equally important are instances in which these strategies fail: when a block of affect (upper left cell) comes in as a blockage against strategically mobilized discourse (lower right cell) and accrues as the intensity proper to its negation (such as when musicians' progressive rhetoric of inclusion

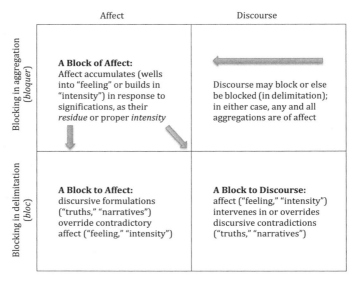

	Affect	Discourse
Blocking in aggregation *(bloquer)*	**A Block of Affect:** Affect accumulates (wells into "feeling" or builds in "intensity") in response to significations, as their *residue* or proper *intensity*	Discourse may block or else be blocked (in delimitation); in either case, any and all aggregations are of affect
Blocking in delimitation *(bloc)*	**A Block to Affect:** discursive formulations ("truths," "narratives") override contradictory affect ("feeling," "intensity")	**A Block to Discourse:** affect ("feeling," "intensity") intervenes in or overrides discursive contradictions ("truths," "narratives")

FIGURE I.1 The blocking of affect and discourse

falls to contradictory discourses of racial difference due to the intervention of feelings of Otherness embodied in musical performance). It is easy to recognize the importance of strong feelings when they arise in contexts of musical abandon, and this book also follows previous scholarship in exploring what happens when affective and discursive responses align (without the negation of either). My aim, however, is to demonstrate that affective restraint, whether realized or merely attempted, is just as central to the interplay of discourse and feeling in music. That such restraint moves people in other ways makes it especially worthy of ethnographic and affect theoretical attention.

The two directions of the dynamic of blocking detailed in the bottom cells of figure I.1 speak to the social usefulness of affective manipulation and map more or less neatly onto Deleuze and Guattari's and Massumi's different conceptions of the potential for representation in becoming. The former's notion that "double becoming" (or becoming-animal) is "affect in itself, [...] and represents nothing" suggests the autonomy from higher-level meaning systems of the lower right cell ([1980] 1987, 259). Massumi, meanwhile, has theorized a possible alternative, an intermediary between absolute null affect and double becoming that he calls "limitative becoming"; this happens when "one of the terms is an abstract identity and the body in question must curtail its potentials in order to fit into the grid," a process suggestive of the affective restraint and residual redirection of the lower left cell of the figure (1987, 94). Thus *affective block* explains the commonly residual, but differently aggregated, affects of double and limitative becoming. It demonstrates how musicians' strategic imposition or subversion of discursive and other significations comes to bear on residual feelings of Otherness in their affective labor.

It is in the residual intensities, in their welling beyond representation (a relation of the symbol, or thirdness, in the Peircean schema), but also in affect's secondary entrance into iconic or indexical signification beyond its primary and forceful physical impact, that intimacy comes into being. Intimacy is not a closeness built solely on positive feelings, though this is certainly a part of it (in much of the former Yugoslavia, getting along with someone is parsed as "being good" [*biti dobar*] with one another). It is also about the sharing of threats and apprehensions, of strange affects. Intimacy, as colleagues of mine and I have argued, "is itself already a kind of violence, a *touching* that makes definite demands of the touched in its very tenderness" (MacMillen, Steingo, and Stirr 2011). The co-delimitation of discursive and affective responses to musical style embeds this violence in a plane of rich significatory and embodied capacities for dealing with social and physical dangers. Approaching this co-delimitation at three levels of discursive scale, in sections devoted respectively to narrative, discourse, and ideology, I examine the intimate, assimilating work that musical affect performs on rational(izing) understanding in the name of race and nation. I demonstrate, ultimately, how dialectical dynamics of co-delimitation between discursive and affective responses to differences in musical style privilege understandings of tambura players as heroic Croatian men, even as the music engenders diverse ethnic and gendered becomings.

DEPTH IN THE SHALLOWS: TAMBURA MUSIC'S PAST IN THE "SOUTH SLAVIC" LANDS

The tambura has been caught up in struggles for territory, security, danger, and national becoming in Southeast Europe for centuries, though that period has been relatively shallow in comparison to the deeper history of the Slavs' habitation in the region since their arrival in the early Middle Ages. In order to contextualize the book's case studies and the broader claims that I make in this introduction, I offer a brief history of tambura music's spread as an ensemble tradition in Austria-Hungary and Yugoslavia.[8] A central premise of this book holds that *feeling* intimately Croatian and affectively transgressing certain racialized ideals often supersede (block) official narratives and discourses, and I next examine the music's more recent history as a spatializing and nationalizing force countering official Yugoslav rhetoric as Croatia pursued independence and its own sovereign public sphere. This was the time when Kosovec was just learning to play; when Grcevich was just making his mark on the transnational tambura scene; and when Croatia, as these musicians' nominal homeland but also a constituent republic of Yugoslavia, was a territory whose national status many intensely desired and even sensed, but only a few would risk constructing apart from the Yugoslav ideal, whether physically or figuratively.

For several centuries, tambura chordophone-type instruments moved throughout Southeast Europe with Ottoman forces during their occupation of the region. The solo tambura (which took a wide variety of shapes and names) became common throughout much of present-day Bosnia and Herzegovina, Croatia, and Serbia by the eighteenth century. Research on the early years of the tambura's diversification into a family of instruments and on its combination in ensemble settings typically cites the small orchestra that the musician Pajo Kolarić founded in Osijek in 1847 as the first documented tambura ensemble (March 1983). Josip Andrić, however, has argued that groups performing on multiple tamburas have existed since the late eighteenth century among the Bunjevci (a group of Catholic Slavs who generally identify as Croats and live predominantly in the northern Serbian province of Vojvodina).[9] According to Andrić, the Bunjevci combined the previously solo instruments in ensembles that they may have modeled after, and intended as a local folklore alternative to, the Hungarian Romani violin and cimbalom bands then popular in the area (Andrić 1958, 13).

Such tambura ensembles were particularly effective at promoting local culture and language in the nineteenth-century nationalist Illyrian movement, which sought to assert Slavic identity (specifically of the local, Catholic Slavs) in the face of Austro-Hungarian cultural and political domination in the middle of the nineteenth century (March 1983, 106). Tambura music's connections to danger-ous, nationalist transgressions of multinational sovereignty date back at least to this period, and Pajo Kolarić, an agitator within the movement, was imprisoned by the Hungarians in 1849 for his actions in support of the Croatian revolutionary Ban Josip Jelačić. Franjo Kuhač, a music ethnologist and childhood admirer of the older Kolarić, would later write that the tambura orchestra leader and other tamburaši "helped a great deal to fire up the Slavonians to support Ban Jelačić and our national politics" (1877, 81; translated in March 2013, 55).

Eric Hobsbawm's introduction to *The Invention of Tradition* (1983) demonstrates amply that practices taken as a culture's connection to the ancient past are often fully modern in being recently introduced, constructed, and woven into national narratives, and that this "historic past into which the new tradition is inserted need not be lengthy" (Hobsbawm 1983, 2). Incorporating an Ottoman instrument, paralleling (and perhaps modeled after) Romani bands, and consciously deployed for nationalist purposes in the nineteenth century, the tambura orchestra was clearly one of those "'traditions' actually invented, constructed and formally instituted" (1). In Croatia, however, the deliberate invention of the tambura tradition was well recognized by tamburaši in the nineteenth century, as it is now, and its lack of insertion into a national narrative predating the Illyrian movement has in no way diminished the earnestness with which musicians assert their nation's historical claim to the instrument. As I argue throughout this book, there is more at work in the invention, acceptance, and mobilization of such a musical tradition than the strategic insertion of a national emblem into histories whose shallowness is obscured in their embedding in spoken and written words. That such politicized mobilization of the music in Croatian media in the 1990s (and in earlier periods of Croatian national organizing) could proceed so quickly and effectively without completely obscuring inherent contradictions in its symbolism suggests that the tambura's role as a Croatian national tradition relies as much on affective responses as on discursive rationalizations: tambura music is Croatian because playing and listening to it *feel* Croatian (while *feeling* Cigan, for instance, transpires through a different set of musical relations). In the current day, however, the emphasis on the emergent affects of race and ethnicity (of "becoming") over their discursive constructions also situates the tambura's impact in experiences of the nation that are less concretely bounded than those of ethnic identification and national signification, a fact that opens tamburanje to manifold transgressions.

Initially, tambura musicians were less concerned with local ethnic distinctions than with opposing Austria-Hungary, and the signification of difference and the affective intensities of shared becomings were neatly aligned in the tasks of building solidarity on the fringes of the empire. Official imperial suppression seemingly only aided the music's significatory and affective appeal to Pan-Slavists and Illyrianists. Even after Austro-Hungarian rule put an end to the Illyrian movement, amateur tambura ensembles continued to spread to other Croatian urban centers such as Zagreb; throughout towns and villages in present-day Serbia and Bosnia and Herzegovina; and by the late nineteenth century to places such as New Zealand, Australia, and North and South America, where many tambura musicians sought to escape poverty and/or political oppression (March 1983, 120–121).

By the time the first Yugoslav state was founded at the end of World War I, diverse amateur, professional, and semiprofessional ensembles throughout the region and abroad were using various combinations of common tambura instruments. These ranged from small, usually round-bodied, lead *prim* tamburas (aka *bisernica*, or simply *tamburica*), to hourglass-shaped secondary melody tamburas (e.g., the *čelović*, the *čelo*, and the *basprim*, aka *brač*), to harmony tamburas (the *kontra*, aka *bugarija*), and finally to the largest, berda (aka bas), which resembles a double bass in appearance and function.[10] A functional tambura group almost always featured a minimum of berda, kontra, basprim, and one other melodic instrument, but many ensembles had one, two, or three additional tamburas. Some bands incorporated violin and/or accordion into their lineups, although this was less common in the East Croatian region of Slavonia, where many Croat patrons associated these instruments with Roma from Vojvodina and with Serbian musical practice rather than with Croatian national identity (see chapter 3 and Pettan 1998, 16–18). Musicians to this day use plectra for all tambura types and, with the exception of berda and kontra players, typically play with tremolo all note values longer than an eighth note.

In the socialist Yugoslav state founded after World War II, tambura ensembles operated in a variety of private and public contexts. Amateur and professional groups performed at private wedding events and at taverns across much of the country (with the greatest concentration in the area triangulated between Zagreb, Sarajevo, and Belgrade/Novi Sad). Official town and city orchestras performed folk, classical, "old-city," and international light popular music. Folklore ensembles also formed as parts of the amateur Kulturno-Umjetnička Društva (cultural-artistic societies; hereafter KUD) that the socialist government established throughout Yugoslavia to promote the folk traditions of its many nations.[11] Alongside older tambura schools founded before the adoption of socialism, in 1954 the Slavonsko Tamburaško Društvo "Pajo Kolarić" (Slavonian Tambura Society "Pajo Kolarić"; hereafter STD "Pajo Kolarić" or "Pajo Kolarić") commenced its educating of young musicians in Osijek, the largest city in Croatia's easternmost region of Slavonia. These KUDs and schools trained many of the musicians who have performed professionally in state folklore ensembles, such as Lado in Zagreb and Kolo in Belgrade, and in the radio tambura orchestras of Belgrade, Sarajevo, and Zagreb. In promoting the musical cultures of the many

Yugoslav peoples to their publics, these ensembles' members traversed much of Yugoslavia's territory and interacted and performed for and with diverse ethnic groups.

In this manner, the ensembles in theory realized the ideal of *bratstvo i jedinstvo* (fraternity and unity) promoted by the Yugoslav state. Yet such staged representations of state ideology and socialist narratives of the Yugoslav federation did not always translate into actual intimacies between or even within the many nations, nationalities, and ethnic groups[12] that contributed the repertoire and members of folklore ensembles, especially following periods of nationalist (re)awakening in the early 1970s and 1980s. Tony Shay notes that even in the early socialist period, Croatian groups in particular, such as Lado, navigated internal tensions arising over members' relationship to the Communist state, from forced dismissals of those whose familial ties or musical tastes suggested sympathies with the World War II Croatian nationalist Ustaša movement to performers' defection while touring Western Europe (2002, 117). As Ljerka Rasmussen writes in her work on newly composed folk music, the socialist period "presents us with both the high points of the quest for 'multiculturalism' and the failure to sustain it by the class-based, meta-ideology of 'brotherhood and unity'" (2002, xxviii).

American tambura players had minimal contact with ensembles in Europe for decades, but in 1950 the Duquesne University Tamburitzans led by Walter Kolar made their first trip to perform in Yugoslavia "at the behest of the [US] State Department to make closer ties with [Yugoslav dictator Marshall Josip Broz] 'Tito' and his brand of communism when he broke ties with Stalin" (Kolar 2009). Although their pan-Yugoslav and -American repertoire suited both countries' ideals for cultural ambassadorship, what resulted was a long-lasting relationship of international tutelage. Concerned about the Tamburitzans' inauthentic, hybridized performances, Yugoslav folklorists emphasized perfecting distinct nations', nationalities', and ethnic groups' repertoires (Kolar 2009). Although this was in keeping with the Yugoslav ideal for multinational diversity, it was these nations, nationalities, and ethnic groups, rather than the socialist ideal of antinationalist unity, that would ultimately draw the affective investments and transnational projects—risky because of their nationalist bent—of Yugoslav and diasporic tambura performance institutions in socialism's final decade.

TRANSNATIONAL TAMBURA
PERFORMANCE, 1979–1989
A North American Tour

Especially since the late 1970s, the Socialist Republic of Croatia's ensembles have traveled to the United States and Canada under the auspices of the Croatian Fraternal Union of America (CFU; an insurance and fraternal organization) and the Matica iseljenika Hrvatske (MIH; the "parent body of emigrants from Croatia," often translated as the Croatian Heritage Foundation). Located in Croatia, the MIH emphasized Croatian ethnicity, culture, language, and transnational connections.[13] Vanja Vranjican, MIH's president through the mid-1980s, wrote of its collaborations with the CFU: "Hosting folklore ensembles and sending our own into emigrant milieus is only part [. . .]. Occupying an important place in this collaboration is help with Croatian language study, textbook printing, organizing courses in our country and the U.S.A." (quoted in Šovagović 1981, 6; my translation). These programs fostered a transnational "fraternal union" of Croats rather than "fraternity and unity" between diverse peoples living across the officially multinational socialist state. Its projects abroad suggest that the MIH accomplished more than "the promotion of the socialist self-management identity of the Yugoslav years" that Francesco Ragazzi attributes to what he calls "an uncritical, ignored organ of the established power" (2013, 68). Admittedly, the MIH did curtail its domestic operations following the 1971 Croatian Spring's suppression, in which MIH leaders such as future Croatian president Franjo Tuđman were arrested for their roles in this movement for political and cultural autonomy (Ramet 2006, 235).

In 1979 the MIH and CFU organized a North American tour for three Osijek acts: "Pajo Kolarić"; the popular singer Krunoslav Slabinac "Kićo"; and Slabinac's backing tambura band, Slavonski Bećari (Slavonian Bachelors), which he had formed with lead prim tambura player Antun Nikolić "Tuca" and which included Rudolf Ergotić (an artistic director at "Pajo Kolarić"). "Pajo Kolarić's" women's folk choir Šokadija (Land of the Šokci [Eastern Croats]) went, too, and programs prioritized the region's Croatian music. Their membership and directorship also included Serbs, however. The orchestra's tour guide noted that "Pajo Kolarić" "equally well performs concert compositions, old-city songs and pieces of the rich folkloric heritage of Slavonia, as well as of the other nations and nationalities of Yugoslavia" (Marija Vukelić, quoted in Šovagović 1981, 11; my translation). Yet journalist Đuro Šovagović describes a much narrower focus in his travelogue. Coinciding with the CFU's eighty-fifth anniversary and geographically distant from official Yugoslav stages, the performances celebrated the Slavonian music, Croatian culture, and transnational contact promoted by the CFU and MIH (23). Šovagović's invitation to document this contact reflects a developing interest in narrating tambura music's travels among Croatian populations, a discursive endeavor whose deep affective power I continue to trace in chapter 1.

Šovagović's celebration of Croatian (specifically, Slavonian) musical activity in a 1981 Yugoslavian text evidences the relaxing of attitudes and policies regarding musical nationalism following Tito's death in 1980. Also in 1981, tambura singer Vera Svoboda released her Marian songs album *Queen of the Croats, Pray for Us* on the official Croatia-based label Jugoton. This album marked increasing openness to Croatian nationalism[14] and Catholicism, which were principally antithetical to the multinational and atheistic Socialist Federal Republic of Yugoslavia (where their representation in official media had rarely passed censorship under Tito). It set the stage for the production of additional Catholic tambura albums such as Slavonski Bećari's *Croatian Christmas Carols* (1982) and influenced the proliferation of even more recordings (see Ceribašić 2000) and tambura Masses a decade later.

The North American hosts of the 1979 tour mostly descended from Croats who had left Austria-Hungary before its disintegration in World War I and had played no part in the Yugoslav project. These ancestors' strategies for deploying tambura music to solidify ethnic identity in the face of oppression from Austrian and Hungarian culture (see March 2013, 40–54) also served them well in resisting musical and linguistic assimilation in North America (113–114). Some even mobilized tambura performance as Croatian resistance to midcentury Yugoslav assimilationist pressures from Belgrade. Ante Beljo, who would later fund Franjo Tuđman and become his party's "propaganda chief" (Perica 2001, 58–59), wrote about how his Sudbury community resisted "Austrian rule," then interwar Yugoslavia, and finally postwar North American Yugoslav clubs, which "discouraged the formation of Croatian organizations" (Beljo 1983, 71). In the 1930s, he recalled, when Sudbury was seeking a tambura and Croatian language instructor, the "Yugo-regime tried to infiltrate the Croatian communities with their own men. The Sudbury community succeeded to avoid such a 'teacher'" (85).

North American Croatian organizations responded to Yugoslavian unity differently. Both the CFU headquarters and the Tamburitzans (at Duquesne University until 2016) are in Pittsburgh, and their Croatian directors differed for several decades over the latter's multinational program.[15] Among the biggest supporters of the 1979 tour, Croatian communities in Pittsburgh also welcomed non-Croat ensembles from Yugoslavia in the 1980s, such as that of famous Rom prim tambura virtuoso Janika Balaž. Peter Kosovec (2008) enthusiastically recalled his father bringing Balaž to their home near Detroit during his (non-CFU) tour. The CFU prioritized nationally conscious ensembles, for which interaction with North American Croats was particularly desirable, if also potentially dangerous for their standing in Yugoslavia.

The affective impact of the ceremonial celebration of relations among the CFU, MIH, musicians, and audience was emphasized on the 1979 tour, which opened with a concert in Brantford, Ontario, and with gift exchanges between "friends" (Šovagović 1981, 23). Osijek's musicians, Šovagović writes,

> act like they still can't believe their eyes that this before them in the full au-
> ditorium is no longer that domestic audience from Beli Manastir and Osijek
> [. . .]. But this, too, is a world that has *felt* the real value of their musicking[16]
> on tamburas, and when Kićo lit up the Slavonian songs with the "Bećari," the
> auditorium pounded from hand[clap]s in the rhythm that the tamburaši were
> giving. (23; my translation and emphasis)

Here musical feeling involved not only conscious musical valuation but also bodily experiences of clapped rhythms, reverberating space, and musical igni-tion. Moving Croatian American audiences to intense affect (embodied feeling) was already a primary concern in Croatian nationalist discourse and helped to naturalize its tenets through somatic experience. In Šovagović's description the Osijek travelers also reveled in influencing audience members' own tambura performance practice. Croatian American folklorist Richard March notes from firsthand experience that "the 1979 tour made Kičo's [*sic*] Slavonian songs and the Slavonski Bećari's tight, transparent music all the rage. Rabid fans drove hundreds of miles from concert to concert to see the show again and again [and] eagerly snatched up" his "records and cassettes" (2013, 205). These releases soon became staple sonic vehicles for Croatian tamburaši's affective labor throughout North America.

For their part, Osijek performers particularly valued the homestays. Vesna, a future STD "Pajo Kolarić" secretary, went with Šokadija in 1979; she recalled fondly to me how enthusiasts and performers in the two countries had con-nected during visits with midwestern Croatian families, including her relatives.[17] These homestays reinforced tambura music's expressive and affective power for celebrating family and homeland across varying degrees of temporal, cultural, and territorial separation.

New Tambura Relations and Projects in the 1980s

Ensemble tours between North America and Socialist Croatia also engendered new transnational familial relations, contributing significantly to the mobilization of national sentiment within and beyond Croatia's borders. The CFU instituted regular North American tours by professional male Croatian tamburaši, many of whom wed Croatian American women. In 1986, for example, Slavonski Bećari invited Miroslav Škoro, then a little-known rock singer-cum-comedian, to tour North America with the band. Škoro met Croatian American Kim Ann Luzaich in Pittsburgh and soon wedded and joined her there.

Škoro's relocation to start a family, while separating him physically from close tamburaši associates Slavonski Bećari (one of whom, Branko Helajz, had been *kum* ["best man"] at the wedding), ultimately advanced his tambura career. Shortly after he returned to the United States in 1989, Škoro met Jerry Grcevich, who had grown up playing with his father, his uncle, and his father's Cokeburg Junior Tamburitzan ensemble. Already an established, virtuosic tambura record-ing artist, Grcevich suggested that they collaborate. The result was that "I started writing songs, and Jerry started composing, and after some time we had an entire album" (Škoro 2010, 71; my translation). The song "Ne dirajte mi ravnicu" (Don't touch my plain) would have a lasting influence on tambura music in Croatia upon its release in 1992, eventually making Škoro and Grcevich popular icons as the genre flourished in the newly independent republic.

The tamburaši who first moved thousands to tears with that song were not associated with Grcevich or Škoro, however, but another band that toured for the CFU in the 1980s. In 1992 Zlatni Dukati (Golden Ducats) rerecorded and released the title track from Grcevich's and Škoro's album. About the different versions, Škoro notes:

"Ne dirajte mi ravnicu" came into existence in 1989, in late fall when the sky and I were both crying. The sky for the waning summer and year, and I for everything[18] that I left in the plain. [. . .] Vlado Smiljanić changed its name [from I Will Return . . .]. [W]hen [Zlatni Dukati manager] Josip Ivanković heard it, he immediately recorded the famous video with Zlatni Dukati in which the late [actor] Fabijan Šovagović lets a tear fall for his wounded Slavonia and this is all mixed with scenes from Schmidt's great films "Đuka Begović" and "Sokol ga nije volio." (2010, 195; my translation)

The latter film (Sokol did not love him) depicts World War II struggles over Slavonia by Yugoslav Partisans and Croatia's Nazi-aligned Ustaša party. Furthermore, the song's "wartime relevance was reinforced by a video with Škoro performing it around an army campfire" (Baker 2010, 26). Zlatni Dukati, and later Škoro, turned what was "originally a typical song about emigrants' nostalgia" (27) into a "teleological narrative of collective displacement and ethnic defiance" during Eastern Slavonia's occupation (26). This realized anew the song's promise of return: Dukati delivered the sentiments of displacement and longing from the diaspora to its newly autonomous country's people and lands, where the song relayed a further promise of return from war to peace (and from refuges to occupied lands) and suggested a narrative for this promise's fulfillment.

This was not Zlatni Dukati's first transplantation of Croatian American sentiments. On the 1988 CFU tour "was born the idea for recording the album of patriotic songs 'Croatian songbook,' which would contribute to popularizing the ensemble and tambura music in general, [. . .] to liberating the national spirit as well as to developing and establishing democratic relations in the then Socialist Republic of Croatia" (Zlatni Dukati 2014; my translation; also cited in March 2013, 223).

Some songs released on the 1989 cassette had been popular in World War II Ustaša campaigns. Although the songs predate World War II, and the "leader of the ensemble modified the lyrics in a way to exclude direct associations with the Ustashas" (Pettan 1998, 12), their patriotic content was potentially problematic in multiethnic Yugoslavia. Rumors quickly spread about a plot by Communist Jugoton leadership to pull the album, and "the affair made tamburica music a politicized product by depicting it as a Croatian value under threat from an expansionist Serbia which was operating through Yugoslav federal structures" (Baker 2010, 60). The democratic relations that the group later noted helping to establish involved partnering with the Hrvatska demokratska zajednica (Croatian Democratic Party, hereafter HDZ), a decidedly Croat-oriented party headed by historian and former general and MIH leader Dr. Franjo Tuđman. The party aimed to liberate not just the national spirit but also the nation from Yugoslavia, and it hired Zlatni Dukati to capitalize on rising nationalist fervor for its successful 1990 election campaigns (Bonifačić 1998). The elections put the HDZ in the driver's seat of Croatia's machine of secession and war the following year, and the band would continue to work for Tuđman, Croatia's first president, throughout the 1990s.

Thus Zlatni Dukati, along with STD "Pajo Kolarić," Slavonski Bećari, Miroslav Škoro, and Jerry Grcevich, at times played integral roles not only in building relations between countries but also in erecting new national barriers. While not all Croats shared the HDZ's sentiments about nationalist organizing, the feeling for the nation (as a territorializing people) that musicians mobilized transnationally proved to be a significant force in reshaping and centering intimate social networks through Croatia's territory. Transgressing the admittedly weakened official Yugoslav ideals of "fraternity and unity" and fostering through such risky performances a "fraternal union" with Croats abroad, musicians made accessing these intimate foreign spaces commonly imaginable, even to those who did not (yet) seek them.

The 1990s, however, also brought something *not* commonly imaginable in the previous decade: the physical violence and danger that escalated between the Yugoslav and Croatian armies and various paramilitary forces. As Jerry Grcevich notes, one could "feel" the tensions between different ethnic groups by the late 1980s, and playing the wrong nation's song in the wrong venue was a risk with repercussions (typically verbal abuse) that he experienced firsthand (Grcevich 2012). However, the force of musical danger, if intensely affective, only rarely threatened lasting physical harm of the nature that musicians would face during the war. I detail the latter more thoroughly in chapter 1 but consider it important to examine here briefly the Yugoslav conflicts' impact on ensembles within the territories and borders of the nascent nation-state. Tambura music's affective facilitation and textual narrativization of the reestablishment of transnational ties with a variety of foreign enclaves test the limits of the concept of diaspora. I suggest here the intellectual merits to extricating from this broad analytic a set of displacements, returns, and intimacies that are sometimes lost in both academic and lay conceptions of dispersion from a homeland.

CROATIA AND ITS INTIMATES: SOVEREIGNTY AND THE TERRITORIALIZATION OF MUSIC SCENES

That nation-states forged from disintegrating republics and empires are messy affairs, always more complex and heterogeneous than their pretensions to homogeneity suggest, is neither novel nor surprising. Purity is an absolute ideal, while the forging of a nation involves not only juxtaposition with external Others but also internal identifications and becomings that are of necessity incomplete (and *de*territorialized as much as *re*territorialized).[19] As James Ferguson demonstrates, however, analysts' "national frame of reference" still oversimplifies such states' structures and societies by assuming (economic) sovereignty and circumscription of heterogeneity within state borders (2006, 64). What an ethnography of a recent nation-state's emergence can contribute to contemporary studies of territoriality and sovereignty, then, is an understanding of the aesthetic and affective attachments to external territories (including those whose most visible connections fall outside of economic relations) that bolster a state's independence yet also thereby limit its sovereignty's territorial boundedness. These attachments comprise a series of intimacies that stand not in opposition to danger but rather as its counterparts. They do not so much compensate for as absorb the threats (small and large, projected and experienced, felt and symbolized) of domestic heterogeneity and of borders' inability to bound all the people and territories that the "nation" would claim.

States deal with such threats in diverse but almost always incomplete ways. Often noted of nation-states forged in the twentieth century are ethnically homogenizing population exchanges with neighboring countries, but these typically bring states new cultural (if not ethnic) diversity and new foreign territorial attachments. Anthropologist Jasna Čapo Žmegač writes that Croat wartime refugees from Srijem, Serbia, who exchanged property with Croatian Serbs saw the tambura as "a [longtime] marker of the Croatian identity of the Croats from Srijem" and compared "with irony [its inclusion] in the list of Croatian symbols in Croatia only in the 1990s" ([2002] 2007, 107). Croatian Croats working at Serbian institutions such as Novi Sad's Radio Tambura Orchestra also returned suddenly to Croatia, where they significantly influenced the emerging neotraditional tambura scene (Benić 2010). Despite their shared ethnicity, dissatisfaction was common among both the displaced and those meant to welcome them, and these migrations were marked by great trauma, even as they jointly fostered the tambura's adoption nationwide and later networked with Serbia's remaining Croatian enclaves.

Other tambura musicians displaced during the Yugoslavian wars resettled among long-established expatriate communities in more distant countries such as Austria and the United States. In Austrian and Hungarian Burgenland towns, South Slavic enclaves had survived since moving north twelve generations before to flee Ottoman forces and join Austria-Hungary in fighting them. In cases such as Parndorf (Pandrof in Croatian), Austria, communities that received Yugoslav war refugees had already had strong tambura traditions in place since the 1930s and had long interacted with music professionals in Yugoslavia (Schedl 2004, 39). The wars significantly affected expatriate communities, too, disrupting patterns of musical interaction with Yugoslavia and sending new waves of tambura musicians and audiences into the midst of older diasporas. However, the musicians' long involvement in Yugoslav politics—through visits in which they fed separatist or federalist rhetoric, acted as political and cultural ambassadors for their countries of citizenship, and financially supported movements such as Croatian independence (Hockenos 2003, 84–85)—was almost completely reduced to sending moral and financial support. Fluent in the Croatian language and connected in their former hometowns, members of the new diaspora often led efforts to reconnect with communities in the newly established Republic of Croatia after the war. Tamburaši played a key role in reestablishing such intimate contacts following the amplification of physical distance through the militarization of Croatia's borders. Rising stars such as Škoro and fellow Osijek singer/tamburaš Vjekoslav Dimter, who lived in Pittsburgh during the war, wrote some of their most successful patriotic songs in North America and subsequently helped to establish Grcevich as a much-sought-after performer in Croatia. Richard March (2013, 213) encapsulates these transatlantic tambura networks' communal strengths with the phrase "My Little (Global) Village," an adaptation of a Vjekoslav Dimter song (played by his and Kosovec's Pennsylvania band Otrov at the 2003 festival in Požega, Croatia), and their reach does indeed span far more than the United States and Croatia. In 1993 Škoro, for instance, became general consul for the large Croatian refugee community in Pécs, Hungary. Many of the public tambura concerts now held in Croatia and within these diasporic communities have developed out of contacts forged or maintained by recent immigrants, and their experiences of war and emigration shaped these connections.

The historical depth and continuity of emigration from Croatia to its various diasporic communities differs tremendously; more distant continents received immigrants intensively but recently in comparison to closer territories. Other foreign Croat enclaves consider themselves not diasporas but simply the casualties of Southeast Europe's balkanization. Croats in Hungarian Baranya (a region continuous with Croatian Baranja) have been national minorities for generations, relating to their perceived ethnic homeland from outside Croatia's border but feeling very much in *their own* territory. Others in Bosnia and Herzegovina and in Serbia have a much shorter history as foreign nationals in the Croatian lands and feel perhaps even more strongly that their cities should be part of what some nationalists envision as "Greater Croatia." Yugoslavia's disintegration added not just more borders but also more kinds of border crossings, informed by different histories. It "deterritorialize[d]" (Deleuze and Guattari [1980] 1987, 269) more fully the lives and livelihoods of many tamburaši across varied, rhizomatic assemblages (263) of dispersion and settlement, even as it reterritorialized their tambura practices upon the states of Croatia, Serbia, and so forth.

The use of "diaspora" to designate a people displaced from a nominal homeland far predates the modern nation-state[20] but has played an important role in theories of "long-distance nationalism" as they pertain to the broader relevance of "imagined communities" (Anderson 1998, 1983). As the nation-state has yielded some of its structuring capacity to processes of globalization in many parts of the world, scholars of migration have embraced more complex ideas of the relationship between displacement and place in studies of decentered diasporas (e.g., Gilroy 1993; Clifford 1997; Stephen 2007). The decentering trend is not irreversible, however, and music has frequently afforded an effective means of "claiming diaspora" within immigrant communities that formerly embraced assimilationist ideologies and rejected their "homelands" as premodern and traditional (Zheng 2010). Moreover, "balkanization" has frequently recentered discourses on nation and displacement for peoples either in diaspora or territorially excluded from new nominal "homelands." Independent Macedonia, for example, became a more relevant homeland for Romani musician émigrés than their South Asian point of origin (India) or even their birth country (Yugoslavia) (Silverman 2012, 40). Displacement and attempts to reconnect through a central territory—particularly one surrounded by "foreign" lands imaginable within the "greater" national cartography—foster identification and commonality among peoples separated by more diverse degrees of time and space than "diaspora" connotes.

I employ the phrase "Croatia and its intimates" to account for the wide range of (musical) communities within and outside Croatia's borders that relate to the Republic of Croatia as a national center (see MacMillen 2011a). These are not all diasporic communities, nor does the entire Croatian diaspora enjoy the same sort of intimate connections with musicians in Croatia as do the Parndorf and Pittsburgh tamburaši mentioned previously. To focus exclusively on the Croatian diaspora would ignore the broader array of displacements affecting the human geography of Croatian communities' wartime and postwar transnational networks and the tambura music and other practices that bolster them.[21]

Since the mid-1990s, moreover, many scholars have questioned the "promiscuous" use of "diaspora," protesting that it stands for too broad an array of migrations and displacements (Tölölyan 1996, 8). Silverman warns of three pitfalls: "essentializing diasporas by attaching them to particular places of origin," "equating all diasporic subjects merely because they are related to a posited homeland," and "diluting the concept so much as to equate it with all migration" (2012, 40). As Hariz Halilovich has shown, furthermore, many residents and recent emigrants of former Yugoslav republics reject "diaspora" due to its connotations of permanence, distance, and successful ethnic cleansing (of home districts) (2013, 120). Given the plurality and "trans-locality" (133) of migrations represented in most Croatian communities outside of Southeast Europe and their diverse practices of visiting and essentializing the "homeland," I find it especially important to eschew utilizing, and thereby broadening, "diaspora." I use "intimates" throughout this book to refer to communities rooted in localities yet continuously building and performing affective attachments to the homeland and, through it, to one another. Particularly through musical endeavors within and on behalf of "their" nominal homeland, Croatia's intimates share in the physical, affective, ideological, and musical constitution of this state's core territory and culture. The concept of "national intimates" accounts for an equalization of investment (though not of the mobilization of power) in this homeland's music, people, and affective capacities across a continuum of displacements not encompassed by "diaspora."

Music and National Intimates

Croatia's intimates' participation in the country's cultural and political affairs also demonstrates more than the familiarity or nostalgic longing for the "old country" typical of many diasporas. Independent Croatia and its intimates keep their connections current through varied means of reciprocal influence and support in political campaigns, insurance networks, religious missions, accessing higher education, tourism, and tambura music (as did the CFU, the MIH, and affiliated ensembles before the war). While Croatia's territory centers these networks, foreign communities function as powerful secondary nodes of attraction and dispersion, maintaining relations with one another (often with reference to Croatia rather than via its nuclear pull). Reverence for Peter Kosovec's and Jerry Grcevich's dangerous performance among musicians in Austria, Bosnia and Herzegovina, and Hungary depends on appreciatively upholding (and cautiously transgressing) tambura music as a Croatian tradition but not in most cases on contact with Croatian American tamburaši within Croatian territory. Shared traditions, affective investments, and personal relationships connecting Croatia and its intimates are facilitated largely by recognition of common heritage that transcends territorial emplacement.

Such geographically dispersed nationalism can be found globally in many transnational musical cultures. As Jane Sugarman shows, the diasporic middle class played an essential role in constructing nineteenth-century Albania's national culture, providing the ideological scaffolding for Albanian musical nationalism in present-day Macedonia (1999, 444). Amnon Shiloah similarly demonstrates the importance of the Jewish diaspora's artistic intelligentsia and of Jewish communities in nearby countries for constructing an Israeli folk music and dance repertoire (1992, 217–218). Christopher Waterman (1990) and Thomas Turino (2000) identify comparable trends within and beyond the borders of Nigeria and Zimbabwe, respectively.[22] Tambura musicians' international nationalist networks are not solely diasporic but are also recognizably transnational and cosmopolitan, contributing to reifications of the nation-state that come into focus across varying gradations of proximity: affective, geographical, temporal, cultural, economic, and bureaucratic.

Contemporary nationalisms owe much of their complexity to migrations and societal changes during the fall of imperial and colonial governing structures. In stable periods, they succeeded in subjecting and organizing populations into diversely mixed societies; Rogers Brubaker argues that subsequently, during imperial dissolution into nation-states, the "unmixing of peoples" was particularly tumultuous and formative (1995). This certainly was true of post–Austro-Hungarian Croatia and post-Ottoman Albania and Israel. Čapo Žmegač extends Brubaker's observation to multinational republican (Yugoslav and Soviet) dissolutions and resultant "ethnic unmixing of hitherto mixed, multiethnic societies" ([2002] 2007, 27).

Yet the teleology of unmixing mixed societies once again assumes the ontological certainty of the nation, overlooking those who do not hold a (single) national frame of reference, including antinationalists, ethnically mixed individuals, and "nationless peoples." For the latter, such as Roma, it is possible to trace, in Philip Bohlman's words, "the alternative historical paths articulated by their music, which are no less political and crucial to the history of European nationalism if indeed they lie beyond the borders fixed by those with the political power and nationalist motivation" (2004, 213). Croatia still has both "nationless" and "nationed" minority communities and still avails itself of Croat minorities in other states. Furthermore, Croats' affective relations to such groups and to one another are not static identifications but ever-emergent "minoritarian" becomings (Deleuze and Guattari [1980] 1987, 291) whose musical flux and embodiments extend back nearly two centuries (MacMillen 2013). "National intimates" encapsulates complexities of nationally charged transnational connections that persist despite governmental, nationalistic, and even scholarly tendencies to reduce these networks to ethnically homogeneous homelands with geographically disparate diasporas.

Tambura music remains a diverse practice and site of contact across racial, ethnic/religious, and geopolitical divides. In playing dangerously, Serbian, Romani, and other non-Croat musicians have greatly impacted tambura music within Croatia, its intimates, and the greater international scene. A closely related study might well consider "Serbia and its intimates" as an overlapping and equally significant, albeit differently structured, zone of tambura performance. Professional and amateur Serb musicians have upheld the tambura as their own folkloric and national tradition in both the socialist and postsocialist periods. The few Serbian tambura ensembles active in Croatia in the 2000s entered the public folklore sphere cautiously (see chapter 3) but participated regularly in semipublic events for Serbs outside of Serbia that celebrate tambura music for rooting them in their territories of residence (Prosvjeta 2010, 3–5). In such cases, Serbia often constituted an "empty" center for its intimates, who solidify Serbian connections outside of—rather than with—their nominal homeland, where the tambura has never achieved true national symbolic status.[23] Yet Croatia, too, remains merely a noncentral locus for music and networking to Serb performers there. In my fieldwork, Croatian ethnicity has surfaced as the single prominent precipitating factor for the intense intimacy examined here between tambura bands and autonomous Croatia.

Intimate Communities

In employing "intimate," I avail myself of the noun's connotation of a close personal friend as a metaphor or metonym that stands for a supportive, closely connected foreign community. In addition, I invoke its many adjectival nuances, expanding the concept's resonance beyond a set of concrete actors to an array of processes and becomings. These communities are intimate with Croatia and its citizens in several respects: in sharing personal relationships; in recognizing closeness through mutual influence; and even through sexual relationships, as young men and women continue to find spouses and raise families in Croatian communities beyond their birth countries.

"Intimates" as an analytic also invokes recent scholarship theorizing these various sorts of intimacy in the close ties of people with shared investments and obligations, as well as at levels beyond personal relationships. Especially important here is Lauren Berlant's examination of the "tacit fantasies, tacit rules, and tacit obligations" that people bring to intimate relationships (1998, 287). Although these tacit understandings often propagate "optimism" about the way things should be, Berlant notes that intimacy "is also formed around *threats* to the image of the world it seeks to sustain" (288; emphasis added). The war that accompanied Croatia's split with Yugoslavia simultaneously assured its status as an autonomous center and threatened its accessibility to Croat communities outside of its borders; the sense of connection that formed or intensified across the new borders between these communities is key to their designation as Croatia's intimates.

The sense of threat that Croats and other peoples experienced, particularly in Croatia, Bosnia and Herzegovina, and Serbia, is also key for understanding the intense feeling that musicians invest through dangerous performance in reestablishing their presence in occupied territories and formerly ostracized church buildings, refostering ties with communities and cultural and religious leaders beyond their state borders, and eliciting from their audiences an affective investment in a national becoming. As Martin Stokes argues in his work on Turkish popular music, postcolonial republics, "amongst which Turkey might be ambiguously counted"—as might post-Ottoman, post-Habsburg, and post-Yugoslav Croatia—have "deployed a sentimental language of affection and intimacy in the forging of independent national identities. This independence would often prove tenuous, provoking retrenchments into fantasies of racial purity and the (always threatened) authenticity of national cultural heritage" (2010, 30). Following Berlant, I might add that sentimental musical performance that effectively locates such a racially pure and independent nation draws its affective capacity from dangers to the very sonic world it seeks to create.

Moving from questions of threat to the realities of loss, Svetlana Boym refers to a "diasporic intimacy" that is not opposed to uprootedness and defamiliarization but is constituted by it (2001, 253). Spanning gaps of physical displacement and cultural estrangement, such intimacy "is rooted in the suspicion of a single home, in shared longing without belonging" (253). I qualify this only by suggesting that such longing and intimacy may also characterize peoples separated by processes other than migration. National intimates such as Croatia's share an intimacy constituted through defamiliarization, dispersion, and separation from their second (symbolically primary) home, whether that separation results from resettlement or from the erection of national borders. This "intimacy does not promise an unmediated emotional fusion, but only a precarious affection — no less deep, yet aware of its transience" (252), whether borne across histories of emigration or within homes that, though not lost, are now in the nominal homeland of another nation.

In his work on "dark intimacy" in Southeastern Europe, Alexander Kiossev notes that connection and identification "take place in an unstable field, where various identity models are in competition; [. . .] such conditions could create a feeling of uncertainty and anxiety [or could afford] individuals more opportunities and more 'free space' for maneuvering" (2002, 178). Some Croats undoubtedly took advantage of separation, exploring alternative or plural models; maneuvering within freer spaces of identification accessible beyond Croatia's borders; and aligning themselves with minority, regional, and broader European organizations. Others, however, readopted models of Croatian national identification from the 1980s, reestablishing physical contact with communities inside Croatia's borders. These latter individuals are largely those who, working with their contacts in Croatia, have kept or made their own communities intimates of the young country.

As I argue elsewhere, however, such "connections are imbricated with conditions of significant economic inequality" (MacMillen 2011a, 107). Croatians' experiences of domestic visitation and foreign concert sponsorship by relatively wealthy diasporic intimates feed narratives of Croatia's geographical and developmental emplacement in between economically still weaker (former Yugoslav) and more robust (Western Europe/North America) countries (107). Moving beyond simplistic national frames to material relations that cause such inequalities, we can recognize that

> while the creation of a sovereign ethnic homeland fed the demand for patriotic music that initially enabled the rise of many tamburaši to celebrity status and commercial success in Croatia, it also eventually fed into constructions both of Croatia's "domestic" problems [. . .] and of foreign enclaves [. . .] as distant, independent sites for sidestepping Croatia's economic policies and bureaucratic institutions. (107)

Intimacy, especially engendered across or within displacements, is neither utopian (as quickly proffered instances of familial, sexual, and spiritual intimacy might suggest) nor "solely a private matter," for "intimacy can be protected, manipulated or besieged by the state, framed by art, embellished by memory or estranged by a critique" (Boym 2001, 253). Thus there also operates within these networks a codependent intimacy with the state's embellishments and estrangements. This "cultural intimacy" internalizes not only national ambivalence over tambura bands but also tamburaši's own "rueful self-recognition" of their complicity with gray economic practices that they see as a sign of the state's inability or unwillingness to match "Western" developments (Herzfeld 1997, 4; MacMillen 2011a, 108).

Music and Public Intimacies

"Intimacy" in music typically conjures up the sights and sounds of physically proximate social or sexual interaction. Such interaction does pervade the musical lives and actions that I examine, yet the intimacies at play here do not merely elide distance; they are constituted through experiences of separation, danger, and even violence. Analyzing how musicians and audiences foster such "dark" relations of closeness at local, regional, and transnational levels, I contribute to a growing body of literature that posits music's claim to intimate experience as persistently enabled through its mediations across physical and cultural spaces that connect but also separate people.

Byron Dueck argues that public space "occup[ies] a middle ground between publicity and intimacy" for Manitoba's First Nations (2013, 8). While contrasting intimacies ("engagements between known and knowable persons") with imaginaries ("acts of publication and performance oriented to an imagined public"), he notes that public space may afford an inclusive "civil twilight" in which strangers easily recruit one another from the "imagined public" into intimate "face-to-face engagement" (7–8). Essential to this capacity for intimacy and to its efficacy in pursuing meaningful musical interaction is an "orientation to a public of strangers" (5), which characterizes both First Nations' indigenous imaginaries and nation-states' "imagined communities" (Anderson 1983).

In Michelle Bigenho's work on Bolivian music in Japan, intimacies depend upon far greater spatial and cultural separation. Bigenho's "intimate distance" emerges through "desire across [geographical and national] boundaries" and maintains a "conceptual tension [in] experiences through which one feels like and unlike others" (2012, 25). Thus diverse nonnatives employ racialized imaginaries of shared genetic heritage but paradoxically do not identify with contemporary natives: a "move of both intimacy and distance [. . .] made through the complicated historical hubris of race and indigeneity" (138).[24]

I situate musical intimacy's spatialization betwixt and between the structures of closeness and distance that these studies model. On the one hand, this book considers how music bolsters intimacy within a community imagined singularly (within rather than spanning national and racial boundaries) but beyond the territorial bounds of the nation-state, on a geographic scale approaching that of Bigenho's study. On the other hand, it analyzes a Croatian public space in which social imaginaries overlap with musical intimacies in ways that unexpectedly make porous the boundaries of race and gender that musicians mobilize from the country's intimates. It thus joins Barry Shank's examination of how such "boundaries of an intimate public are often charged with affective intensity, where different values or ways of being that can't be ignored can spark a struggle between the ordinary and the unjust" (2014, 49). Roma are the objects of an unjust, essentializing discourse (sometimes self-perpetuated) of hereditary musicality. Their perceived ability to play dangerously solicits intimate distancing as Croatian musicians aspire to this skill as a potential source of national pride, yet channel its affective capacities toward affirming rather than destabilizing national intimacies and insular values. Roma, Serbs, and additional musical Others, such as African Americans in Pittsburgh, variously enjoy these musical intimacies, perceivably endanger them through territorializing presence, and elicit desire within Croatian communities for transgressing racialized musical sensibilities. Music's claims on intimacy as interior affect, public sentiment, and (trans)national relation are bound to its enticing transgressions: "the danger of music," the "suspicion" and "control" that it provokes among authorities, and the resistance to oppression that musicians have mobilized in the circum-Mediterranean for centuries (Taruskin 2008, 168).

SCALES OF SPACE, STRUCTURES OF ANALYSIS

This book situates affect's interactions with systems of meaning—narrative, discourse, and ideology—by dedicating pairs of chapters to each of three corresponding geographical scales of intimate spatialization. It takes up the scalar analytics of Lila Ellen Gray, who notes of *fado* that a "sentimentalizing aesthetic" and representations of place "echo a geopolitical strategy of scale" through which the state produces a "cartography of both the enormous and the miniature, where social and geo-spatial structures of intimacy and interiority (of neighborhood, of family, of faith) symbolically st[an]d in for the expansive reach of the nation and the imperial, corporate, totalitarian state" (2014, 113). Expanding the scope of ethnographic research to scales well beyond the state, this book similarly examines the structuring of musical intimacy, social danger, and racializing affect within and through the nation-state in three interconnected scales of spatialization: the transnational and diasporic, the regional and urban, and the proximate space of ritual and bodily contact. The progressive contraction from "enormous" to "miniature" geography (and from more elaborate to more ingrained forms of meaning into which musical affect transgresses) foregrounds important histories of tambura's transnational movement at the book's outset. It also deliberately cuts across the grain of standard analytic narratives of intimacy as a quality of local, face-to-face interaction that may then spiral outward into larger spaces. Instead I posit intimacy as intrinsically spatialized and spatializing at multiple levels of scale and examine its role in small and large ensembles, thereby representing the range of ensemble types while also considering how intimacy accrues and is mobilized within different scales of human organization.

This introduction and the following chapter elaborate the history of the STD "Pajo Kolarić" and related city and professional ensembles and examine the work of musical and affective responses to danger in generating and blocking narratives of race and mobility since the Yugoslav-Croatian conflicts. Chapter 1 focuses on "Pajo Kolarić's" youth orchestras, tracing further their musical travels into militarized and demilitarized zones and abroad after the outbreak of war in 1991. Connecting wartime concerns over neighborhood, family, and faith to both emergent narratives of national awakening and affective experiences of danger, the chapter takes up affective block in its less disruptive sense of tambura ensembles generating new blocks of becoming (affectively shoring up the public disavowal of Yugoslav identification). It also begins to examine affective block in its second instance: the curtailing of certain counternarratives via the intensities of musicking in sites of racialized fear and danger as ensembles (re) connected Croatia's intimates to the country's core territory.

Two subsequent chapters address the capacity for affective responses, in turn, to be blocked through strategic or incidental discursive maneuvers. They examine music as a spatializing and socializing force (Krims 2007) that brings diverse populations into contested territories and racialized sentiments at the level of urban centers (Pittsburgh and Osijek) and the regional territorial assemblages in which these cities' tamburaši most often perform (the American Rust Belt and Eastern Croatia). These assemblages are neither geographically static nor culturally monolithic, despite discourses of racial difference that suggest otherwise. In order to demonstrate these discourses' spatializing power over and simultaneous susceptibility to material processes of physical urban relation and the tactility of tambura technique, these chapters examine discursive responses to the sensational knowledge (Hahn 2007) of racialized becoming. Chapter 2 analyzes Pittsburgh's semiprofessional bands in relation to local Croatian Homes' junior tamburitzans ensembles and to professional musicians from the former Yugoslavia. Taking up questions of sincere feeling, it examines bands' staging of jokes and humorous musico-textual translations as an anti-affective strategy. It shows how this block to affect privileges meanings of racial difference but also produces residual feelings of Otherness, shoring up whiteness as a form of limitative minoritarian becoming in the face of intimate contact and even conflict among Croatian, Serbian, Romani, and African American residents. In contrast, chapter 3 examines limitations of discursive strategies in staving off such feelings. Turning to Roma bands in Croatia and how they delimit practices among Croat bands and the orchestras and folklore ensembles with which they train, it argues that bands and orchestras that play dangerously risk transgressing a postwar Croatian aesthetic for the musically "clean" and adopting the "dirty" technique of Romani musicians. The inaccessibility of this feat both blocks (delimits) affective states that Croatian musicians might otherwise hold in common with racialized others and blocks (delimits) discursive counters to constructs of Roma as nonthreatening nomads and of Serbian presence as a dangerous incursion on East Croatian territory.

Two final chapters consider ideologies of belonging and intimacy and their co-delimitation of physical human relations as felt and embodied in the space and time of musical ritual. They build upon previous chapters by addressing tensions that emerge within racialized groups (thus narrowing the scope) but that concretize around distinctions of gender and religion, which themselves often intersect with race-thinking and -feeling. They thus bring into focus the internalization of power structures that at times contradict dominant orders of inclusion and exclusion, demonstrating new possibilities for blocking chauvinistic ideologies in delimitation through socially, intercorporeally, and even supersensorially distributed affect. Turning to the all-women band Garavuše and to both male and female fans of male (semi)professional groups, chapter 4 examines the particular gendered relations of (semi)professional bands[25] and their audiences. It demonstrates how physical blocks (of both affect and assembled human bodies) can successfully mobilize to counter restrictive ideologies, arguing that performances have their own structures of power that draw on racialized dynamics of performative interaction. These structures simultaneously threaten musical intimacy with a block of intense aggression and build affectively on the intimate nature of threat itself. Chapter 5 returns to questions of faith introduced in chapter 1, analyzing supposedly fixed hierarchies among the officiators of Catholic-oriented tambura services (typically priests), the mostly adult orchestras/folklore ensembles that perform for them, and those in attendance. It also returns to affect and meaning's cogenerative dialectic, examining how the slippage and potential blockage between sensorial and ideological understandings of space allow musical worshippers a flexibility to move beyond structures of architecture and dogma. The chapter thus delineates the ways in which hierarchies are jeopardized or reinforced through musical performance, the affective intensity of which often relies on a para-Christian metaphysics of space and energy and on participants' mutual physical constitution of Croatia as a racially musicked nation and core territory.

ONE

Tamburaši and "Sacral Buildings" on a Balkanizing Peninsula

The tambura is silent now, the rifle tells the tale.

Radovan Milanov and Antun Nikolić, "Tell the World the Truth about Baranja"

Spring 2010: Drinking tea in a moderately lit, below-ground café in Osijek, I mentioned to Antun (president of the STD "Pajo Kolarić") the existence of a youth Farkaš tambura orchestra in Ruse, Bulgaria.[1] I knew from visiting Ruse in 2009 that its leaders were seeking additional international collaborations, and Antun suggested the possibility of the "Pajo Kolarić" children's orchestra traveling to Bulgaria. Several parents, however, expressed "fear" at the prospect of sending their children to Bulgaria. Antun attributed this reaction to concern about the musicians' young age. Yet one of the orchestra's directors told me that she, too, felt "fear" at the thought of leaving Croatia for unknown countries. All were happy to welcome the Bulgarians if they came to Osijek. However, anxiety over travel to proximate foreign territories among this generation of young adults (who had been children or youths during the war) was strong enough to prevent a trip to Bulgaria, despite the "Pajo Kolarić" orchestras having recently traveled to such destinations as Hungary, Austria, Serbia, and the Netherlands.[2]

The orchestra's director, furthermore, had grown up in the nearby Croatian region of Baranja before being evacuated to the country's interior during the war. She thus had witnessed firsthand the fact that living within Croatian territory did not guarantee a secure, fearless existence; intermittent ethnic tensions and problems with untripped landmines and buildings weakened by shellfire keep the threat of further destruction alive even today. Under what conditions, then, would this director and the parents travel to foreign territories that presented no such physical threats? Nearly two decades after the war, how did experiences and narratives of daring movement into war-torn territories interact with the affect of a fear that has persisted despite attempts to rationalize it into insignificance?

Such a dissonance between thought and feeling is affective block at its most basic: the ability of feeling to block (in delimitation) a conscious, rationalizing, and contradictory understanding of the world. It does so through an accrual of embodied intensity that in its generation is "disconnected from meaningful sequencing, from narration" (Massumi 1996, 219). Yet this chapter also examines the "interanimation" (Gray 2014, 9) in musical spheres between affective and narrative registers of security and risk. Probing under what wartime and post-war conditions affective attachments, tales, and eventually traveling musicians themselves reached beyond the boundaries of secured Croatian lands, it shows how a nation-state's core territory emerges physically and discursively through the common site of the body. It argues ultimately for a new way of understanding the emergence of terms of becoming and of Otherness (a national "we," a racialized distinction of "us" and "them") through intimate, musical relationships with dangerous areas and presence. It thus demonstrates how this affective block is also an aggregation of feeling, a building of intense intimacy as individuals begin to feel like a "we."

One of the first dangerous areas abandoned was Baranja, whose refugees saw both themselves and tambura traditions as passive wartime victims and did not immediately hear in this music the potential for responding physically to the realities of warfare. The particular poignancy of this northeast Croatian region's capture for its residents instead often inspired tambura music composition as a form of communication from afar. Ballads such as "Tell the World the Truth about Baranja" ("Istinu svijetu o Baranji reci") connected narratives of threat, endangered traditions, and calls to armed engagement. Released in 1992 by Slavonski Bećari, it tells of the peaceful village life of food, wine, family, and tamburaši that the Šokci, one of the easternmost groups of Croats, had enjoyed in Baranja before its occupation by an "evildoer" (the Yugoslav People's Army).

A resonant song for Croatians during Baranja's 1991–1998 occupation, it was, however, only partially accurate in its claim that the tambura had fallen silent while the rifle narrated (and caused) the falling of "cold steel" and other wartime dangers. Certainly from the perspective of Croats such as the "Pajo Kolarić" director (then a child), who had fled from Baranja, the rifle and not the tambura was sounding in their home villages. This likely rang true despite the fact that their Serb neighbors or the Yugoslav soldiers positioned there could have been playing instruments at the time. As Kruno Kardov notes, Croats in nonoccupied cities such as Osijek imagined towns and cities in Eastern Slavonia and Baranja not merely cleansed of Croats but altogether devoid of residents, though many Serbs remained throughout the occupation (Kardov 2007, 66). Yet as this song demonstrates, tambura music was also an effective sonic medium by which to "tell the tale" of war to nonoccupied Croatia and the world beyond. In this respect, the tambura remained decidedly outspoken throughout the war.

In 1992, however, tambura performance was also becoming important for reclaiming Croatian territory, establishing postconflict transnational networks, and other material processes that, like the advance of riflemen, have reconfigured musical performance's human geography in Croatia and beyond. Tambura music's connection to danger became most concrete during this period as some tamburaši, far from playing it safe, used songs and performances to confront not only discursively but also physically the actions of Yugoslavian forces. Prominent tambura ensembles' movement during and after the war and the conflicts' narrativization in publications, song texts, and other media illuminate the resonance and affective capacities of war, danger, and aggression for tambura performance in independent Croatia.

I consider these processes' material and spatial dimensions by examining diverse divisions and intimacies in relation to national musical belonging, which has intensified since 1991 through tambura networks centered in Croatia. The chapter focuses on the regional and international activities of the STD "Pajo Kolarić" as a primary case study while also examining affiliated or comparable professionals such as Slavonski Bećari and the tambura/rock singer and songwriter Miroslav Škoro. All hail from Osijek, which Yugoslav forces bombarded but never occupied. I consider their performances and discourses on tambura music during and after the war, both in Croatia and abroad. The chapter further elaborates "national intimates" as an approach to transnational nationalism, its tambura narrativization, and the intersections of secession, militarization, diaspora, affective block, and constructions of national music.

In examining the flows and disjunctures in ensembles' movement across these territories to reconnect to intimates beyond Croatia's new national borders, I also consider the nature of Yugoslavia's disintegration, or "balkanization," as it has of course also been labeled. This term, which emerged from studies of Southeastern Europe, has come to connote rupture and fragmentation in geopolitical entities the world over. Its use reflects the focus of much political discourse, journalism, and scholarship on the creation of separate, often mutually hostile or fearful nation-states out of larger republics such as Yugoslavia, Ethiopia, Micronesia, Indonesia, and Sudan.[3] Just as notably, however, national independence has often been cause for intensification of communal ties and intimacy across the very borders it has erected.[4] I consider the affective work of making and narrativizing border crossings through musical performance in contexts of wartime danger and fears.

DANGEROUS PERFORMANCE

The most pressing territorial concern for such ensembles throughout the 1990s was the return to lands where tamburas had perceivably fallen silent. Armed conflict and bombing severely limited transport of passengers and mail via car and train, and Croatian media saturated their programs with fear-inspiring reports on the dangers of accessing contested regions (Povrzanović 1993, 140). Even for those in areas not directly affected by the encroaching Yugoslav forces, occupied Slavonian territories and cities in danger of capture and destruction became objects of longing tinged by threat. Several prominent tambura ensembles took advantage of opportunities to fight for, return to, and reclaim these territories. Their efforts to stabilize the state's outlying lands and borders were important not only for physically and symbolically instituting Croatian sovereignty but also for resurrecting access to communities in neighboring states, Central Europe, and North America.

The act of pushing toward the front lines and borders responded to the perceived and, for many tamburaši, physically experienced dangers of war. Svanibor Pettan notes that the war "brought together musicians and musical genres that would otherwise hardly be considered compatible. The shared necessity to neutralize the threat made folk musicians, opera singers, and rappers perform on the same occasions" (1998, 14). Music fulfilled three functions: encouraging "those fighting on the front lines and those hiding in shelters," provoking and humiliating "those seen as enemies," and calling on "those not directly endangered—including fellow citizens [and] the Diaspora" (13).

Often situated or originating in East Croatian regions that felt the war most heavily, tamburaši themselves spanned the spectrum of endangerment. Their responses often extended beyond such discursive functions to include direct physical, musical, and affective engagement with the war's dangers. Analyzing music's relationship to territories and deterritorialization, Deleuze and Guattari write that musical expression is "inseparable" from a minoritarian becoming "because of the 'danger' inherent in any line that escapes, in any line of flight or creative deterritorialization: the danger of veering toward destruction, toward abolition" ([1980] 1987, 299). "Music," furthermore, "has a thirst for destruction, every kind of destruction, extinction, breakage, dislocation. Is that not its potential 'fascism'?" (299). In taking up the call to arms (to arm themselves with instruments), tamburaši engaged affective, embodied flights toward the destruction of dangerous performance. Through the musical deterritorialization of wartime milieus and their own minoritarian becomings (Yugoslavs were becoming Croats), they simultaneously reterritorialized themselves as citizens of the new nation and physically assembled these milieus into a sovereign state.

Dangerous Media

In 1991–1992 many prominent professional tambura bands released war-themed musical media, such as Škoro's and Zlatni Dukati's videos for "Ne dirajte mi ravnicu," one of the period's most iconic tambura songs (see the introduction). The tambura band Dike (The Glories) released a similar video for "Oj Hrvatska Mati" (Oh Mother Croatia). They paired lyrics telling Croatia to "grieve not" (for the "falcons" will sacrifice themselves for *her*) with war footage and shots of the band in camouflage fatigues.[5] They reinforced their image as protective "falcons" by posing with helmets in a trench for a publicity photograph (reprinted in Ferić 2011, 259). Three of them hold their tamburas outstretched over the trench's lip, aiming them like rifles, while one reaches an arm overhead as though throwing a grenade. Another holds a tank ammunition round raised upward from his pelvic area, which along with the butt of the round remains hidden behind his nearby tambura bass. This suggestive image of wartime virility responded to "Serbia's 'masculine' and warlike [musical] self-representation," defending Croatia, which was symbolized as a "mother figure [who] is proud but also worried for her son/ defender" (Ceribašić 2000, 226, 230).

A number of tambura bands, including Agrameri, served in the war (Baker 2010, 36). Zlatni Dukati's members also attempted to enlist (Bonifačić 1998, 138), reinforcing tamburaši's perceived duty to protect and reclaim Croatian lands by any means at their disposal. The "rejection of their applications confirmed [. . .] the powerful propaganda role of patriotic songs and the activities of the *Zlatni Dukati* in a war-time situation," and the government instead had them perform "on the very front lines, and at numerous charity concerts" (138), mobilizing them as a political instrument, a territorializing machine of martial affect.

As numerous studies demonstrate, discursive and other symbolic practices concerning wartime musical performance significantly impacted Croatian ideologies and actions during this period (Bonifačić 1998; Pettan 1998; Hadžihusejnović-Valašek 1998; Ceribašić 2000; Bogojeva-Magzan 2005; Baker 2010). Catherine Baker in particular has privileged the discursive framing of the past and present in musical texts, devoting an entire chapter of her book to what she calls the Presidential narrative of the war (2010, 11). I examine here how musical affect and related material forces mobilized individual and social bodies in wartime and postwar territories, blocking and otherwise impinging on discourses (subalternating ubiquitous representations) and ultimately "circulating and transforming official and unofficial historical narratives" to render history "as a feeling" (Gray 2014, 9). I begin with discourses on danger, or *opasnost*, that emerged in popular music—and acutely in tambura music. I reexamine narratives and other discursive formulations cited by tamburaši (and earlier scholarship) through the lens of race and show how these contributed associatively to the affective capacities of playing dangerously and coalesced into narratives of territorial reclamation and heroism. Taking up Lila Ellen Gray's observation that "tidy chronologies and official historical narratives are sometimes displaced, giving way to a version of history that is such because it *feels* so" (9), I examine the particular dynamic of affective block that allows such feelings to dominate.

Narratives of the Push toward the Front Lines

Popular music groups referenced "danger" frequently in both wartime lyrics and discursive framings of their work for the armed resistance. For example, the rock band Opća Opasnost (Common Danger, a reference to Yugoslavia's shelling of Croatian cities) sang numerous songs about Croatia's war heroes. The band began forming in 1992 when two members were serving in Croatia's 131st Brigade, uniting poetic textual address with physical military action (Radio Našice 2011). Marko Perković "Thompson," whose rock career also started while he was serving in the Croatian Army and who, like Opća Opasnost, has collaborated with tamburaši, was criticized for lyrics suggesting aggressive military retaliation in Serbia in his hit war anthem "Bojna Čavoglave" (Čavoglave Battalion). Catherine Baker quotes a Croatian journalist defending the song as "'*not* giv[ing] off an atmosphere of malign aggressiveness' but just reflect[ing] the reality that 'life is dangerous'" (Kuzmanović 1992, translated in Baker 2010, 38). Aggression and atmosphere (see chapter 4) were already common descriptors of musical affect, suggesting the author's awareness of music's potential to move beyond representation to something more pernicious, even as she denied this particular song's culpability.

Opasnost and opasno ("dangerously") became closely associated with the war's effects during this time. In a wartime ethnography of Croatian public culture, Maja Povrzanović deemed fear "one of the most basic and intensive emotions" that "arises as an accompaniment to actual or anticipated danger" (1993, 121). Fear's intensity as a response to wartime dangers imbued musical performance in Croatia during this period with capacities for aesthetic and affective elaborations of trauma. In tambura and other popular music genres, opasno and opasnost registered as a theme for compositional response to the destruction of battle and bombardment, as one way in which "culture redefines objective situations of danger and threat" and "the terrifying become[s] domesticized, 'tamed', or, at least—familiar" (147). Yet even as fear and danger yielded some of their intensity through mediation, the musical vehicles for this redefinition simultaneously became less domesticized, tamed, and familiar, participating in an excitingly dangerous intimacy "formed around threats to the image of the world it seeks to sustain" (Berlant 1998, 288).

Alongside invading Yugoslav forces, whose government and peoples they came to represent, neotraditional Serbian "folk" genres such as newly composed folk music (Novokomonovana narodna muzika) and turbo-folk became common targets. Croatian musicians, critics, and journalists denounced these musics' encroachment on Croatian territories as dangerous. These genres have been popular among some Croats since before 1991. Yet as Catherine Baker demonstrates, Croatian media and society in general denigrated venues that played these musics as "dangerous places populated by gangsters, footballers, prostitutes and celebrities," and journalists "employed various strategies to mark folk clubs as other and dangerous, such as the use of flood/invasion metaphors" (2010, 149, 153). The tamburaš Veljko Škorvaga restarted Požega's "Golden Strings of Slavonia" tambura song festival in 1992 "to 'create new Croatian music' as 'a substitute for folk music, especially the newly-composed music we were bombarded with for years,'" "warn[ing] of 'a danger such a melos might return'" (Baker 2010, 67, citing Škorvaga in Topić 1992). "Pajo Kolarić's" directors restored their own festival with specifically Catholic overtones, citing Marin Srakić, assistant bishop of the Đakovo-Srijem diocese, on this beloved music's importance as an alternative to what he called the "racket" (*buka*) of the discotheques (STD "Pajo Kolarić" 1995, 51).

This music's perceived threat depended closely on its association with Serbs, whom official media often racialized as biologically foreign during this and earlier wars. Tomislav Longinović writes that the "abject position" of Serbs due to their historic colonial subjugation as "serfs" or "servants" (cognates of "Serb") "makes them 'black' despite their genetic 'whiteness' in the eyes of the West" (2000, 642). Although "Serbian treatment of the Ottoman colonial heritage [. . .] manifests European fear of contamination with an alien, 'oriental' civilization," their "turbo folk features the 'oriental' sound as the essence of racial being and belonging, which it appropriates from the culture of Ottoman invaders as a metaphor of its own colonial power over other Yugoslav ethnic groups" (642). Associations of such invasive, destructive power with Serbian popular music registered in a primary-school textbook's story of a boy who "had just started school when 'they', 'some kind of bearded army', arrived with 'strange songs' (as in the familiar news image of bearded Četnik paramilitaries occupying Vukovar) and 'destroyed my city'" (Baker 2010, 44, citing Pilas 1997, 102–103).

Allusions to beards drew on reinvigorated constructions of ethnic difference. These harkened back to stylistic and military opposition between World War II–era Ustašas (extreme Croat nationalists with clean-cut visages who resembled their Nazi allies and Catholic clergy) and Četniks (extreme Serb nationalists sporting beards styled after Ottoman-era Serbian *hajduk* bandits and Orthodox priests) (Hayden 2013, 7–8). Emphasis on Serbs' distinct physical features, including facial hair, dates back to the Ustašas' "aggressive, militant language [. . .] permeated by biological (and, therefore, materialistic) concepts, such as blood, race, and instinct" (Djilas 1991, 114). Though never formalized into a coherent racist theory, such language racialized Serbian enemies "in the same way in which the Nazis treated people they considered both racially inferior and racially dangerous" (119).

In Croatia in the early 1990s, similar sentiments registered beyond neo-Ustaša circles in popular songs about Četniks' physical, biological, and therefore racial or even taxonomic difference. "[P]*rimitives, non-humans, savages, hoofs* are common denotations in [sung] statements about the enemy, whose behavior is explained as an animalistic or demonic nature" (Prica 1993, 53). The cover of Zlatni Dukati's 1995 EP *Nema više suživota* (There's no more coexistence) similarly represented Serbs as horned demons whose long, pointed teeth merge into beards as the monsters writhe upward from a can bearing a Serbian banner and resting on a map of Croatia. In turn, Serbian sources sometimes demonized returning Croats as "vampires" who, for instance, reentered Vukovar "like a dance macabre" with "horns, songs and provocations" (Berić 1998, 92). In challenging what they perceived as the combined encroachment of Serbian propaganda, turbo-folk, and neo-Četniks, several tambura bands working within official media advanced a particularly effective discourse: the narrative reclaiming of Croatian lands from Serbia's physically dangerous army, politically dangerous media, and culturally dangerous music. As these and amateur ensembles confronted their fears and faced such external(ized) threats, feelings of intimacy and otherness also began to accrue around state media narratives of resisting Serbia as a racially dangerous people.

MUSICAL NARRATIVE AND AUTHORITY

To what extent, then, did such narratives also arise from the bottom up? Julia Kristeva notes that in much of Hannah Arendt's political philosophy, she distinguished from the ideological tyranny of the thinker-cum-politician an important form of "authority no longer based on the notion of domination but on that of a nature composed of differences" (2000, 67). Kristeva reminds us that "the discourse proper to this other authority [. . .] is, quite simply, narrative" (67). Narrative arises in service not of a sovereign singularity but of a unity of disparate subjects whose authority rests on a commonly analyzed and projected historical trajectory. As I argue here, the narrative of overcoming dangerous Others and their music using both rifles and tamburas resonated with Croat citizens for the authority and responsibility that it recognized and demanded at lower (nongovernmental) levels across the new country.

Philip Bohlman argues that "music intersects with nationalism not simply to narrate the past, but rather to contribute profoundly to the ways we perceive and understand the history of the present" (2008, 261). Michael Largey similarly writes that each of several "modes of cultural memory—recombinant mythology, vulgarization and classicization, diasporic cosmopolitanism, and music ideology—produces narratives that connect the present with an idealized past" (2006, 19). In 1990s Croatia, musicians', ideologues', and diasporic communities' narratives of reclaiming territories recognized internationally as Croatian, and of pushing beyond to proximate intimates constituting a projected "Greater Croatia," connected back to several periods embedded in nationalist cultural memory, each more idealized than the one succeeding it (see March 2013). In reverse chronological order, these include the short-lived, Axis-aligned Independent State of Croatia, formed in 1941; the Party of Rights's mid-nineteenth-century self-determination project, which inspired later, Nazi-aligned separatists; and the medieval reign of King Tomislav, whose territories the Party of Rights sought to reconstitute as a sovereign state (Gow 2003, 229n8). The authority and responsibility vested in Croats through such narratives in the 1990s were rooted in reflections upon this succession of actions and near-successes.

Bohlman also argues that music "expressed national aspirations even before the rise of the modern nation-state" and "charted the landscape of struggles and great events that would inscribe the fate of the nation on its history" (2008, 253). Croatia's past national movements were commemorated in nationalist musics long before it achieved independence. "[M]usical genres become narrative the moment they are enlisted in the service of the nation," and such service rather than the realization of national aspirations enables this inscription of fate (250). With the advent of nation-states, however, national music, in which "reinforcing borders is not a primary theme," shifted to nationalist music, which "often mobilises the cultural, even political, defence of borders" (250). The concern with territory and borders has certainly been a primary stake in Croatian musical nationalism and its engagement with the past. Yet Bohlman's own narrative of evolving deployments of musical national narratives warrants an additional observation that I proffer throughout this chapter: narration of (and via) musical events inscribes the nation's fate not only on its history but also on its present, which in war is lived and felt in service of the future (when the nation expects to fulfill its promised territorial defense or expansion). As suggested in Dubravka Ugrešić's evaluation of Croatian wartime ideology, this required narrative as well as physical violence: "In the name of the present, a war was waged for the past; in the name of the future, a war against the present. In the name of a new future, the war devoured the future" ([1995] 1998, 6).

The emphasis on futurity in both pushing through occupied territories toward Croatia's borders and narrating attempts and successes at realizing territorial sovereignty responded to physically proximate dangers and perceived threats. The fearsome, bearded, turbo-folk-driven, and sometimes racialized Četniks whom many Croatians perceived as threats certainly had their counterparts in actual Serb militiamen encountered in person or in official media. Their existence, however, frequently took on mythic qualities as racialization developed into animalization and demonization, paralleling the projection of a lack of human life onto Baranja and Eastern Slavonia (where only dangerous creatures were conceivable). The "fear of small numbers" provoked by minority Serb militias was all the greater for their perceived "cellular," nonvertebral organization, which "destabilizes [society's] two most cherished assumptions—that peace is the natural marker of social order and that the nation-state is natural guarantor and container of such order" (Appadurai 2006, 32–33). Narrations of musical and militaristic counters to perceived threats from within the nation-state, as well as actual armed attacks from the much larger Yugoslav army invasion, drew their force from the increasing intensity of experiences of fear (Povrzanović 1993). As Brian Massumi writes, "fear is the anticipatory reality in the present of a threatening future. It is the felt reality of the nonexistent, loomingly present as the *affective fact* of the matter" (2010, 54). Feeling the affective fact of threat as fear lent urgency to the actions (and their narration) through which musicians and other agents sought to create a future alternative to that which loomed in the presence of bearded Četniks. While actual histories of Četnik and Ustaša violence inflect narratives of future security, musical affect affords alternative moments of historical listening that block the rationalizable constructedness of cultural truths. This simultaneously makes cultural truths an aggregate of experience and understanding separate from (even subaltern to) affective fact and obstructs such truths' surfacing for conscious deconstruction.

The abundance of narratives of Croatia's push to reclaim and move beyond borderlands should not suggest a dwindling role for spatiality and materiality. Rather, discourse became imbricated with physical endeavors that must be considered simultaneously in order to ascertain their combined affective work in Croatian tambura music. As Michel Foucault has argued, "the production of discourse is at once controlled, selected, organized and canalized in every society [. . .] by way of certain procedures whose task it is to subdue the powers and dangers of discourse, to evade its heavy and threatening materiality" (1984, 10–11). Such materiality, I argue, threatens not merely in accompanying discourse (unless properly controlled) but also in organizing discourse, especially narrative, with a force that states may not ultimately succeed in canalizing. It is to nonstate actors' imbricated actions and narratives and their inspiration and divergence from official strategies that I now turn.

THE INTERNATIONAL FESTIVAL OF
CROATIAN TAMBURA MUSIC

Of the "Pajo Kolarić" children's and youth orchestras' several concerts in Croatia and nearby countries during the 2009–2010 school year, my longest fieldwork period, the most ambitious program was the society's weeklong International Festival of Croatian Tambura Music. Organized each summer in Osijek and in other Croatian cities and enclaves (such as Sombor, Serbia; Pécs, Hungary; and Parndorf, Austria), this juried, noncompetitive festival brings together numerous tambura choirs and children's, "junior" (youth), and "senior" (adult) tambura orchestras to perform for gold, silver, and bronze plaques.[6] I attended most of the 2010 festival's ten consecutive evening performances (May 14–23) and researched its history in archives in Osijek and Zagreb.

In 1961, seven years after its own founding, the STD "Pajo Kolarić" organized its first biennial Festival of the Tambura Music of Yugoslavia. Its eventual name change reflects a shift in the festival's orientation from pan-Yugoslavian outreach to an embrace of Croatia and its intimates that closely parallels political events in the late 1980s and 1990s. This history held particular weight for the festivals' organizers and participants, who quickly began to narrate its accomplishments in print.

In 1989 the festival still carried its original name, and booklets distributed to participants and audiences in the final years emphasize representation of ensembles from across Yugoslavia. The 1987 booklet states: "Our amateur-tamburaši from Subotica [Serbia], Varaždin [Croatia], Samobor [Croatia], Drniš and Posedarje [Dalmatia: Croatia's coastal region], even all the way to Artiče in Slovenia, have demonstrated a high level of professional musicianship" (STD "Pajo Kolarić" 1987, 1). The 1989 festival booklet welcomed "one more *druženje* of tamburaši from our entire dear homeland" and noted representation for most Yugoslav republics (STD "Pajo Kolarić" 1989, 5). The gerund *druženje* derives from *družiti se* ("to be friendly") and connotes "friendly associating." The booklet's author stressed active processes of mingling, but *druženje* may also have the more general quality of "intimacy," as it is also sometimes translated. Its root is *drug*, a noun used in Yugoslavia and later the Republic of Serbia to invoke a "comrade," though Croats would abandon the term in favor of the synonym *prijatelj* ("friend") as part of the Croatian language's cleansing in the early 1990s.[7] Having programmed ensembles from Croatia, Serbia, Slovenia, and Tuzla, Bosnia, the 1989 festival's organizers celebrated broadening Yugoslavia's tambura movement despite the growing financial crisis across Eastern Europe (7–8).[8] Their booklet's public articulation of *druženje* among Yugoslavia's many regions and peoples was in keeping with STD "Pajo Kolarić's" multiethnic composition and compliance with Yugoslav doctrine.

The 1991 festival did not convene, as militarization and violence that escalated from late 1990 led to full-scale war following Croatia's declaration of independence in June 1991. In 1992 the festival organizers and "Pajo Kolarić's" directors—with the exception of ethnic Serbs, one of whom told me that he could not work at "Pajo Kolarić" after the war's outbreak due to assumptions that he supported "Četnik" militias—moved the event to Križevci, near Zagreb, which unlike Osijek had not been heavily shelled. The festival's president, Professor Frano Dragun, wrote about their affective resilience, despite not being able to meet in Osijek, "the cradle of Croatian tambura":

> [B]arbarian hordes from the east and domestic Serbian highway robbers have disabled us [. . .] devastating all that which not one army had ruined since the Roman Empire and its Mursa [Osijek's antecedent.] Osijek has lost more than 800 of its Osijekans, and it has left more than 4,800 cripples on the conscience of those who have none at all. After all that our spirit is not destroyed. (STD "Pajo Kolarić" 1992, 6; my translation)

The event's name—XVth Festival of Tambura Music of the Republic of Croatia in Osijek—emphasized its now explicitly Croatian orientation while connecting it to its previous fourteen meetings in Osijek and downplaying the alternative location. The "idealized past" (Largey 2006, 19) of this festival's Croatian nature, implicit in the titular change, and the "inscri[ption of] the fate of the nation on its history" (Bohlman 2008, 253), evident in Dragun's narration of Osijek's enduring "spirit" over centuries of conquest, established an important connection between Croatian culture and spirit (whose Christian overtones I also explore in this chapter). These immaterial essences had remained and, Dragun suggested, would continue despite the physical destruction of buildings and people.[9] The short 1992 festival comprised three concerts featuring nine orchestras from unoccupied Croatian regions. The only foreign ensemble was Slovenia's group from the previous two festivals: the largely Croatian orchestra "Oton Župančić," which performed as a guest of the festival. The festival's geographically and ethnically narrower focus functioned as a bastion of Croatian culture, identity, and resilience in the midst of wartime violence.

REEXPANSION OF THE FESTIVAL

During the 1990s the festival's media outlined an agenda for, and narrated, its expansion in two successive stages: (1) the festival's return to Croatian cities ravaged and/or occupied during the war and (2) the inclusion of ensembles from Croatia's intimates. I examine the second of these in a later section. The first stage began in October 1992, when the organizers arranged a special, nonjuried performance in the church on Osijek's main square by three of the festival's participating orchestras: "Pajo Kolarić," Križevci's ensemble, and "Ferdo Livadić" from Samobor. Reflecting on the event the following year, president Frano Dragun wrote that the

> performance in the Church of Saints Peter and Paul (popularly [known as] the Cathedral), the speech and the holy Mass of the illustrious bishop [. . .], will remain permanently in the hearts and memory of numerous Osijekans, church dignitaries, the government and other guests. At last the tamburica, as our Croatian national instrument, has very successfully entered the sacral building. (STD "Pajo Kolarić" 1993, 6; my translation)

The festival's return to Osijek reclaimed not only the bombarded city but also the Croatian Catholic Church. Religious institutions' ostracism and official separation from socialist society had largely prevented public church concerts for decades. It had also been difficult to perform concerts honoring only Croatian musicians, instruments, and folklore within the doctrine of multinational Yugoslavian folklore, and "enter[ing] the sacral building" for a nationalistic concert doubly reclaimed space formerly under Yugoslavian legal and military control. Local Serbs, furthermore, were unlikely to attend a performance in a Croatian Catholic church, and selecting the "Cathedral" for the principally public concert effectively placed it in a space out of reach of the "enemy," whether construed as Orthodox Serbs or atheistic Yugoslavs.[10]

This concert in Osijek's largest Catholic church took place just four months after the bombardment of the city had ceased, and the war's dangers and destruction were readily apparent to all who resumed playing there. The Croatian National Theater, which hosted many of the 1989 festival's concerts, was heavily damaged by bombing in November 1991. Its position almost directly across Županijska Street from the "Cathedral" made its ravaged halls a poignant reminder of Osijek's yearlong devastation. As ethnologist Lela Roćenović of the Samobor museum notes, the tambura orchestra "Ferdo Livadić" changed performance sites for her city's 750th anniversary that year because the organizers were "well aware that public opinion would condemn playing and singing near the commemorative board" of the borough's fallen soldiers (Roćenović 1993, 161). "Ferdo Livadić" and other participants' subsequent performance in Osijek's main church thus fit a broader pattern of relocating celebratory music from sites attesting to the war's human and architectural casualties. Significantly, they chose a church: a space that had endured, both physically and spiritually, the socialist period and Yugoslav conflicts and that contrasted with the secular, physically compromised theater.

Osijek's theater was only restored to performance condition in 1994, and several alternative spaces, often literally underground, harbored Osijek's musical activity even before the bombing's cessation. Recording and airing new pop songs symbolically resisted the bombing, and particular "importance was placed at that time on the creative act of composing" (Hadžihusejnović-Valašek 1998, 169). A "rich palette of musical events [. . .] took place at that time," developing further in the months after the bombardment with events such as the festival's culminating "Cathedral" concert (176).

The symbolic reclamation by STD "Pajo Kolarić" of Croatian territory continued in May 1993, when the event (now larger and renamed the Festival of Croatian Tambura Music in Osijek) returned home. It has continued to meet there annually ever since (twice as often as before the war). Affirming the connection between musical activity and the war effort, Frano Dragun wrote of the "massive" 1993 festival that "in spite of the proximity of the [war's] front line, economic hardships, and internal and international tensions, WE are showing them our Croatian supremacy, so on the front line, thus also in culture" (STD "Pajo Kolarić" 1993, 6; my translation). The 1993 festival also featured a Mass with tambura music in the "Cathedral." Duško Topić, who prepared a special tambura accompaniment (Hadžihusejnović-Valašek 1998, 180), directed the performance by the Folklore Choir and Orchestra of his recently renamed Croatian Cultural-Artistic Society "Osijek 1862" (hereafter HKUD "Osijek 1862").[11] The festival's many orchestras from all over Croatia, even Dalmatia (where tambura music historically was not prominent), evinced widening interest in the tambura as a Croatian instrument within "national integration ideology" and in reviving Croatian patriotic and religious songs banned in Yugoslavia (Bogojeva-Magzan 2005, 108–109). As Ruža Bonifačić argues, this growing interest was due in part to the military and political involvement of professional bands such as Zlatni Dukati, whose service helped establish them as Croatia's most popular musicians (1998, 138).

Such ideology and support for military and political resistance to Yugoslavia are also evident in Dragun's selection and capitalization of the pronoun "WE." This term held a particularly territorializing capacity in 1990s Croatia, since "boundaries and territory, the key issues at stake in Eastern Slavonia, were fundamental to establishing or reinforcing a distinctive Croatian national identity—a means of defining the distinctions between 'us' and 'them'" (Klemenčić and Schofield 2001, 48). The pronoun "I" largely disappeared from Croatian popular music, becoming associated with Serbian romantic songwriter subjectivities (Crnković 2001, 38), while "us," "we," and especially "our" strongly encapsulated "the abstract nation" during the 1990s (45). Citizens' common term of endearment for Croatia became *lijepa naša* (our beautiful), an abbreviation of the Croatian national anthem "Our Beautiful Homeland."

In this way citizens constituted discursively and through physical acts of proximity and intimacy what Alexei Yurchak has termed a "public of *svoi* [ours]" (2005, 116).[12] In postsecession Croatia, however, the result was not the deterritorialized milieu of Yurchak's Soviet public but a territorialization of public sociality through the state, its lands, and its borders. Discursive formulations of "us" and "them" in the former Yugoslavia most typically connote racial or ethnic (as opposed to gender or age) distinction. Interlocutors frequently asked me *Jesi li naš?* ("Are you ours?"). This question can pertain to shared ethnicity or shared citizenship, but the latter is folded into the former, since Croats abroad acquire citizenship by virtue of ethnicity. Croats who learned that I was not from the Croatian diaspora often expressed surprise that a non-Croat would research "their" music. As I argued previously, this territorialization itself was a means of becoming by virtue of setting the minoritarian "WE" onto new lines of flight from the majoritarian Yugoslav collective. This went hand in hand with racializations of Serbian Others, surfacing both in explicit discourse on biological difference and in more broadly interpretable commentaries on belonging based on ethnicity and citizenship ("WE are showing them our Croatian supremacy").

This division into a culturally supreme "us" and a musically, militarily, and at times racially inferior "them" paralleled popular songs' emphasis on religious and ethnic differences (Baker 2010, 25). Following Ceribašić (2000), Baker notes that gender, too, framed important distinctions, though implicitly (within narrative roles rather than within "us" and "them" narratives); women mostly sang emotional and prayerful rather than expository songs, though they "were more likely to be 'expository' than men purely 'emotional'" (2010, 28). Of Meri Cetinić's famous "Zemlja dide mog" (My granddad's country), Baker comments: "Cetinić's narrator remembered her grandfather telling her about 'people not like us' and looked to a day when a well-known person (presumably a euphemism for an enemy who did not need naming) would want to take the land. 'We' would not let go of it" (28). The juxtaposition of an unnamed, hostile Other with a specified "us" parallels the contrast in detail between an unspecified *zlotvor* (evildoer) and the concrete agents "we," "Šokci," and "peaceful people" in male artists' recordings such as "Tell the World the Truth about Baranja" (whose call for the Drava and Danube Rivers to address the world draws closely on "Our Beautiful Homeland's" plea for the Drava, Sava, Danube, and sea to tell the world of the Croat's love for his people).

For Arendt, as Kristeva writes, the "essence of narration" is not "coherence intrinsic to the narrative, that is, as the art of storytelling"; what matters instead "is to recognize the moment of the achievement and to identify the agent of the history/story" (Kristeva 2000, 55). The emphasis on "us/we/ours" in narrative songs, festival publications, and government proclamations and agendas recognized and proclaimed the agents of Croatian wartime resilience. History is necessarily idealized as the narrator constructs a narrative out of "true history"; as Kristeva herself argues, the "art of narrative lies in its ability to condense the action down to an exemplary period of time, to take it out of the continuous flux, and to reveal a who" (55). Thus the "who/we," through this revelation, becomes separated from "them." Idealized histories of past distinction interject to confirm the truth of racial and religious difference, despite or perhaps in response to the decades-long propagation of alternative truths in Yugoslavia. The created agent's remainder—the Other—becomes an all-too-familiar, perhaps intimately known, yet ultimately unnamable enemy or barbarian, for to name it would be to create another "who." At most, such media reduce enemies to the pronoun "they" (*oni*), which in Croatian and Serbian is also the deictic "those" and thus "function[s] in a heightened indicative way" (Tomlinson 2015, 311n1). Only intimate, wartime knowledge of the Other makes the term sensible. Unlike "we" (*mi*), *oni* implies distance, either physical or personal, for to apply this pronoun rather than proper names to those present is considered rude (Đurašković 2007). "We" is the agent of an ever-new narrative and the subject of an intimate becoming that generates closeness with others who are "ours" and distances those who are not, while "they/those" is the term of an intimately distant minor presence.[13]

Yet an agent—a "who"—does not suffice to generate narrative. As Kristeva writes: "The actor alone, no matter how heroic his exploit, does not constitute the marvelous action. Action is marvelous only if it becomes memorable. [. . .] It is the spectators who bring the story/history to completion, and they do so by virtue of the thought that comes after the act, and this is accomplished via recollection" (2000, 54). The constant acts of spectation, audition, and recollection that contributed to the narratives of independent Croatia involved, first, the narrators themselves: pedagogues and tambura promoters such as the festival's president, Frano Dragun, and songwriters such as Antun Nikolić "Tuca." Yet they soon sought ever broader publics: festival participants, local audiences (the public of *svoi*), the state, its citizens, its intimates (near and far), and finally the "world." Reaching spectators beyond the local and prompting their thoughts and recollections required further acts: moving into occupied lands and reestablishing physical contact with communities beyond territories under Croatia's legal or practical sovereignty. These acts in turn warranted further recollection and narration. Thus within narratives of Croatian resilience and territorial reclamation we can recognize deep dependence on physical acts, not just as sources of histories/stories, but also as a means of producing actors and spectators. In this oscillation between discursive and physical endeavors, musicians and audiences heightened and blocked in aggregate one another's divinely guided affective resilience (spirit) as they reterritorialized themselves on the Croatian state.

FORMERLY OCCUPIED TERRITORIES AND CROATIA'S INTIMATES AT THE FESTIVAL

Building a resilient population and state demanded new spectators and agents, and the widening of participation in tambura music within Croatia also extended to involving Croatia's intimates. Starting in 1993, the CFU provided general sponsorship for the festival. For the 1994 festival, which officially convened "under the auspices of the Republic of Croatia's president Dr. Franjo Tuđman," CFU president Bernard Luketich wrote: "We are especially honored that this year's Festival theme is 'all for one, one for all' because it has also been the slogan of our Union for one hundred straight years" (STD "Pajo Kolarić" 1994, 69; my translation). Luketich specifically mentioned Osijek as an important guardian of the Croatian tambura tradition, and he had a close personal connection to its festival; Željko Čiki, assistant to the festival's president (later its president, and executive director of the HKUD "Osijek 1862"), was also godfather to Luketich's grandson, Derek Luketich Hohn, who became a well-known semiprofessional tambura musician and instructor in Pittsburgh.

The war was not over in 1994. The Yugoslavian Army would shell Zagreb in 1995 in retaliation for Croatia's Operation Flash offensive, which retook lands held by the Republika Srpska Krajina (Republic of Serbian Krajina, or Borderland). Battles were renewed over parts of the Krajina along the Bosnian border, which significant Serbian populations had assisted in temporarily seceding from Croatia; these eventually terminated with the signing of peace agreements in Erdut, Croatia, and Dayton, Ohio. Osijek's troops participated in these efforts, but the violence was now no longer close to their own homes.

As Osijek's own wartime suffering subsided, songwriters and festival publications refocused their attention on nearby territories recently occupied by the Yugoslavian army and subsequently (until 1998) controlled by the United Nations Transitional Authority in Eastern Slavonia, Baranja and Western Sirmium (UNTAES). As Baker notes, during the siege of Vukovar, Zlatni Dukati and its manager/arranger Josip Ivanković began releasing new songs about this severely damaged East Croatian city, which was close to their hometowns. They declared in the magazine *Arena*: "We will be the first to enter Vukovar with tamburas! We played in that holy Croatian city last and that power does not exist that can impede us in this intention" (Stažić 1995; also cited in Baker 2010, 41; my translation). The description of Vukovar as "holy" is significant, as the reestablishment of religious practice was closely associated with Croatian independence and tambura music and resembles Frano Dragun's earlier statement about the tambura reentering Osijek's "sacral building." Using music to reclaim occupied territories, make these achievements audible on Croatian media, and hail a public of spectators/auditors to validate these feats through their narration became a common and religiously charged endeavor in the mid-1990s.

The 1996 festival booklet discusses the organizers' desire to move the festival into occupied territories. Frano Dragun noted that they were holding the festival under

> complicated socio-political and economic conditions. A part of *Lijepa naša* that is situated immediately alongside us still is not free. Consequently we cannot also present part of our Festival's program in our Croatian and once beautiful [city of] Vukovar, the picturesque Ilok or the rich Beli Manastir.
>
> But, we firmly believe that we will realize our idea [. . .] in 1997. (STD "Pajo Kolarić" 1996, 9; my translation)

To support this idea and tambura music's further spread throughout Croatia, the organizers of the festival decided to reinstate the Croatian Tambura Alliance

(CTA) in Osijek. They emphasized *renewing* rather than *creating* the 1937 Alliance, which had ceased to exist after World War II "due to well-known reasons"—a reference to the abolition of specifically Croatian institutions in postwar Yugoslavia, whose coded nonrecognition (non-narration) resembles the non-naming of well-known enemies in 1990s Croatian songs (STD "Pajo Kolarić" 1996, 8). Plans for the upcoming festival's move into occupied territories were foremost among the renewed CTA's concerns.

The publication's other stated purpose, however, was supporting ensembles that at that time largely had to secure musical and financial resources on their own. Many school, amateur, and professional ensembles in Croatia that had received direct or indirect institutional support and financial subsidies from the socialist Yugoslavian state struggled to remain active in the postsocialist era. Naila Ceribašić explains that "folkloric amateurism" received "various funds at state and local levels," but that companies also

> formerly had an obligation—whether in the sense of a dictate or an unwritten rule—to aid cultural activities in their region financially, including folkloric ones. Today's businesses, however, are entirely independent in deciding whether, how much and under what conditions to aid financially this or that cultural program. [. . .] [T]hey are led by interest in their own promotion, which in practice results in aid to *folklorni amaterizam* being almost negligible. (2013, 153; my translation)

"With decreased financing," Ceribašić continues, "it often happens that members of a society themselves cover some part of these expenses" (154). Maša Bogojeva-Magzan argues that with the transition to private enterprise, the state could not take on more of this support itself "because of economic instability and great damage after the recent war in Croatia, [and] many amateur and professional cultural and/or folk societies ceased to exist" (2005, 77–78).

The war sometimes caused this change even more directly: factories that had supported performing ensembles with leadership and rehearsal space closed due to damage or workforce losses in the early 1990s. Topić's HKUD "Osijek 1862" was able to continue because the socialized sugar plant that hosted it survived, transitioning successfully to a limited liability company structure within post-1989 Croatia's somewhat more capitalistic system (HKUD "Osijek 1862" 2014). By 2009, however, the society also needed to collect annual dues from my fellow performing members and me. STD "Pajo Kolarić" similarly benefited from association with a software company then run by this society's president (and employing one of its directors), although this more informal relationship began after the wars' end. Many schools and KUDs lacked necessary materials, despite promises from purportedly supportive state employees such as a Croatian television editor's statement that his "mission [would] be over when each school [would] have a *tamburica* orchestra" (quoted in Pettan 1998, 16). This posed a challenge to the state's canalization of narratives of Croatian national development, bringing to bear a "threatening materiality" on official support proclamations. Ultimately, the CTA's support of ensembles without state funding or wealthy industrial benefactors became essential to implementing the pan-Croatian festivals that the organization hoped to realize in 1997.

The CTA and "Pajo Kolarić" leadership achieved the return to eastern Slavonia not in 1997 but in 1998, when territorial sovereignty passed from UNTAES to the Croatian government, enabling the organizers to hold the festival in Beli Manastir and Ilok, in addition to Osijek. Frano Dragun utilized the CTA's new journal, *Croatian Tamburica: Organ for the Promotion of Tambura Music*, to secure further audiences for his society's ongoing actions and narrations. He called the Beli Manastir and Ilok concerts great successes and noted that the congregation of Croatian tamburaši in Ilok was particularly memorable because 90 percent of the musicians were able for the first time in their young lives to see Ilok's famed Bulwarks and Church of St. John of Capistrano (Dragun 1999, 17). They had also planned to perform in Vukovar, "the symbol of Croatian opposition," but practical realities of playing in war-ravaged buildings prevented this (17). The return to formerly occupied territories and their war-ravaged tambura venues often stopped short of placing performers, particularly children, in actual physical danger. As Catherine Baker notes (2010, 41), mediated rather than live tambura performance returned as Radio Vukovar relocated to the "holy city" after broadcasting patriotic songs in the unscathed city of Vinkovci for five years (commencing in 1992 with Zlatni Dukati's lament "Vukovar, Vukovar" and concluding in 1997 with Dike's "Good Morning, Wonderful Vukovar," the station's first postwar Vukovar broadcast). The fact that some of these professional musicians played and served on the front lines helped to reinforce the significance of youth orchestras playing in formerly threatened, dangerous, and therefore all the more precious national regions and performance halls when they returned in 1998.

Croatian Tamburica also included entries from directors of participating ensembles on the importance to themselves and to their students of performing in formerly occupied cities. They discussed their ensembles' nonfestival activities, too, including performances for wounded and disabled veterans. The unifying theme of the journal's first issue was how ensembles moved throughout the now fully sovereign republic, connecting musicians from disparate regions with one another, with locations damaged and/or kept distanced by war, and with soldiers who had protected and regained Croatian territories.

Croatian Tamburica's mention of veterans and foreign/occupied communities reflects a broader, national media trend of invoking them as inspiration for the fight for Croatian territorial sovereignty within its post–World War II borders (more rarely for the Greater Croatia envisioned by the Ustaša regime). The HDZ mobilized occupied territories and wounded veterans alongside tambura music throughout the 1990s to foster nationalist sentiment and garner electoral support (see Ottaway 2003, 117–129; Baker 2010, 26). The CTA actions that *Croatian Tamburica* celebrated fully supported the state's "strategic narrative" (Price 2011) of actively rebuilding the country through military and cultural programs that the CTA believed would reunite separated territories and heal the population's physical and emotional traumas.

INTERLUDE: CULTURAL INTIMACY AND TWENTY YEARS OF EUROPEAN ASPIRATIONS

The fact that such ensembles typically still supported this narrative and reified the state as a noble monolithic entity in their narratives suggests an enduring "cultural intimacy" (Herzfeld 1997) wherein discontent with waning state structural and financial support ultimately reaffirmed cultural organizations' "national frame of reference" (Ferguson 2006, 64). Sustaining this intimacy in part was a shared vision of an independent Croatia connected to *its* foreign enclaves. By the late 1990s, professional tamburaši were supporting this agenda in nonstate capacities: playing for weddings in Herzegovina and recommencing North American CFU tours. The high demand for them among Croatia's intimates and access there to cheaper goods and higher, untaxed, gray-market incomes have bolstered musicians' cultural intimacy with a Croatian state that has successfully grounded the affective and cultural attachments of a large national network but not secured the idealized financial independence to which its government and citizens aspire (MacMillen 2011a).

Striving for the comparative economic and political stability of the West European and North American countries that house its wealthier intimates was also closely tied up in Croatia's projected destiny to "be one of Europe's stars," as Tomislav Ivčić described European Union (EU) accession in his famous pop ballad "Stop the War in Croatia" (1993). The ambivalent, culturally intimate affection among state, tambura players, and public came to a head around this very issue two decades later. On June 30, 2013, the eve of Croatia's accession, I stood among thousands who had gathered to count down to midnight at the official music and dance celebration in Zagreb's central square. It became strikingly clear that official culture now also at times specifically excises tambura music's potentially embarrassing side from public displays (see MacMillen 2011a). Of the many popular, folk, classical, and avant-garde groups that performed short segments that night, the only appearance of a tambura was a very brief performance during a procession of *kraljice* ("queens") by a folk musician on a *samica*. Tamburaši consider this solo tambura closer to the tambura's pre-nineteenth-century form than the modern, guitar-shaped Srijem tamburas. The organizers did not bring out a tambura band to sing nostalgically about the country's rural past or embracing of conservative sentiments in the 1990s; rather, the ceremony featured a solo instrumental tambura player who, along with other folk instrument performers but distinct from the evening's globally oriented rock acts, celebrated folklore as the nation's eternal wellspring.

The moment when the country finally completed its long-projected teleology was evidently a time for the state to present internationally, including to foreign Croat enclaves, a version of itself that is musically compatible with Western Europe. Yet this version excluded the very bands whose tours had helped sustain CFU donations—for example, humanitarian aid to Croatia's war victims, totaling more than $150,000,000 by its own estimates (Croatian Fraternal Union 2014)—and thus facilitated the country's path to independence and accession. Then president Ivo Josipović would meet just a few days later to discuss further donations with CFU leaders, who were in Zagreb for their Junior Cultural Federation's tambura festival (see chapter 5). Tambura bands' and the government's parallel turning to resources from Croatia's intimates and mutual embarrassment over one another's "backwards" (*naopako*) politics and structures (MacMillen 2011a) shored up their culturally intimate relations with the state as the assumed agent of national organization.

OUTREACH TO CROATIA'S INTIMATES
IN THE LATE 1990S

Croatian Tamburica highlighted its affiliated ensembles' work for such national and European aspirations in the form of outreach to foreign territories. This project served HDZ's aims, as it relied heavily on financial investments from Croat populations abroad (see Hockenos 2003). Frano Dragun writes:

> A special interest of last year's Festival [. . . was] to watch and listen to Czech performers [. . . the ensemble from] Artiče (Slovenia), a TO [Tambura Orchestra] from Nuremberg and the small ensemble "Senjo" from Kreševo (Federation of Bosnia and Herzegovina). [. . .] Osijek is once again recognized as the very source and center of an international tambura movement. (1999, 17; my translation)

The narratives of reclaiming Croatian territories through musical performance and of Osijek's reemergence as an international tambura music hub went hand in hand. Of the nine concerts held over the now lengthier festival, this Osijek performance featuring foreign orchestras and two Croatian orchestra concerts in formerly occupied cities received special attention in the festival booklets and the journal.

Most foreign orchestras that again began participating in Osijek's festival were themselves largely Croatian in membership and orientation, including (in 1998) those from Slovenia, Bosnia and Herzegovina, and Germany.[14] Their involvement was growing; two of them had performed in 1995 and only one in 1992. Tambura music practice's deliberate broadening throughout Yugoslavia's lands and peoples evolved into a practice of selectively inviting Croatian ensembles from beyond the country's borders. These were mostly situated among Croat enclaves in the diaspora or in lands now foreign but once more easily imaginable as Croatian. Rare exceptions, such as the Czech orchestra, were from lands and ethnic groups of relatively little political consequence to the former Yugoslavia.

In 1995 the festival's organizers called attention to the war's ongoing hardships and dangers. These had reduced the festival's international scope but then been overcome by bringing ensembles from "two independent and internationally recognized states, our neighbors: Bosnia and Herzegovina (Tuzla) and Slovenia (Artiče)" (STD "Pajo Kolarić" 1995, 9). Noting that Tuzla's group had participated in 1989, the program highlights how "in 1992, the aggression against B[osnia] and H[erzegovina] interrupts their inbound trajectory [with] grenades, hunger, power outages, [but] soon they are back to work and onstage. In 1994 at the first New Year's 'Liberated' concert, the tamburaši demonstrate how the tambura sounds in the hands of those who love, feel and experience it themselves" (51). The narrative of overcoming wartime dangers through sonic liberation emphasizes tamburaši's musical feeling and experience as a block to aggression and to counternarratives of Serbian domination, reframing the latter as a brief physical interruption outlasted in affective continuity.

TRAVEL TO CROATIA'S INTIMATES

In the late 1990s many Croatian tamburaši also began to cross their young country's borders, visiting once again the communities of support and patronage available to them in Croatia's intimates. One case of a prominent musician's activity in a nearby foreign enclave particularly warrants consideration here before I return to the development of amateur orchestras' international programs. In 1995, after hearing him speak on the radio, President Franjo Tuđman invited tambura singer Miroslav Škoro to serve the HDZ, naming him first general consul of the Republic of Croatia in Pécs, the capital of Hungary's Baranya County (Škoro 2010, 138–142).

The consulship began less than two months after the bombing of Zagreb and the escalation of violence in other regions that Yugoslav or militia forces controlled. Pécs and other southern Hungarian cities with long-standing Croatian communities were providing refuge to Croatian citizens newly displaced by the war. At the 2010 festival's concert in Pécs, a member of the leadership of "Pajo Kolarić" whose son played in its orchestra recalled seeing more Croats than Hungarians on the streets there during the war. Škoro worked with Pécs's Croatian residents and war refugees, and he describes seeking funds to bus the Pécs Croatian Theater into Croatia on a guest trip (2010, 143–144). "There's no [money], it was always the same answer. Several times I paid out of my own pocket. I didn't understand how there was always [money] for cheese, prosciutto, ash trays and neckties, but never for a bus" (144). Heavily bureaucratic and seemingly arbitrary distribution of funds and associated problems with corruption, around which he notes maneuvering in the diplomatic service (144), sometimes hindered programs between Croatia and its intimates. Yet HDZ-appointed patriotic artists such as Škoro facilitated connections among Croatia, parts of the broader Croatian geography once continuous with Croatia in Austria-Hungary (Croatian Baranja and Hungarian Baranya formed a single region through World War I), and diasporic communities such as those of Škoro's Croatian American in-laws. While shoring up culturally intimate conceptions of the state as embarrassingly corrupt yet essential, however, these material shortcomings also threatened its discursive control. This placed greater responsibility on local music ensembles throughout Croatia and its intimates to constitute themselves as an authority "of a nature composed of differences," not of state domination, and to employ their own narratives as "the discourse proper to this other authority" (Kristeva 2000, 67).

The directors of "Pajo Kolarić," their festival's organizers, and other Croatian ensembles also began to seek collaborations abroad and turned to Croat communities. A number of Croatian orchestras partnered with individual Croat enclaves' religious or musical institutions. The Tambura Orchestra of Zagreb's Matija Gubec Elementary School, in addition to making appearances at the Festival of Croatian Tambura Music and charity concerts for war veterans, performed a tambura Mass in the Croat Burgenland town Jarovce (known to Croats as Croatian Jandrof) near Bratislava, Slovakia (Ećimović 1999, 11). "Pajo Kolarić" partnered with ensembles in Mohács (also in Hungarian Baranya) and in the Croat enclave in the Burgenland town of Parndorf, Austria.

One of the most significant steps, however, came about through a relatively recent development in "Pajo Kolarić" and the CTA's annual festival. In 2009, for the festival's thirty-second meeting, the CTA held concerts in Parndorf and Pécs and renamed it the International Festival of Croatian Tambura Music in Osijek.[15] For each of these concerts, a local Croat host ensemble secured performance space, advertised the event to Croat residents, and performed. The festival became "international" by networking with ensembles in Croatia's intimates: one in the diaspora (Parndorf) and one in a geographically proximate intimate (Pécs). The narrative of reclaiming occupied territories and Catholic churches as spaces for tambura performance and of reuniting with Croats displaced by dispersion or geopolitical boundaries culminated with replacing the festival's former pan-Yugoslavian reach with a new network spanning Croatia and several intimates.

ETHNIC DIVERSITY

May 2010: The thirty-third festival featured concerts in Pécs and Sombor. The latter city is situated in Vojvodina, Northern Serbia's semiautonomous province, in the ethnographic region of Bačka, and has a sizable Croat minority. The Parndorf ensemble continued to participate in the festival and also performed nonfestival concerts (with "Pajo Kolarić" members in attendance) in Parndorf. The festival organizers, however, wished to build upon the festival's international character and sought out contacts in Sombor rather than repeating the Parndorf festival meeting.

I traveled to the Sombor concert by bus with "Pajo Kolarić's" president Antun, his wife Gordana, the society's secretary, Vesna, and Junior Tambura Orkestar Krste Odaka from the city of Drniš in Croatia's Dalmatian hinterland. Milka, the Drniš orchestra's director, led the bus in a prayer to the Virgin Mary for safe travels. Most passengers participated, alternately reciting in tandem with her and responding with brief confirmations of faith to passages that she alone delivered.

The other festival performers at Sombor City House's Great Hall were the Tambura Orchestra of Sombor's Music School "Petar Konjović," the senior orchestra of KUD "Oton Župančić," and the junior orchestra of Zagreb's KUD "Gaj." The Sombor orchestra was hosting but not officially participating in that evening's juried performances, so they played only three short instrumental (classical and arranged folklore) pieces. The other orchestras each performed three similar numbers from or styled after the common practice era. These fulfilled the festival's requirements for "a composition from the concert tambura literature"; "A premiere of a concert composition for tambura orchestra"; and "one of the recommended compositions," which included fantasias, symphonic movements, romances, fugues, and symphonic poems by Croatian composers with 2010 jubilee birth or death anniversaries (STD "Pajo Kolarić" 2010; my translation).[16] Each group accompanied a vocalist, an essential jury criterion.

Ensembles commonly contributed nonjuried performances at additional festival stops to fill out an evening's worth of music. In Pécs, both the junior tambura orchestra of "Pajo Kolarić," which had already been judged, and the hosting Tambura Orchestra of the Croatian School "Miroslav Krleža" gave such performances. Ensembles from Našice and Virovitica, Croatia, played nonjuried festival programs at other Croatian sites. Thus groups congregated musically and socially on multiple evenings, often in several countries.

Most instrumental compositions and song arrangements performed at the festival are by Croatian composers of the past two centuries. Four of the ensembles participating in Pécs and Sombor played pieces by tambura composer, conductor, musicologist, and festival organizer/jury member Julije Njikoš (1924–2010). These included symphonic poems (e.g., portraying the Drava River), settings of Croatian poetry, and arrangements of classic Croatian songs. Njikoš spoke after the performance about the tambura as the Croats' national instrument (which he claimed predated Russians' adoption of the balalaika as such); the Bačka region's significance for this music; and the importance of increasing the festival's international scope to include the Burgenland and now, happily, Sombor. In Pécs he had similarly expounded on the tambura's nineteenth-century spread from Croatia to Bosnia, Slovenia, the Burgenland, and Hungarian Baranya; its importance to the Croatian subgroups Šokci and Bunjevci; and his hope that Pécs's ensemble would participate fully in the 2011 festival by performing for the jury in Osijek.

Following the Sombor concert, we dined with the other ensembles, including the "Oton Župančič" orchestra director from Artiče, Slovenia, and soon a discussion of ethnicity started among them and our Sombor hosts. Many of Sombor's Catholic Slavs identify as Šokci (singular Šokac, feminine Šokica). This Croatian subgroup lives primarily in Western Vojvodina and Slavonia (where they appear in numerous song texts such as Slavonski Bećari's "Istinu svijetu, o Baranji reci"), and the stage backdrop that evening had read *Urbani* (Urban) Šokci Sombor. "Šokci" likely derives from a name that Orthodox Serbs invented for their Catholic neighbors; although the latter considered it a derogatory name as recently as the eighteenth century, by the twentieth century the Šokci had appropriated it proudly as a marker of distinction from both Serbs and other Catholic groups, even Croatian ones (Fine 2006, 503).[17] In Sombor the "Pajo Kolarić" president, Antun, proclaimed his Šokac background, while the secretary, Vesna, indicated coming from different Croat stock; it was evident from Antun's affirmation of commonality with Vojvodina's Šokci that while Vesna's heritage was no source of tension, Šokac identity played a role in collaborations between Croatia's and Vojdina's Croat musicians. Upon our arrival at the concert hall our hostess, the Sombor orchestra director, had introduced herself as a Šokica, and Antun added to me that she was the "greatest Šokica." Later, when welcoming the various ensembles to the performance, she repeatedly mentioned connections among the various communities of Šokadija, despite most of that evening's performers having traveled there from beyond this "land of the Šokci" (which straddles Croatian Slavonia and Serbian Bačka).

The Sombor organizer who brought up the issue at dinner also noted the frequent ill will between Šokci and Bunjevci. The Bunjevci also reside in the Sombor area; although they mostly identify as Croats, some have suggested that they are Serbs, with whom they associate closely and share some religious observances, despite generally practicing Catholicism rather than Orthodoxy (see Hofman and Marković 2006, 316). Antun agreed with the organizer's assessment, commenting that it had been easier to coordinate this concert with the Music School "Petar Konjović's" Tambura Orchestra because of the Šokci there.

To a certain extent, people in central and coastal Croatia associate tambura music with the Šokci, who in Croatia are prominent only in Slavonia. This region has the greatest concentration of tambura bands and orchestras actively performing in public, including each weekend at the Šokački Disko "Tom Tom" in Đakovo, Croatia. The Sto Tamburaša (One Hundred Tamburaši) concert that the Croatian Tambura Orchestra performs annually in Zagreb similarly is titled "Šokac Rhapsody." Šokac identity is particularly important to tamburaši in Osijek, the site of a recurring international round table, "Urban Šokci." In 2007, participants from Slavonia, Zagreb, Vojvodina, and Pécs, including Julije Njikoš and other "Pajo Kolarić" leaders, gathered to present their research and thoughts on the second annual round table's theme, "Šokci and the tambura" (Erl and Njikoš 2008, 4–5).

Subsequently, however, the round table has explored ethnically more diverse themes, such as "Earth, Forest, Šokci and Bunjevci" in 2009. Scholars from elsewhere in the former Yugoslavia, including Belgrade (situated in Serbia proper, several kilometers to the south of Vojvodina), have also participated. Large public tambura events similarly include participants from across Croatia and its intimates, and tensions between groups within the same overarching ethnic category have largely subsided as the momentum for bridging geographical divisions has increased through public and institutional support. Especially since the war's outbreak in 1991, the "WE" that has advanced Croatian musico-territorial expansion and sovereignty has been more of an affective agent, a becoming, than a bounded identity with fixed inclusions and exclusions (albeit one consistently constituting itself in relation to Serbian/Yugoslav Others). Antun himself put the matter in affective terms, telling me that one "Pajo Kolarić" director who "is of Jewish descent" serves as one of theirs because "he feels [*osjeća se*] like a Croat."

Bridging differences within and between various ensembles and countering wartime dangers that exacerbate them require significant investments of time, money, and physical—and often emotional—effort. Rather than discourage such relationships, these investments add value to the intimacy fostered on performance trips. In this respect, the tambura ensembles that connect Croatia with its intimates have reformulated on a transnational, monoethnic plane the Yugoslavian model of multiple nations performing diverse repertoire (for one another, on a single stage) and its ideal of "brotherhood and unity." On this transnational plane, Croatian tambura ensembles cultivate fraternity and intimacy through (and for) a sense of unity based on ethnic heritage rather than national citizenship.

RELIGIOUS SOLIDARITY

This network's connections typically consist not only of official, public relations but also of strong camaraderie and religious ties. The president of "Pajo Kolarić" is close to Zoran, a tamburaš who moved his family from Vukovar to Parndorf in the 1990s. Their relationship extends beyond festival coordination to include frequent personal visits. I first met Zoran in 2008 during a preliminary visit to Osijek, when Antun hosted me on an excursion to a festival in Bački Monoštor, a Vojvodina town with a considerable Šokac population. Zoran and his wife had friends there and had come to see them, Antun, and the festival. Antun took advantage of Zoran's connections with musicians there to discuss possible musical exchanges (similar to those between "Pajo Kolarić" and Zoran's "Ivan Vuković" tambura society in Parndorf) with a Monoštor tambura ensemble's leader.

As happens at many such festivals, a performance in the town's Catholic church followed. This afforded one of the afternoon's primary moments of Catholic (Croat) congregation and one of the only ones held indoors, separating old and new acquaintances from the more diverse public outside.[18] In this instance a women's choir performed sacred and folk songs, though often a tambura orchestra and choir will perform an entire Mass. In September 2009 I accompanied the "Pajo Kolarić" leadership, including Antun and Julije Njikoš, to a tambura Mass played by "Ivan Vuković"' in Parndorf's Croatian Catholic church. For several years "Pajo Kolarić" has supported Parndorf's ensemble with encouragement, sheet music, and artistic evaluation, and this visit strengthened their relationship in a specifically religious context. The service included a sermon delivered in Croatian and then German, readings and prayers given alternately in Croatian and German, and classical and popular tambura settings of the Mass's Proper. Following the Mass, Njikoš addressed the locals and visitors in Croatian and then German, praising the orchestra's technical expertise. The day concluded with a lunch in honor of the Osijek guests and much relaxed repartee over food and alcohol, before Zoran saw us off on our drive home.

That churches afford places for Croat minorities to congregate outside Croatia's borders is naturally no surprise. Notable, however, is that churches in Bački Monoštor and Parndorf, as in Croatia, provide free, publicly open spaces for performing and listening to tambura music and serve to ritualize musical congregation. In doing so they articulate zones of practical intimacy in theoretically or officially public contexts (the Catholic Church is, after all, an international institution with a nominally universal outreach). In this respect, in Croatia and its intimates, specific Croatian Catholic churches' practical intimacies, as manifested through musical rituals, are closer to the "musical intimacies" that Byron Dueck (2013) describes among Canada's First Nations than what Lauren Berlant terms "intimate publics" (2008). Like Dueck, I accept that intimate publics may "presume that they share with one another certain kinds of emotional knowledge," but "such connections can be distinguished from forms of acquaintanceship that exist between more immediately knowable and engageable others" (Dueck 2013, 17). Churches can facilitate practical separation from theoretically accessible (and accessing) publics.

At the same time, sequestering musical intimacies in churches builds on the Croatian Catholic Church's role as a sanctuary of Croatian nationalism under socialism, when it provided spaces accessible to but largely avoided by Yugoslavia's atheistic and officially multinational regime (and facilitated connections across a broader, intimate Croatian public). The Church encouraged and harbored the performance of national music, including "Our Beautiful Homeland," in socialist-era church services (Bellamy 2003, 156). As Barry Shank argues, "by focusing the attention of the singing members on their common object of identification, anthems can increase the intensity of the boundary marking beyond the needs of the intimate public and toward what is necessary for true political formation" (2014, 49–50). Intimate publics' boundaries, moreover, "are often charged with affective intensity, where different values or ways of being [. . .] spark a struggle between the ordinary and the unjust" (49). While Croatian Catholic churches today often emphasize practical musical intimacies of face-to-face interaction, they historically have defined intimate publics, sparking within them musically the affective intensity needed for political organizing leading up to independence in 1991.

Catholic churches in Croatia's intimates similarly preserved and propagated Croatian community and culture. A Croatian priest in Tuzla, for example, opened a tambura school in his church during the Bosnian war and trained such future luminaries as Vedran Čičak, a devout Catholic who leads the tambura orchestra of Radio-Televizija Sarajevo (Čičak 2010). In Parndorf, Austria, the priest who hosted my research visit was also hosting Croats traveling through from Romania, and his promotion of tambura music in the church community extended to sharing local Burgenland traditions with his guests. Churches, as spaces of education, performance, and wartime and postwar refuge, imbricate faith, becoming, and national musical practice (see chapter 5); tamburaši who play in them simultaneously celebrate increasing religiosity, national consciousness, and the ability to express these in independent Croatia.

Church performances also facilitate ensembles' recruitment of Croat tamburaši, not through any official means of segregation but through the practical, tacit, and even unintentional means that are intrinsic to intimacy at any level. When I asked a "Pajo Kolarić" children's orchestra director whether Serbs played in the ensemble, he replied that they were welcome but that it could be a problem when performing in churches. He added that they do not inquire about the children's ethnicity, but he assumed that they were all Croats. Whether or not ensembles are as ethnically homogeneous as some of their leaders assume,[19] one of their main functions is performing repertoire, particularly Croatian folk songs, that demarcates intimate zones in churches whose congregations continuously constitute and connect Croatia's intimates. In these spaces, musicians and audiences are freest to assume both religious and ethnic commonalities (that they are all Croatian Catholics and not, say, Austrians) and to kindle intimacy even before beginning the affective gestures of recognition, introduction, and acquaintance.

TAMBURA STYLE: GEOGRAPHY, NARRATIVE, AND AGGRESSION

"Pajo Kolarić" plays diverse repertoire, but its folklore performances (often accompanying an affiliated girls' choir) mostly comprise East Croatian Šokci folk songs, such as "Ej pletenice" (Hey, plait of hair; see figure 1.1). As is characteristic of much Croatian traditional music, especially Slavonian, the song employs what analysts of South Slavic folk music call a diatonic tone row (*tonski niz*—in this instance a B-G# hexachord), with the row's second tone (C#) acting as center and providing the final, cadential tone. Tamburaši tend to harmonize this and similar melodies according to Central European tonal harmonic practice, and thus to hear "Ej pletenice" in B major with several returns to the tonic preceding a half-cadence on scale degree 2 (as tambura accompaniment tonicizes the dominant via a II7–V progression). Such songs have several verses and, according to the prominent tambura arranger and composer Josip Ivanković, former manager of Zlatni Dukati, the cadence on scale degree 2 with dominant harmony prepares for the immediate melodic repetition and return to the tonic typical of this area's folk music (Ivanković 1993).[20] As leading Yugoslav ethnomusicologist Jerko Bezić noted, folk songs with tone rows commencing with the (major-sounding) *whole tone—whole tone—semitone* tetrachord, but emphasizing the second tone as central, are found throughout Croatia, Bosnia and Herzegovina, and Montenegro; they are distinguishable from the narrower intervals and nondiatonic sets found in Croatia's more western regions of Međimurje and Istria (1981, 34–35). More specific to Croatia's Drava and Danube River regions (and distinct from

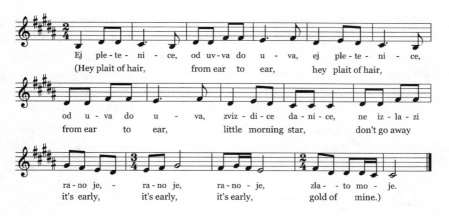

FIGURE 1.1 "Ej pletenice"

other domestic regions and foreign republics) is the sudden triple meter in a piece otherwise characterized by duple division (notated in mm. 13–14 with a change to 3/4 time signature).

"Pajo Kolarić" uses Šokci songs in forming and strengthening relationships with Croatian ensembles of diverse culturo-geographical location and/or origin. Performing Šokac repertoire identifies its particular subgroup and region, situating the group as a musically and culturally distinct, yet noninsular, node in Croatia and its intimates' broader musical and ethnic network. The celebration in performance of historical, cultural, and musical differences between other Croats' repertoire and "Pajo Kolarić's" own emphasizes the breadth and diversity of the network that the group has painstakingly reestablished since its wartime disruption.

It is within this network that "Pajo Kolarić" has once again reunited with other musical Croat communities and that various ensembles have refamiliarized each other with their respective styles. Thus performances of Šokac repertoire by "Pajo Kolarić" are not most important for their ability to represent the cultural and musical distance to be bridged by the network but for their capacity to aid this bridging process. To groups less familiar with Šokac repertoire, "Pajo Kolarić" makes this music not only familiar but also present as the groups meet and draw one another into their respective sonic proximities.

At the festival, however, "Pajo Kolarić's" repertoire is decidedly more tonal. It includes Julije Njikoš's compositions, which strategically advance an agenda of elevating tambura concerts and musicians' technique to the sphere of art music.

Njikoš's writings—both musical and musicological—are as narrative in form as was his Sombor speech about the tambura's dissemination. His tonic-driven settings of patriotic poetry have spread among geographically far-flung festival participants, somewhat homogenizing their repertoire and bringing them stylistically as well as physically and socially into the fold. One of his best-known compositions, "Legenda o tamburici" (Legend about the tamburica), relates through Stjepan Jakševac's text and Njikoš's customarily lyrical chromatic part writing a mythic story of the tambura's origin and attainment of a soul in the hands of Slavonians. Njikoš counted it among the "compositions dedicated to the figure of Pajo Kolarić" in his book on this famous originator of Croatian orchestral tambura music and namesake of Njikoš's Slavonian Tambura Society (1995, 143–162). He thereby situated Kolarić within the "great events" of the legend that, through musical narration, "would inscribe the fate of the nation on its history" (Bohlman 2008, 253).

Njikoš's book contains a biography of Kolarić, his arrangements of the latter's songs, and other tambura works narrating the life and death of Osijek's greatest tambura legend. Mostly arranged by and/or dedicated to Julije Njikoš, the founding conductor of "Pajo Kolarić," these latter pieces include Franjo Kuhač's "Osijek Galop" and Josip Andrić's "Pajo Kolarić Overture," "Cantata about Kolarić," and "Diptych about Kolarić." Njikoš and fellow musicologist/composer Josip Andrić's choice of the preposition "about" (*o*) indicates these instrumental compositions' descriptive, narrative engagement of the tambura legend. Festival participants have performed all but Andrić's cantata since the early 2000s; "Legend about the Tamburica," though not featured—likely because it is texted but much longer than the songs they usually perform—remains an important part of the repertoires of "Pajo Kolarić" and other Slavonian orchestras (STD "Pajo Kolarić" 2001, 50; 2002, 44; 2003, 54). Collectively, such pieces bolster the festival's narrative of the tambura's rise and dispersion among Croats.

LINEAR PROGRESSIONS

"Pajo Kolarić's" orchestras have also long played local tambura bands' popular songs, especially patriotic wartime ballads.[21] Although these enter the festival repertoire less often, the Croatian songwriting style that concretized in the 1990s played an arguably even larger role in placing goal-driven tonal music (over regional modal folk songs) at the center of a canon of specifically Croatian transnational performance. The festival's art music entries had nurtured tonal stylization in a similar manner in Yugoslavia, and the flurry of composition and stylistic concretization in independent Croatia picked up much more quickly in the ballad tradition. Drawing upon older Yugoslav and "traditional" (anonymous popular) compositional models, the canon of new tambura ballads bears what I identify as "a number of recurring, archetypal harmonic and melodic structures"; their tonally static verses yield to refrains that harmonically tonicize the subdominant, relative minor, or VI chord and then melodically elaborate (often via sequences) linear progressions to scale degree 3 or 1 (MacMillen 2011a, 110).[22]

While these archetypes vary somewhat melodically and harmonically, they share basic structural descent beginning a fourth, sixth, octave, or tenth above the lower tonic (scale degree 4 or any note higher than it by one or more stacked thirds). For example, the refrain of Miroslav Škoro's "Ne dirajte mi ravnicu" moves to the subdominant and elaborates a simple progression: the first two lines of text begin melodically on scale degrees 4 and then 3, and the third and fourth lines end on scale degrees 2 and 1, respectively (see figure 1.2A).[23] This upward modulation followed by melodic descent mirrors the common regional folk song practice of melodic repetition via transposition between upper and lower tetrachords (in the tonal schema of modern tambura arrangements, between tonic and subdominant modalities or, as in "Ej pletenice," alternation of dominant and tonic modalities). Anonymous Šokac refrains progressing from scale degree 6 to the tonic (see figure 1.2B), such as "Vesela je Šokadija," a 1975 hit for Slabinac and Slavonski Bećari, represent an intermediate step between bimodal folk songs and the tonal melodic and harmonic complexity of new tambura ballads with scale-degree-6 progressions (e.g., Škoro and Grcevich's "Moja Juliška"[24] and Željko Barba's festival hit for Zlatni Dukati, "Slavonijo, jedna jedina" [Slavonia, one and only]).

Such ballads diverge significantly from the tonal melodic and harmonic structures of Njikoš's through-composed tambura works, which typically elaborate the linear progressions from scale degree 3, 5, or 1 that Heinrich Schenker identified in nineteenth-century European art music. Yet the tonal direction (rather than modal fluctuation) is similar. When Zvonko Bogdan, a Vojvodinan Bunjevac tambura singer, rearranged Bane Krstić's popular "Tko te ima, taj te nema" (He who has you has you not) with Jerry Grcevich on their eponymous 2007 CD (Croatia Records), they rewrote the refrain melody, articulating with only slight elaboration a descent from scale degree 4 to the tonic. Bogdan explained that the original "melody doesn't pull anywhere" (2017). While not necessarily modeled after "Ne dirajte mi ravnicu," their version's refrain now "pulls" to the tonic in

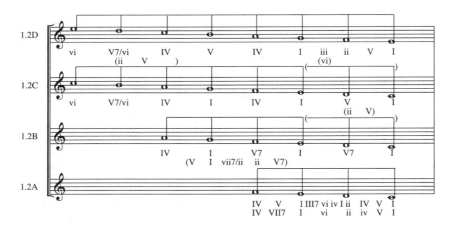

FIGURE 1.2 Archetypal refrain structures. The linear descents are in reverse order from the textual analysis in order to facilitate visual comparison of how the longer descents extend linear descent A (the most basic).

the same manner as Škoro's hit, and the melody of each refrain's third line is practically identical, suggesting the lasting tonal melodic dominance of songs from twenty-five to thirty years ago. Other influential songs' refrains elaborate progressions from the upper octave (e.g., Slavonski Bećari's "Istinu svijetu . . ." and Berde Band's "Oj hrastovi Slavonije Ravne"; see figure 1.2C) or upper tenth (e.g., Zlatni Dukati's "Tena" and Crni Šest's nearly identical "Laže selo, lažu ljudi"; see figure 1.2D);[25] due to their similarly methodical, often sequential, and harmonically modulating descent and their frequent conclusion on scale degree 3 rather than the tonic, I group them with the other archetypal refrain structures. These "pull" the music toward the tonic but in structurally different, more repetitive ways than Njikoš's narrative compositions.

Uniting the folk songs, tambura ballads, and classically styled compositions were not just performances by the same 1990s bands and orchestras but also the development and pervasive application of a Slavonian "sound." During the sharpest wartime isolation from other Yugoslav republics' tamburaši, this sound developed characteristics including three-part baritone vocal harmonies (doubled by tamburas in several octaves); heavily chromatic melodic embellishments by the lead prim tambura, "including short, stepwise fills between successive notes of the vocal melody and longer runs when the vocals are silent," potentially earning a virtuosic primaš the reputation of playing dangerously; and what tamburaši call "an 'aggressive' plectrum technique consisting of hard attacks, quick tremolos, and stricter duple division than one tends to hear in northern Serbia or Bosnia" (MacMillen 2011a, 110).

My interlocutors' descriptions of Slavonians playing not only *opasno* ("dangerously") but also *agresivno* registered a hard, masculine aesthetic resonating with wartime notions of heroism. On the one hand, *agresija* ("aggression") was strongly linked with Yugoslav forces and "Serbian aggression" (territorial encroachment and bodily harm) that threatened newly independent Croatian territories (Jambrešić 1993, 75). Domestic aggression by *Croats* was decried in Croatian discourse as a sign of xenophobia (Povrzanović 1993, 122) and malignance unbefitting heroic Croatian musicians (Kuzmanović 1992). On the other hand, as Maja Povrzanović writes, aggressiveness was "one of the most frequent responses to the fear experienced in battle," and "depending on the side in this war which we consider to be our own, we can also see it as *bravery*" (1993, 146). Audiences sometimes deemed aggressive performance an appropriate response because, as the website for the 2017 documentary film *Louder than Guns* puts it: "[O]pen aggression on Croatia in Fall 1991 incite[d], like never before or since, an impulsive reaction from [. . .] tamburaši" and other musicians (Factum 2017; my translation). "Aggressive tambura music," I came to understand, was desirable for hard metric articulation's capacity to territorialize bands' musical resistance to invasion. Playing aggressively brings a physical, affective force into the picking arm, lending the virtuosity of dangerous performance a heroic strength.

Croat tamburaši's widely, if not universally, aggressive playing during and following the war helped to unify the purposeful, even forceful "pulling" of patriotically deployed tonal compositions. Availing themselves of "the indexicality of the refrain, its alliance with territoriality," Croat tamburaši served to remake "musicking-as-virtual" into "the effect[s] of the refrain-as-actual" (Tomlinson 2016, 168). This reverses musicking's typical deterritorialization, bringing aggressive performance into tension with improvisatory lines of flight from dogmatic meter and refrain, which transgressions can sometimes make a performance most dangerous.

This partially explains the ambiguous appeal of Roma performers (see chapter 3) and musicians from Croatia's intimates who have embraced their style, such as Grcevich and Peter Kosovec; Others internal to Croatia's sovereign territory and Croats deterritorialized through diverse musical practice and livelihoods in foreign lands potentially undo (sonically, affectively, symbolically) the aggressive musical territorialization of Croatian repertoire. If narrative's art "lies in its ability to condense the action down to an exemplary period of time, to take it out of the continuous flux, and to reveal a who" (Kristeva 2000, 55), then performances supporting the emergent national narrative needed to fashion refrains out of the continuous flux of musicking (which might not "pull" anywhere). This involved not only Zvonko Bogdan's melodic revisions but also the aggressive, driving playing more typical of Slavonian musicians than Bogdan's Vojvodinan tamburaši. These performances standardized within Croatia and disseminated to its intimates a performance practice built around shared narration: of present war efforts (in tambura ballads) and of histories of national awakening (in through-composed works). This practice produced a shared narrative position (a "who," a "WE") and generated an affective block, a becoming that aggregated aggressive feelings toward fear and physical danger, allowing this narrative position still to admit and recognize plurality in its folk history and songs. In other words, common feeling affectively blocked (delimited) counternarratives of cultural, geographic, and musical fissure, making such representations of difference stand in a relation of alterity to shared musical experience.

DIVERSE PERFORMANCE IN INTERNATIONAL EVENTS AND TRANSNATIONAL NETWORKS

Croatia's ensembles perform in ethnically varied contexts today, and these provide instructive points of comparison to the tambura Masses and Croatia-oriented festivals. Along with Osijek's KUD-affiliated tambura ensembles such as the HKUD "Osijek 1862" and Batorek Tambura School orchestras, "Pajo Kolarić" orchestras attend numerous Croatian tambura gatherings and international (mostly public) tambura, folklore, and orchestra festivals. Croatian events tend to be much more intimate; musicians spend preconcert hours competing in football (soccer) tournaments, dining together, and rehearsing for combined orchestra concerts, and they often meet up afterward at the Šokački Disko to hear professional bands together. International festivals (with the exception of the "Pajo Kolarić" noncompetitive festival, whose international scope involves incorporating foreign *Croat* communities) tend to be competitive, juried events at which interaction happens largely among those already acquainted, reproducing intimacies that already exist.

Many professional Croatian bands formed while playing in these youth orchestras. As final examples, I turn to two such professional groups: Sedam Osmina (Seven Eighths), which emerged mainly out of Batorek's orchestra and began participating in international festivals in the late 2000s, and Vučedolski

Zvuci (Sounds of Vučedol, named for an archaeological site near Vukovar), the self-declared solitary, permanently established tambura orchestra composed of Croatian Serbs, who otherwise play tamburas only in ad hoc wedding ensembles and a few Serbian KUDS (though part of Vukovar's Serbian Cultural Society "Prosvjeta," Vučedolski Zvuci operates like a professional band).

Fall 2009: Sedam Osmina took awards for best ensemble and best soloist at a juried international tambura festival in Serbia. I attended with Vučedolski Zvuci and spent several hours with the band before the competition. Like Sedam Osmina, the musicians seemed content to keep interactions within their own group during the performance and the dinner afterward.

Mirko Delibašić, the multi-instrumentalist leader of Vučedolski Zvuci's eight-man ensemble, was my *bugarija* (harmony) tambura instructor throughout my 2009–2010 stay in Osijek. One of many Serbs who remained in Vukovar during the war and the subsequent UNTAES period—as he said, "I never had to leave my home"—he performed actively there throughout the 1990s, even playing for Jacques Klein, the American UNTAES administrator. Mirko and his fellow bandmates were among those performing tambura music during the instrument's alleged silence (and the rifle's domination) in Baranja and Eastern Slavonia. Not all Croats there overlooked this fact; Serbs' ability to stay and perform in Vukovar during the Yugoslav Army/Serb militia occupation, when groups such as Zlatni Dukati could not, drew hostility from some non-Serbs who returned in 1998. Once, when a man passing us on the street waved unconvincingly, Mirko explained that he had played with Mirko's group before the war but had since performed in a somewhat chauvinistic Croat ensemble. "There, you see that that antagonism still exists," he commented (Delibašić 2010). Later he told me that such "tension" between Vukovar's Croats and Serbs had evolved into mere "polarization," which also pervaded some international festivals (Delibašić 2015). Although they maintained (and sought to expand upon) ties with certain Croat tambura musicians, Mirko and his bandmates largely kept to themselves and their own, distinct zones at festivals with groups of known ethnic/national origin but unknown politics.

The festival audience in Serbia similarly kept their interactions at their own groups' tables, calling out only occasionally to musicians onstage whom they had come to support. The event was not exceedingly formal, and the lack of interaction among groups was striking in comparison to other events that I had attended. The festival was competitive, however, and the musicians, it seems, accepted the competition as the event's primary focus and single interactive dimension.

According to Franjo Batorek, founder of the Batorek School, Croatian ensembles ceased participating in Serbian festivals during the war and only recently started attending again (Batorek 2010). He added that organizers sometimes asked him to serve on juries and to nominate potential Croatian band entries, largely because this could qualify festivals for EU funding for multiethnic events. Otherwise, he indicated, there might not be much interest in Croatian bands participating.

Still, organizers and tambura leaders in Croatia and Serbia alike are making attempts on their own. Batorek organizes a summer workshop for tambura students of many ethnicities and from as far away as Macedonia and the Czech Republic, and the Tamburica Fest in Vojvodina's administrative seat of Novi Sad (formerly in Deronje) draws many Croatian bands and judges. Antun and I tried for more than a year to organize a first meeting of the Bulgarian Farkaš tambura orchestra and the "Pajo Kolarić" children's orchestra in Osijek or Ruse. The parents' and director's expressed fear of foreign territories (with no ethnically intimate hosts) meant that it would have to happen in Croatia, and the Ruse group nearly came to Osijek for the 2011 festival (they withdrew after communication and translation difficulties delayed receipt of their admission). Non-Croat performers from foreign countries—including Czechs but mostly excluding Serbs—occasionally participated in Croatia's nominally "international" tambura music festivals at this time. Yet the lands in which these performers reside remain sources of discomfort for Croatian musicians who have grown (up) comfortable within their networks of personal familiarity (or at least ethnic familiality).

CONCLUSION: CROATIA'S INTIMATES AS NEW MUSICAL POTENTIALITIES

Being among intimates abroad seems to allay Croatian parents' fears of such proximate, foreign, and potentially dangerous territories. "Pajo Kolarić" often visits Croat enclaves in Austria, Hungary, and the Netherlands, and Antun frequently mentioned his desire to repeat the 1979 North American CFU tour. These endeavors are a direct continuation of late Yugoslav and wartime efforts. While the racialized "they" have often been more of a domestic than an international concern, having the national "we" abroad has helped to alleviate a similar level of insecurity over otherness and territorial belonging as cross-border enterprises have shifted from more political to more intimate (and touristic) relationship building. The generation who entered adulthood and fought in the 1990s wars has at times approached such risky (or at least fear-inducing) prospects with a caution likely balanced against the relative stakes of the physical dangers they faced decades earlier and the concern for preserving the security that they fought hard to assure for their children.

Foreign Croat enclaves typically interact regularly with non-Croat musicians, making them significant intermediaries for Croatia's musical travelers and underscoring their (especially recent emigrants') importance for international connections. Time spent in Croatia's intimates facilitates (re)acquaintance with newly and long-foreign territories alike, and within these sometimes affords opportunities for interaction with other ethnic groups (the topic of the following two chapters). While tambura musicians there prioritize building relationships with Croats from Croatia, they also take advantage of "more 'free space' for maneuvering" (Kiossev 2002, 178) outside Croatia's borders. They listen to and sometimes collaborate with other ethnic groups, including Roma and Slovaks, who are represented as minorities in Croatia and typically participate there in separate systems of official minority festivals. Such interactions increasingly make Croatia's intimates important sites for Croatian citizens to encounter the ethnically and geographically foreign, affording spaces that promise both the comfort of intimacy and the excitement of danger.

Furthermore, these territories' special role for Croatian tambura groups and the different interactions that they enable beyond Croatia's borders demonstrate the need to readdress in two ways the processes of balkanization in the term's own region of origin: by examining how divisive actions actually foster intimacies across emergent borders and by examining how in subsequent years these intimacies have fostered new (not simply geographical) zones, both exclusive and inclusive, frightening and intimate. Balkanization is itself a narrative, one whose narrators and audiences have largely resided apart from the actors who allegedly realized its fractured geopolitics on the ground. The war separated Croatian enclaves in other Yugoslav republics from their nominal homeland and caused them, the Croatian state, and many of its citizens, including musicians, to rely heavily on Croatian diaspora support and patronage in nearby Austria and farther abroad in North America and Australia (rather than on one another), yet the STD "Pajo Kolarić" and other institutions' activities have begun over the past twenty-five years to equalize the roles and relations allotted to these two types of foreign enclaves. Yugoslavia's division and Croatian ensembles' subsequent attempts to reconnect with Croats across newly minted borders have created more complex geographical connections than those for which "diaspora" or balkanization narratives can account. This demands an expanded conceptualization of musicians' movement and migration within and beyond the nation-state. It is in the narratives of risky movements that the threatening materiality of discourse, its affective intensity and instrumentalization of racialized, biological lives, weighs most heavily on Croatian citizens' beings and imaginations, producing new becomings that are simultaneously territorialized on the new agents of history: the "WE" that demonstrates "our" cultural and military supremacy and that is intensely blocked from counternarratives of both state and enemy.

TWO

Whiteness and Becoming among Tambura Bands of the American Rust Belt

[F]or almost fifty years now my French taste has not always been able to
resist the jolts of an early music coiled around a memory that is still vigilant.
From these connected vessels there emerges a strange language, a stranger to
itself, neither from here nor from there, a monstrous intimacy.

Julia Kristeva, Crisis of the European Subject

On the brink of socialism's collapse and Yugoslavia's violent disintegration, Miroslav Škoro and Jerry Grcevich's 1989 album (released in 1992 as *Ne Dirajte Mi Ravnicu*) launched their respective careers as tambura virtuoso and popular music icon. It also raised several questions about musicality and ethnicity/race in intimates of Croatia such as Grcevich's Croatian enclave near Pittsburgh. In this chapter I reconsider their album, in particular the hit song "Moja Juliška," and examine performances of this and other tambura music as spatializing and socializing forces (Krims 2007) across Pittsburgh and beyond to Toronto and Chicago. This "music's power to 'compose' situations" (DeNora 2000, 9) arises most intensively in variously securing and preventing contact and intimacy over racial, ethnoreligious, affective, and physical boundaries, particularly across the thresholds from which intimate interiors open onto dangerous urban expanses beyond.

Like Julia Kristeva in the harsh essay ("Bulgaria, My Suffering") on her native country quoted at the beginning of this chapter, many Rust Belt tambura musicians relate to music from the homeland with affective ambivalence regarding such boundaries. Their attachments span a strangely "intimate distance" (Bigenho 2012) from the homeland's language and culture as well as a jarring, at times traumatic separation from fellow citizens where they reside. Such "strange language" and "monstrous intimacy" are indeed emergences, translations between the elusive security of an inner alleyway, chamber, or self and the potential risks but also mobility of the outside. On the brink—looking out, looking in—this is where intimacies become strange, even monstrous, indeed where society's "stranger" becomes "an element of the group itself" (Simmel 1950, 402).[1] It is also where new agencies take hold, where musicians and listeners develop new subjectivities and capacities for blocking (and blocking) musical affect.

I hone in on musical insincerity, a cutting of affective work on the self and on audiences, in one of Croatia's most musically and economically influential intimates. Communicating sincerity is often as important as demonstrating authenticity in the diaspora, where becoming-Croat is understood to require effort and choice (MacMillen forthcoming). Yet strategically subverting sincere, intense feeling is equally important to the maintenance of racialized, affective boundaries, and involves a blocking of affect (in delimitation) while also accruing a strange, residual intimacy. Narrowing the scope of analysis from narrative to racialized discourse, I consider instances of musical and linguistic "translation" that facilitate the performative and affective dimensions of (in)sincerity. In doing so, I illustrate an affective experience of whiteness that is essential to understanding the risks and pleasures that musicians take across the postindustrial Rust Belt's urban interiors and geographies and the anxious, sometimes derogatory, and competing discourses regarding these musicians' belonging (as "honkies") or separation (as "Hunkies") within white America. These discourses' humorous translations generate planes of indeterminacy across the affective block— a precarious teetering between a block *of* affect and a block *to* affect—upon which musicians transgress into the sincere embodiment of Others yet adopt strategic insincerities for racio-musical maneuvering. At stake here is a racial immanence, an emergent exteriorization of whiteness, but of a whiteness that is itself minoritarian and thus, unlike Deleuze and Guattari's interpretation of the positionality "white-man" ([1980] 1987, 291),[2] not the subject proper but the object of a becoming. Trapped apart from Whiteness, this white subjectivity opens to its own objectifications and desires, a barred ~~subject~~-cum-object that undergoes what I term becoming-~~white~~.[3]

TRANSLATING "MOJA JULIŠKA" IN NORTH AMERICA

Pittsburgh was a center of dissemination as much as attraction for tambura musicians of the Midwest United States, and the success of Grcevich and Škoro's album was boosted by their association in Chicago with touring Yugoslavian star Zvonko Bogdan. Škoro (2011) noted with some irony that this 1989 meeting (when he was twenty-seven years old) was his first time seeing and speaking with Bogdan, though he had grown up listening to the tambura composer and singer, who worked in Novi Sad, scarcely one hundred kilometers from Škoro's Osijek. Škoro and Grcevich had just finished their album of new Croatian-language songs, sung by Škoro with multitrack tambura accompaniment by Grcevich. Uncertain of what to do next, they traveled from Pittsburgh to Chicago to seek the advice of the more experienced Bogdan, whom Grcevich knew from visiting Yugoslavia with his father in the 1970s and was thus able to visit at the house of a mutual friend.

Škoro doubted his own suitability for tambura songs, citing his distaste for and inexperience with folk music, and suggested that Bogdan consider performing them. Bogdan responded that the recording was not bad for a first attempt, and that Škoro ought to continue working with the material himself. Škoro quotes Bogdan as saying: "You sing how you sing, there's no help there. Our people [*narod*] loves repetition and if you play this for them a number of times, they will fall in love with it and will even emulate you" (Škoro 2010, 193; my translation). Škoro took Bogdan's advice and, following the success of the album's title track "Ne dirajte mi ravnicu" and Zlatni Dukati's 1992 cover version, joined the forefront of the emerging popular tambura band movement in Croatia.

Bogdan, however, concluded his advice with a warning: "Don't you [two] write any more Hungarian lyrics to Russian Music" (quoted in Škoro 2010, 193). He was referring to another future Croatian hit from the twelve-song album, "Moja Juliška" (My Julie). The song addresses Juliška, a young woman whom the narrator knew as a youth. Sung in Croatian, it recalls how they danced crazily to the čardaš, a Hungarian couple's dance (*czardas*) whose name relates to taverns (čarde) where it was commonly played and danced by Hungarians, Roma, and Slavs in Northern Yugoslavia.

When I spoke with Bogdan about this song, he laughingly confirmed that it has always sounded Russian to him: "That's how Jerry wrote it" (Bogdan 2013; my translation). The song shares a number of musical features with Russian romances and folk dance melodies then popular among Yugoslavian tambura

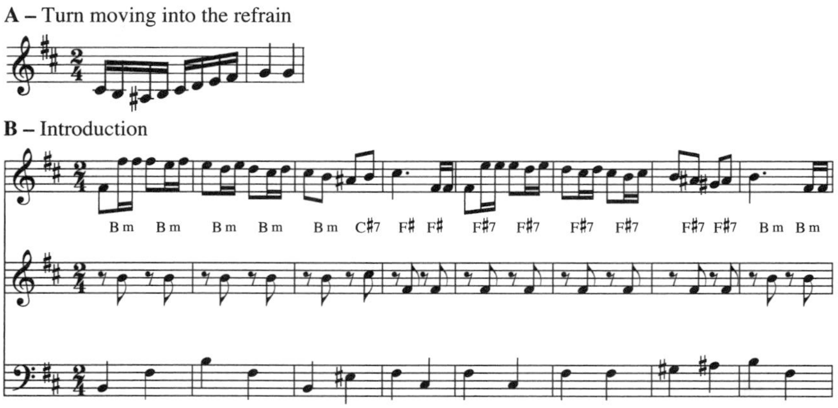
A – Turn moving into the refrain
B – Introduction
Bm Bm Bm Bm Bm C♯7 F♯ F♯ F♯7 F♯7 F♯7 F♯7 F♯7 F♯7 Bm Bm

FIGURE 2.1 "Moja Juliška" (1989). Text by Miroslav Škoro; music by Jerry Grcevich.

Bm Bm F♯7 F♯7
F♯7 F♯7 Bm Bm

FIGURE 2.2 Čardaš transposed into B minor (often performed in E minor in Croatia)

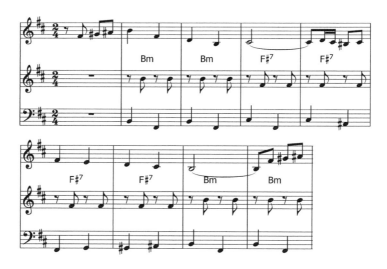

bands,[4] though other elements resemble the čardaš music played in Croatia and Serbia. Grcevich's instrumental breaks, for example, employ the ornamental turns with raised lower neighbor tones found in nearly every čardaš (compare the turns leading into scalar runs in figures 2.1A and 2.2). The instrumental introduction also employs the general harmonic pattern i–V7–i (figure 2.1B) typical of čardaš minor passages (see figure 2.2).

The melody of the introduction, however, is simply sequential, employs mostly stepwise motion, and holds to a nearly parallel phrase structure over the harmony. In contrast, čardaš pieces played in Croatia and Serbia usually employ sequences less systematically, pair stepwise motion with arpeggios, and feature answer phrases that mirror the question phrases less faithfully. Also common in čardaš are chromatic passages in the main melody and modulation to the relative major ("Moja Juliška" stays in the minor). "Moja Juliška," in departing from standard čardaš formulae, does bear similarities to Russian tunes such as "Kalinka moya" (figure 2.3). "Kalinka moya" utilizes similar descent, mostly stepwise, from scale degree 5 to 1 over accompaniment with nearly identical harmonic rhythm (3 bars of V7 followed by 1 bar of i, rather than 2 bars of each as in figure 2.2). Still, Škoro and Grcevich's original recording of "Moja Juliška" makes use of turns and offbeat, rhythmic vocal calls of "op, op, op" typical of Southeast European čardaš music. Škoro's 1992 music video for the song emphasized this connection, with shots of a young couple dancing čardaš, and audience members and amateur folklore performers, who have contributed alike to making this a classic, frequently dance the čardaš to its accompaniment. As an experienced songwriter, however, Bogdan may have felt that these elements and the Hungarian lyrical references were superficial details at odds with the basic Russian structure. From Grcevich's (2018) perspective as the composer and performer of the melody and all the accompanying parts, however, the details are what really make the song, as he took unusual care in crafting each part to accentuate the song's driving dance nature, which was inspired by its *czardas* theme.

Beyond the issue of how to interpret such melodic and harmonic data, Škoro's first encounter with Bogdan highlights the complexity of conceptions and experiences of ethnicity and the fragmented geographies of tambura music performance. Bogdan's playful critique of "Moja Juliška" placed value on ethnic purity and the matching of musical character and lyrical content in songwriting. Although not proscribing the writing and performance of non-Croatian or even non-Yugoslav material (e.g., Hungarian and Russian songs), his reference to "our people" located performance and the arbitration of musical taste among com-

FIGURE 2.3 "Kalinka moya" transposed into B minor
(often performed in D minor)

munities of South Slavs. (Given the Croatian-diaspora context of the conversation, he likely meant Croats.)[5] These communities, however, were quite distant from one another geographically. In this meeting alone there were Croats (and importantly, close male friends) present from at least four different areas: Bogdan and Škoro hailed, respectively, from Vojvodina and Eastern Croatia, and their meeting was made possible by movement between Pittsburgh and Chicago, two nodes in the Rust Belt tambura performance network that Grcevich and the friend who was hosting Bogdan called home.

In sharing with me Bogdan's mild rebuke, Škoro was emphasizing humorously but seemingly also proudly the song's purportedly inappropriate, even transgressive nature. Pairing "Hungarian lyrics" with "Russian music" constituted, in a sense, a translation: a "carrying across" of elements from one people's tradition to another's. That the lyrics were entirely in Croatian, with only a few Hungarian cognates, further underscored the inappropriateness of this musical and linguistic translation. If Hungarian lyrics and Russian music presented ill-fitting elements, their pairing was no more natural for these elements' *translation*— which Bogdan had implicitly projected onto the song's genesis—into Croatian-language text and the timbres and texture of a Croatian tambura ensemble. Škoro and Grcevich may ultimately have followed Bogdan's advice, in the sense that they did not continue to write songs precisely in the style of "Moja Juliška," but Škoro has greatly expanded the transgressive capacities for translation in his recent performances of this one early "čardaš" song. In the process, he has raised significant blockages to affective sincerity that I address in this chapter's concluding ethnographic section.

It is important to note, however, that Bogdan's comment also suggested a tension over a mixing of musical and linguistic elements that is specific to immigrant communities in this region of North America. Croats' scattering across the industrial belt brought them into contact with other migrant populations, including Russians and Hungarians. As I discovered in my fieldwork, they even came to appropriate the somewhat derogatory term "Hunky" (derived from "Hungarian"), by which WASP populations sometimes disparage them collectively with Hungarian and other East European immigrants. While interaction with Hungarians and other ethnic groups was neither an uncommon nor a vexing experience for Bogdan and others in northern Yugoslavia, his critique implied that Grcevich and Škoro were losing their musical and national specificity in the jumble of East European communities that have cohabited in Rust Belt cities for decades. Historically, furthermore, Hungary and Russia are far from neutral geopolitical entities for the South Slavs: Austria-Hungary long controlled Croatia and Vojvodina and, though tensions between Croats and their Hungarian governors were common in the nineteenth century, this membership in a Central European empire also purportedly justifies their perception of Croatia as a Western nation (see MacMillen 2011a). Russia, for its part, aided Serbia in battles against Austria-Hungary's Croatian factions following the assassination of Archduke Franz Ferdinand at the outset of World War I. The Soviet Union later played a decisive and forcible role in stabilizing state socialism in the region, notably through its 1956 military intervention in Hungary. Both Russian and Hungarian influence could thus suggest imperial transgression onto a musical tradition that by 1989 was serving in Croatia and Vojvodina to advance a form of Croatian nationalism long suppressed within empires as well as state socialism but that, despite gaining ground in Yugoslavia, could once again be lost in the North American context.

In Yugoslavia, while professional tambura bands might play various nationalities' repertoires, folklore groups typically showcased national musical traditions as equal yet distinct on the stage in terms of repertoire and instrumentation. In North America, however, the mixing of repertoires and ubiquitous use of tamburas (at the expense of purity and traditional instrumentation) is common in folklore practices as well as in compositional efforts like that of Škoro and Grcevich.[6] This performance trend parallels the physical intimacies—sexual, familial, communal, but also, and significantly, those of male camaraderie—in which members of various enclaves engage as they draw into one another's spatial proximities at work, in adjacent and overlapping neighborhoods, and at shared music venues. It is in these proximities that tensions over translation and mixing arise most noticeably. I approach these two closely interrelated sources of both concern and intensely pleasurable affect in somewhat distinct sections before considering their joint assemblage into musical productions of intimacy and whiteness.

(Z)BROKENLY FLUENT

The problematic of "Moja Juliška," of course, actually lies in its nontranslation, a particularly touchy issue for many in Croatia's intimates who struggle to speak and understand the Croatian language. The implicit projection of a history of translation onto a song whose melody Jerry Grcevich authored but for which, unable to compose fluently in Croatian, he wrote no text belies the fact that Miroslav Škoro, in supplying lyrics, worked directly with Grcevich's melody rather than from some imagined original Hungarian text. This points, furthermore, to the already complexly imaginative processes of linguistic translation. As Paul Ricoeur has argued, "in a good translation, the two texts, source and target, must be matched with one another through a third non-existent text" ([2004] 2006, 7; also cited in Bohlman 2011, 507). Philip Bohlman points to the inherent interplay in song translations, which "multiplies meaning" and "realizes the interplay between the familiar and the unfamiliar" (2011, 507, 503). Both the "source" and the theoretical third (ur)text are nonexistent in the case of "Moja Juliška." The latter's multiple meanings arise not so much from a specific history of its own translation as from a sociocultural context of multilingual and multicultural encounter between Yugoslavia and North America shaped by long and complex histories of interpretive translation.

This song, however, points to an important practice entirely apart from the symbolism and imaginings that it has elicited. Rather than working from an urtext, even a conceptual one, Škoro and Grcevich seem to have entered into a process of composition with one another, an idea that is borne out by other aspects of their early partnership. As Grcevich related to me on several occasions, he learned to sing Croatian songs and play the tambura with his father at home and in the Junior Tamburitzans of the Croatian fraternal lodge in Cokeburg, Pennsylvania (near Pittsburgh). He did not speak much Croatian in either context, however, nor certainly did the non-Croatian members long admitted to such groups (I therefore refer to them as "Croatia-oriented"[7] rather than "Croatian American"). When Grcevich and Škoro began to interact, perform, and record on a daily basis in 1989, the two new friends developed a practice of what Škoro has called *razgovara[nje] na "zbrokanom" engleskom*: "convers[ing] in 'zbroken' English" (Škoro 2010, 106). *Zbrokan* (the nominative adjective from which one derives the locative *zbrokanom*) is an example of broken English as much as it is the title: the insertion of the prefix modifier "z-" before the root and the replacement of "-en" with "-an" transforms the English word "broken" into a Croatian-like past participle. In fact, the resulting "zbrokan" comes to resemble very closely the Croatian past participle *zbrkan*, meaning "confused."[8] The hybridized language that the two men composed and adopted combined English and Croatian words in humorous and inventive ways that made up for gaps in their knowledge of their respective second languages. Much of the humor they situated in incomplete (or nonexistent) translations of words, as in the following exchange (Škoro 2010, 106–107):[9]

	[Miro]	do you	see		there	some'ere?
JG—	"Majro [. . .]	da li	seejaš	something	tamo	neđe?"
			vidi<u>š</u>	nešto		

	I don't	see	anything,		Do you?
MŠ—	"No, ja ne	seejam	ništa,	Jerry.	A ti?"
	Ne,	vid<u>im</u>			

[. . .]

	We'll		[chicken.]	You	like	[chicken?]
JG—	"Mićmo	get	čiken.	Ti	lajkaš	čiken?"
	[Mi ćemo]	uzeti	pile.		voli<u>š</u>	pile?

	In the		shop?!
MŠ—	"U	tobacco	shopu?!"
		trafici	_____?!

	[Miro,]			They	there	have a	very	[nice]
JG—	"No,	Majro,	shit!	Oni	tamo	imaju	jako	najs
	Ne,		sranje!					lijepo

		[place.]		let's go,	screw it!
(JG continued)	food	plejs.	Let's go,	idemo,	jebiga!"
	s hranom	mjesto.	Idemo,		

Grcevich is famous in Croatia for his inventive and humorous hybridizations of Croatian and English. While Škoro's re-creation of this conversation for his autobiography twenty years later could itself have required some inventiveness, the phrases that appear there are representative of sayings that I heard Croatian tamburaši attribute to Grcevich well before the book's publication.[10] The difficulty with which he and many other Croatian American tamburaši in Pittsburgh speak Croatian places a severe limitation on their participation in tambura musicianship in Croatia and its intimates: for the most part they do not write new songs, as they cannot write Croatian lyrics.[11] Many of the new tambura compositions that have emerged from Pittsburgh are instrumental, including the solo recordings of Peter Kosovec and Jerry Grcevich, which are now famous in Croatia as well as its intimates.[12] Yet in Grcevich's case this limitation has also motivated creative forms of musical and linguistic co-composition; in addition to soliciting song texts from Croatian songwriters, he once wrote his own lyrics by stringing together short lines that he knew from other songs, resulting to his pleasant surprise in relatively few grammatical mistakes (according to a Croatian friend who reviewed the text).

Such instrumentalization of linguistic particles and strands speaks to the composition of more than just song text. Through strings of such particles, the interpretive acts of translation, and perhaps especially the incomplete or nontranslations that Grcevich and Škoro jokingly yet effectively employed, he and his Croatian friends pushed creatively into new and multiple meanings and into the co-composition of their own relations. They broke in and out of a "third space" between the sociolinguistic paradigms of Croatian and English communication (Bhabha 1990, 211).[13] Within this third space, they were not merely feigning cross-cultural communication but were actively translating in new and inventive ways through which they mutually assembled a new and intimate plane of understanding.

Constituting this plane are relations that move beyond imitation and representation to affective simulation — what Deleuze and Guattari call "becoming." This drive draws the subject into a "zone of proximity" with a specific term, such as "Croat" or "Hungarian": a minoritarian "medium or agent" that "rends him from his major identity" as "white-man, adult-male, etc." ([1980] 1987, 274, 291). Thus, to Croatian and other East European Pittsburghers, musical performance is "ethnic"; it enables a becoming-ethnic via an entrance into a zone of proximity with ethnicity (what non-"ethnic" white Americans sometimes term "Hunky") and an intimate withdrawing from the racialized white majority, an affective blocking of representations of whiteness.

Translation, not merely language, is key to this withdrawing. In becoming, one does not "borrow 'disguised' words from foreign languages. Rather, he snatches from his own language particles that can no longer belong to the form of that language" (Deleuze and Guattari [1980] 1987, 273). The recombinatory particulation of Grcevich and Škoro's hybridized words, which could no longer belong (solely) to the forms of their respective languages, facilitated their own destabilizing from "molar" categories of identity (Croatian American, Slavonian Croat, etc.) and emissions of their "molecular," co-composed selves (274–275). Words themselves served as the vital "something else" with which they entered into co-composition and became-Other (became-one-another's-terms) in Pittsburgh (274). Although humorous and, to a limited extent, imitative, their conversations were performances of necessity, of creative composition, and from their own descriptions of these exchanges to me, of great affect; they were becomings.[14]

TECHNIQUE, IMITATION, AND MUSICAL BECOMING

North American tamburaši such as Jerry Grcevich, however, by no means confined their compositional practices to discursive and linguistic parameters. Playing tambura, recording instrumentals, and attendant physical phenomena constitute essential Croatia-oriented activities and experiences for many Croatian Americans in Pittsburgh. The affect and embodiment of ethnic and at times racialized roles are equally significant in informing people's interactions and negotiations of difference and sameness, comfort and discomfort. Playing tambura was a vital part of Grcevich's relations to Škoro during these early years of their collaboration and friendship.

Škoro writes: "Our emigrants, especially in the U.S.A., nourish Croatian tambura music, and appeared to do so even when we all consequently were thinking that we were Beatles and Stones" (Škoro 2010, 12; my translation). He continues:

> They teach their children how beautiful it is to be your own and love your own, they take pride as well in tamburica. In America that is the most normal thing and it doesn't bother anyone—really because of the freedom by which you express your own [culture]. To my question "why are you a Croat[?]" Jerry Grcevich completely calmly and with deep conviction answered: "Because I play tamburica." (12; my translation)

Škoro connects his celebration of Croatian Americans' veneration for tambura music to a central critique of Croatian Croats' lack of respect for the music.

Viewed from this perspective, his statement (and citation of Grcevich) speak to concern over the music's Croatian reception as much as to its promotion in North America, where many Croats similarly ignore the tradition. Playing tambura, however, has occasioned many of Grcevich's social interactions in and around Pittsburgh through gatherings coordinated by nominally Croatian organizations. Those Croatian Americans, who likewise orient themselves to their heritage through these most financially powerful of Croatian diasporic institutions, almost inevitably take part in the tambura milieu that they finance.

In Škoro's words, "What is nice about Jerry is that he both was born and became [postao] a Croat" (2013; my translation).[15] Grcevich, he continued, "became a Croat in both a sociological and biological [sense]" and his Croatianness is something that "he has both genetically and sociologically" (2013; my translation). He and other Croatian musicians also sometimes recognized this potential to become Croatian in a sociological sense among those who did not claim "biological" or "genetic" Croatianness; Bob Sestili, who long played with Grcevich in a number of ensembles and performed with him and Škoro in the early 1990s, "does not have Croatian roots" but, in Škoro's words, "is politically and sociologically a Croat" because he grew up living and performing with Croats outside of Pittsburgh (2013; my translation).[16]

Expanding on the commentary on Grcevich's tambura practice begun in the autobiography, Škoro also suggested that the Croatian American's playing eventually enabled him to move beyond mere imitation to a deeper feeling of personal style and being. When he went to the United States in 1989, he found that Grcevich could play like famous tambura musicians such as Antun Nikolić "Tuca," with whom Škoro first toured the United States in the late 1980s, and Janika Balaž, the Rom tambura player who led the tambura orchestra for Radio Novi Sad for many years (Škoro 2011). Grcevich had learned to imitate the musical styles of Tuca and Balaž by listening to recordings and hearing them live in Yugoslavia and in the United States when these famous musicians had toured there during Jerry's youth. He didn't know what "his own style" was like, he told Škoro, who claimed that only in working through their first album did Grcevich really come up with something that was his own (2011).

In the spring of 2009 I studied basprim (a melody tambura) and kontra (a rhythmic/harmony tambura) with Jerry Grcevich for two months, and in our lessons together he regularly asked me to record his playing so that I could emulate it while practicing. In my tambura education, as in his, recorded music facilitated copying closely the playing technique and emulating the physicality of performing in a certain style. Grcevich had first mastered the style of Tuca, then arguably the most famous Croat tambura player in Yugoslavia. Grcevich's ability to switch from this style to that of Janika Balaž opened up additional directions of performance and musical relation to others (see later in this chapter). His education in the style of a particular male Croat musician, however, allowed him to experience musically the "ways of the hands" (Sudnow [1978] 2001), head, and body associated with *his own* ethnic performance practice.

Yet his imitation of legendary recording musicians also appears initially to have limited Grcevich's musical relations with Yugoslavian performers such as Miroslav Škoro and Zvonko Bogdan, who consistently urged him to invent a style of his own so that they could collaborate more creatively. Noting that Grcevich was a "genius" (*genijalac*) and that "in America, only Jerry can accompany me," Bogdan told me that he had recognized in the young performer the rare potential to play tambura professionally and had worked to convince him to pursue this career (Bogdan 2013; my translation). He also encouraged Grcevich to stop simply imitating Balaž and other players and to adopt a playing and compositional style of his own—something that Bogdan, too, had had to do when starting out as a singer and composer (2013).

Grcevich's own philosophy on this matter—which surely drew as much on his experiences learning to play from his father and uncle and on writing and recording his own songs as on the advice that he received from Škoro and Bogdan—distinguished compositional practice from playing style.[17] He located the latter in the embellishments that he added to preexisting songs. When he demonstrated this virtuosic, semi-improvisatory style on the song "Evo banke, Cigane moj" (Here's the banknote, my Gypsy), his basing of ornamentations on the original melody was both visible and audible. As his hands shifted positions on the neck of his basprim in order to produce the changing registers of the "main" melody, each of the four playing fingers of his left hand would hover above the string and fret against which it would soon press to produce its allotted upcoming melody note. It was largely of these positioned note-fingerings that he availed himself for the embellishments. His turns, mordents, and short diatonic or occasionally chromatic runs diminished the duration but not the salience of the "main" melody's notes and for the most part preserved its conjunct phrases (rather than introducing additional registral leaps). His "danger" as a virtuoso lay precisely in his ability to play such embellishments at tempos and in quantities (of sixteenth notes) that constantly threatened to break into free improvisation, but through which he consistently articulated the basic melody (he was considerably freer, however, in solos and during the main melody's pauses).

Grcevich conceived of the song to which he added such improvised flourishes as a musical work that an author (whether a known songwriter or the anonymous "folk") had composed in a certain way. Musicians, consequently, ought to identify and honor this original work in their performances, embellishing it in a limited fashion without actually changing the basic melody (Grcevich 2009a). He offered as an example Romanian composer Richard Stein's "Sanie cu zurgălăi" (Sleigh with bells): Zvonko Bogdan "had to be true" to its melody when he "changed the words" into "what we then called Serbo-Croatian. . . . I guess we can call it Croatian" (Grcevich 2009a). This commentary both speaks to melody's primacy in his conception of composition and raises an interesting point of comparison with "Moja Juliška." Although Bogdan did not work with Stein as Škoro worked with Grcevich, neither did he simply translate the original text by Liviu Deleanu; he composed and copyrighted new lyrics for it that, aside from a general winter theme, have little to do with the original or with Romania.[18] Grcevich's philosophy on the issue of melody also parallels Croatian copyright law, which assigns intellectual property rights for songs in a tripartite fashion: for the music, text, and arrangement.[19]

In playing the music of legends such as Janika Balaž, Grcevich himself embellishes the basic melody in his own virtuosic (dangerous) style and, to the extent that he recomposes anything, adjusts in creative ways the piece's structure and accompaniment. Thus when in March 2009 at Pittsburgh's Gypsy Café Grcevich asked me what they could play for me and I requested "a Jerry Grcevich original," he responded by suggesting "a Janika Balaž piece with a Jerry Grcevich touch to it." He proceeded to lead the group Gipsy Stringz in a Balaž instrumental composition that he both ornamented lavishly and medleyed into short virtuosic breaks of his own composition. He thereby balanced adherence to the original with a compositional and stylistic approach that staked out his own, nonimitative practice.

Grcevich's development of a personal style in collaboration with Škoro realized this creative turn in his musicianship. Just as their conversations together opened up spaces between their respective languages for inventive hybridization and improvisation, each developed musically in the process of recording their first album. Where Škoro and their joint recording project prompted Grcevich to develop a personal style, Grcevich as the older and more experienced songwriter pushed Škoro, who was "very talented" at writing song texts and "learned a lot from Jerry" about compositional technique (Bogdan 2013; my translation). The interplay between the familiar and unfamiliar enacted in their translations expanded beyond the emulation of difference and similarity (and the qualities of certain other musicians, performance styles, and ethnic types) to a space for creative relation to the sonic and tactile experiences of "ethnic" performance.

This space—both the smooth proximities of their composing and the sonic-architectural interior of Grcevich's parents' basement where they collaborated—was an intimate one. When Škoro accepted the slightly older musician's invitation to come play some music since their houses were only ten minutes apart, "thus began our intensive, everyday socializing. A beautiful time that will never repeat itself again. I was concentrated on Kimica, music and Jerry. That was my world" (Škoro 2010, 71; my translation).

Grcevich, for his part, fondly recalled writing melodies and arrangements for his near neighbor Škoro. He contrasted this experience with his situation at the time of our lessons, when Bob Sestili, Peter Kosovec, and the latter's cousin David Kosovec (the kontra player who with violinist George Batyi filled out the Gipsy Stringz lineup) each lived more than forty-five minutes away (Grcevich 2009b). Recollections from this time resonate with sonic descriptions: Škoro "composed 'Ne dirajte mi ravnicu' in my basement" while Grcevich "wrote the arrangements, the chords" (Grcevich 2009a); Škoro had "to get used to his rhythm" of joking around in the daytime and working at night (Škoro 2010, 71; my translation); they "listened to [Grcevich's] recordings" and "put on the [new] recordings for Kimica" (71). Nostalgic and idealized, these recollections nonetheless evince what Lauren Berlant has called a "live intimacy": an interpersonal relation that "reminds me that I am not the subject of a hymn but of a hum, the thing that resonates around me, which [. . .] involves getting lost in proximity to someone and in becoming lost there, in a lovely way" (Berlant 2010, 102). Their rhythms of living, resonating, and listening with one another suggest, in Berlant's words, the affect of

> a hum not where "we" were but all around, and that hum is a temporizing, a hesitation in time that is not in time with the world of drives and driving; nor is it in a mapped space, but rather a space that is lost. What intersubjectivity there is has no content but is made in the simultaneity of listening. (102–103)

The rhythms and resonance of Grcevich and Škoro's intersubjectivity were the product not only of musical collaboration but also of the intimate relations of male, heterosexual friendship. Berlant's comments concern John Ashbery's poem "Ignorance of the Law Is No Excuse" and the loveliness of two men in love rather than bonded in friendship. Berlant uses Ashbery's passage to introduce "cruel optimism": "a relation of attachment to compromised conditions of possibility whose realization is discovered either to be *im*possible, sheer fantasy, or *too* possible, and toxic" (2010, 94). In transplanting this reading to a homosocial context, some of that cruelty is lost, though perhaps not all of it, as Škoro's description of the impossibility of the return of their "beautiful time" (following the birth of his two children and the advancement of his and his wife's careers) suggests.

Yet the creative, musico-textual relations and co-compositional becomings enabled in this intimate, intersubjective resonance were precisely what led to the men's writing and recording their Russian-Hungarian-Croatian hybrid, "Moja Juliška." If humorous particulation of language and intensive composing (they wrote the album's twelve songs in twelve days) in a Croatian national style could bring the Yugoslavian rock singer and the Croatian American tamburaš intimately into one another's zones of proximity, these activities could also open them dangerously to composing with—not merely imitating—the musics of other nationalities. As Bogdan made clear in his equally humorous yet pointed critique, at issue here was not their abandoning of Croatian performance practice per se but the transgression of the stability of *distinction between* practices. While such a concern for purity naturally raises questions of musical authenticity, I argue here for the centrality of sincerity. As Croats, Serbs, Hungarians, and other East European communities increasingly drew into zones of neighborly proximity with one another and with broader "white" and African American communities, these intimates faced new challenges to sincerely affective relations with their own specific ethnic term. The very difficulty of separating such terms as pure entities out of the jumble of "ethnic" whiteness in which tambura music circulates gave rise to a new, racial sincerity that blocks and supplants objectifying discourses on authenticity as their intersubjective excess (Jackson 2005). Neither ignoring Bogdan's critique nor letting it stop them from performing "Moja Juliška," Škoro, Grcevich, and the many tamburaši who perform the song embrace its humorously translative capacities. They do so with an intensity that, with certain exceptions that speak to race's dangerous affect (and the need to block it before it goes too far), becomes this sincerity in lieu of authenticity as they perform for audiences who traverse increasingly complex geographies of musical contact. It is to these changing zones of proximity and their fostering of racial sincerity that I turn now.

MUSIC AND PITTSBURGH'S
POSTINDUSTRIAL SPATIALIZATION

Such mixing of immigrant cultures, in combination with their persistent distinction from African American as well as more assimilated white communities, has led many tamburaši to appropriate "Hunky" and, somewhat less commonly, the more broadly intelligible slur "honky" in describing their music. Many of my interlocutors used these terms regularly and sometimes interchangeably, although they have distinct origins: "honky" is a term for white Americans more broadly whose use is often associated with African Americans; "Hunky," as one interlocutor noted to me, likely derives from the word "Hungarian," but many East European peoples in Pittsburgh who are active in "ethnic" events use this word reflexively. Although some musicians in the tambura scene apparently conflated the two words, likely due to their phonetic and semantic similarities, the two terms referenced similar yet actually distinct anxieties over essentialisms and distancing experienced in relation to African American and white Anglo-Saxon Protestant (WASP) populations, respectively. Both experiences are integral to tambura music's affective work in racializing and spatializing musicians' lives.

The appropriation of "Hunky" by Croatian and Serbian Americans suggests an openness to subsumption under a homogenized (Hungarianized) grouping conflating East European peoples whose neighborhoods and performance practices have intertwined. Far from remaining a spatially stable and demographically homogenous East European entity, however, this jumble of nationalities was very much in flux in the final decades of the twentieth century. The precise geography of multinational tambura performance in cities such as Pittsburgh that musicians traversed in the late 1980s and that Bogdan's critique seemed to reference would soon change dramatically.

The wars of Yugoslavia's dissolution that helped to popularize Grcevich and Škoro, whose nostalgic lyrics resonated with a public longing to return to peaceful times and to occupied territories, also divided North America's Croatian and Serbian communities. In Pittsburgh, the geography of their respective communities and venues facilitated this separation (see figure 2.4); many Serbian tambura music events took place in the American Serbian Club on Pittsburgh's South Side or in centers affiliated with Serbian Orthodox Churches even farther south. Croatian gatherings, meanwhile, happened primarily at clubs and centers north of the Monongahela River or even beyond the Allegheny River, on Pittsburgh's North Side. During my fieldwork in 2009, many Serbian and Croatian

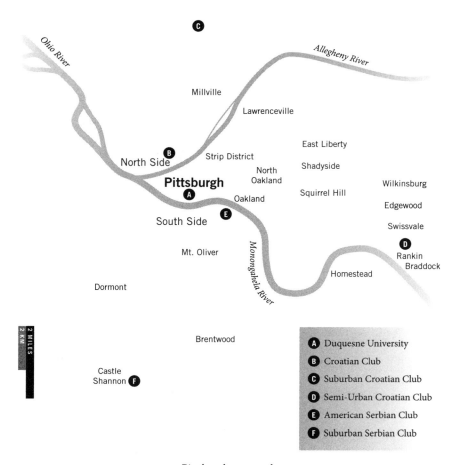

FIGURE 2.4 Pittsburgh area tambura venues

American interlocutors noted that they had ceased attending one another's events during the war. They had resumed attending only recently (around 2004) and were still less likely than before the war to cross over the Monongahela River for this purpose.

They also noted, however, that Croats and Serbs had reconciled much more successfully in Pittsburgh than in cities such as Chicago, where waves of new immigrants from the former Yugoslavia had brought fresh memories of violence. The Duquesne University Tamburitzans, though directed largely by Croatian musicians and situated just north of the Monongahela, arguably contributed to the relative speed of tambura players' reintegration.[20] Their scholarship opportunities, repertorial diversity, and geographic centrality within the nexus of tambura performance venues continued to make them attractive to Serbian American students during and after the war. Reintegration has not proceeded symmetrically, however, and Serbs, whose presence is sometimes taken as a territorializing force (see chapter 3), less commonly crossed into Croatian performance venues to listen or play than did Croats into Serbian locations.

The issue of territorialization is often exacerbated by the fact that many families affiliated with ethnic centers and clubs for generations have needed or chosen to move from their vicinities. As in other Rust Belt cities, Pittsburgh's steel industry suffered dramatically in the 1970s and 1980s, and the mill jobs that had attracted thousands from Southeast Europe in the 1890s were not available a century later when Yugoslavia's war refugees immigrated. As mills closed, many South Slavic families moved away from their long-standing communities nearby and, transitioning to white-collar careers facilitated by educational opportunities such as those offered at Duquesne University, began settling diffusely in various suburbs. According to George Batyi, a prominent Rom violinist who performs regularly with tamburaši, Pittsburgh's Roma made an even more substantial exodus, departing nearly en masse for the then still-plentiful industrial opportunities in midwestern cities when Pittsburgh's steel industry began to suffer with the onset of the 1973 oil crisis (Batyi 2013). Batyi himself moved to Michigan and attempted to make a living playing music there and in neighboring Ontario, Canada, but he quickly returned to Pittsburgh's East European neighborhoods; there he found better professional musical prospects, even during the 1990s, when he notes having had to weather the souring relations between his Croatian/ Serbian publics and collaborators and the latter's sudden refusals to play for or with one another (2013).[21]

Several formerly East European neighborhoods are now in disrepair, offering low-income housing that is inhabited by sizable African American populations. Pittsburgh's industries drew thousands of black workers from the South during the Great Migration after World War I (Gottlieb 1991, 70), and nearly a century later, in the 2010 census, 27.7 percent of Pittsburgh's population self-identified as black or African American (US Census Bureau 2010). Following the steel industry's decline in the late twentieth century, interracial tensions flared over employment, upward mobility, and territorializing habitation of urban space. Yet churches, clubs, and lodges in the old neighborhoods remained important community centers to which Croatian and Serbian Americans returned, especially for tambura training and performances. Many musicians and fans, even as they stopped frequenting other peoples' venues during the war, became accustomed to commuting long distances to visit their musical centers. On these trips they increasingly sensed their distinction from local majority populations more racially and musically distant than their formerly close fellow Slavs.

In 2009 Croatia-oriented musicians (many of whom lived in wealthier neighborhoods but commuted to the Croatian Homes, clubs, and churches for music, services, and other social events) exhibited an anxiety arising over social separation yet also over encounter and musical competition with African Americans. This anxiety registered in comments that several interlocutors made (with intended humor), ranging from self-deprecating remarks about tambura music's "Hunky/honky" nature to jokes about potential interracial violence. I discuss anxieties about physical, racialized danger in the next section.

The connection between anxious discourses on whiteness (and on racial distinction) and Croat-Serb relations warrants some consideration first. The annual Tamburitza Extravaganza, organized by the Tamburitza Association of America (TAA), meets in a different North American city each year and since the 1970s has been the premiere event bringing together ensembles of Croatian, Serbian, and mixed membership. As Richard March argues, the program's inclusion of "both Orthodox and Catholic observance opportunities for Extravaganza festival participants is an indication of the TAA's clear intent that the event welcomes both Serbians and Croatians" (2013, 166).[22] The event also welcomes musicians of non–South Slavic descent, if in tellingly different ways. Held in downtown Pittsburgh (a geographically intermediary position), one particular Extravaganza featured George Batyi's band Gipsy Stringz, a regular participant in the event. The Extravaganza's master of ceremonies (a member of a mixed Croatian and Serbian band) drew particular attention to its Romani orientation, asking Batyi with evident earnestness: "Are you the one who brings the Gypsy element to the group?" There followed a long, uncomfortable pause during which Batyi stared back at the MC with an uncertain expression. The MC then added, "because of your violin," to which Batyi responded with a nervous chuckle: "I guess so."[23] The MC's deflection from the question's potentially racial connotations via a stereotypical invocation of the violin as the marker of Romani or "Gypsy" difference within tambura music did little to ease the essentializing terms of the introductory question. Batyi has since remarked to me that he feels that some tamburaši expect him to supply such a "Gypsy element" in their bands (Batyi 2013).[24] In contrast, the MC introduced Trubaduri—a Croatian American rock band specializing in Croatian patriotic popular music that on this particular occasion featured no tamburas in its lineup — by jokingly praising the musicians for their "contribution to this music and other 'honky' stuff." Singling out neither its difference in instrumentation nor its questionably nationalistic repertoire, he placed this band in a broader category of white performance distinguished anxiously, if humorously, by its presumed negative reception among (or in comparison to) African American musicians.

In North America, the term "honky" has a number of important associations with white musical culture beyond tambura practice. Contemporaneous with honky-tonk saloons and the eponymous brand of country music that emerged in association with them, Polish American bands developed a "honky style" of polka in the 1950s (Keil 2005, 119). Polka has long played an important part in American tambura bands' live dance repertoires. Richard March, whose Croatian heritage and experience with bands have made his scholarly output popular among American tambura circles, has paired Croatian American tambura recordings immediately alongside Chicago-style honky Polish American bands on a number of Midwest polka compilations.[25] Croats' and Serbs' common anxiety over being lumped together musically and racially with the progenitors of polka and country (and being considered similarly less adept or fashionable than blues/soul musicians) have paved the way for reestablishing their common bonds and commutes across the Monongahela River since the early 2000s.

In Croats' and Serbs' evolving relations to and through urban space we can, in the words of Adam Krims, "see music as both part of the spatialization of social relations and also as a consequence of that spatialization" (Krims 2007, 31). Tambura performance has both facilitated the maintenance of churches and clubs as centers for dispersed communities and also caved to the spatializing pressures of industry and nationalism. These localities, though used at times for resistance against both ethnically close adversaries and racially distant competitors brought into proximity through the flux of urban space, acquire symbolic and economic value that contributes to the urban spatialization of East European interaction. (Ethnic) place and urban space, "far from being separate and opposed realms in which we can cheer one side against the other [. . .] increasingly merge in the contemporary world, becoming two different faces of a single, overarching hegemonic process" (35). Such economically driven diffusion continues to privilege the intercity and international musical networks that facilitated Bogdan's 1989 meeting with Škoro and Grcevich.

This diffusion has also made networking with amicable groups outside one's own ethnicity but situated within the same city or a shared regional network of ethnic culturo-economic cooperation quite advantageous, leading to the mixing that Bogdan critiqued in "Moja Juliška." For tambura musicians, especially during the Yugoslav conflicts, this mixing very often happened along religious lines: Croats turned to their fellow Catholics (Slovenians, Hungarians, and Lithuanians), and Serbs often looked to other Orthodox Slavs who go in for similar styles of music (e.g., Ukrainians and Macedonians). Many of the "Croatian" families that I met in Pittsburgh also had Scottish and Irish American members who had married in, and my introduction to the Rankin Croatian Home on the east side of Pittsburgh and to its Junior Tamburitzans ensemble actually came about through a woman named Anne, who noted that she and I were alike in claiming mostly Anglo-Saxon/Celtic heritage. Her husband, though not a tambura player, is of Slovenian descent, and this provided a connection for their children, who grew up playing in the ensemble. Anne had involved herself deeply in organizing and fund-raising for Rankin's Junior Tamburitzans, and once her son joined Duquesne University's Tamburitzans, for that larger coeducational ensemble (which like its feeder groups instructs all its youths in the dances, songs, and tambura performance of diverse ethnicities).[26] My welcome into the group and the Croatian Home seemed to have been precipitated by the joining of many Irish and Scottish spouses.

That Croatian Americans still felt separate from the white majority population, not only as a distinct ethnic group but also as part of the broader "Hunky" demographic, became clear as they and I negotiated the limits of my own acceptance and distinction within the tambura scene. In March 2009 I became a member of the Tamburaški Zbor Svete Marije (the Tambura Choir of Saint Mary's), an adult amateur tambura ensemble based in a Croatian Roman Catholic parish serving the Rankin community. The group was preparing for an upcoming performance at the 2009 Tamburitza Festival ("TamFest") at the Cokeburg, Pennsylvania, Croatian Lodge where Grcevich had grown up performing. At my first rehearsal, when a female ensemble member and leader introduced me as "Ian MacMillen," several members began joking in heavily stylized Greek accents that it would have been appropriate if my name had been "*Eee-awn Mee-lehr*." This was neither the first nor the last time that Croatian American musicians made this humorous reference to "Ian Miller," the groom character in *My Big Fat Greek Wedding*. Over the course of that 2002 film, Miller's distinction from his bride's Greek immigrant family becomes increasingly evident, both in the extent of their ritual festivities vis-à-vis his own white (Anglo-Saxon) American family's dearth of traditions and in their heavily accented pronunciation of his name.

Employing this as a humorous script for not just encountering but also accepting an ethnographer within their ethnic enclave (as they had done with Scottish and Irish American spouses), tambura players simultaneously mobilized it for a further distancing from white America in which musical separation translated into reappropriating the accents of their immigrant ancestors.

At stake in these encounters and in the humorous acts of accentation and translation that they at times require and at times enable is, I argue, sincerity. This sincerity marks a becoming similar to that previously discussed with respect to Škoro and Grcevich but operating on broader spatial and communal planes. The affective investment that such sincerity demands from musicians and other tambura participants who are willing to become-"honky" or -"Hunky" (and yet objectify this process in humorous discourse) points to the capacities of tamburaši to influence directly the opening or closing of their affective blocks to one another. These capacities involve the musical spatialization and racialization of the intimacies into which they enter with their audiences—processes that I examine in two case studies from my fieldwork that again involve the song "Moja Juliška." I begin by considering the affective and discursive dimensions of sincerity in Rust Belt experiences of "Hunky" musicality, returning to the discussion of translation via the case of a recent live performance of "Moja Juliška" at a Croatian concert held in a Lithuanian banquet hall in the Toronto area. I then examine discourses and feelings of racial anxiety among professional musicians navigating "honky" subjectivity and their musical and spatial proximities to African American communities in Pittsburgh, analyzing the involvement of a semiprofessional tambura band from that same part of Ontario, Canada. These highlight, respectively, how humorous significations can serve strategically to block off (delimit) the sincere intensities otherwise privileged in tambura performance and how the corresponding block (aggregation) is, however, again that of a resilient affect (discourse and signification block off but do not block as an aggregate).

ŠKORO'S MISSISSAUGA CONCERT, NONTRANSLATION, AND A BLOCK TO/OF BECOMING

To the time-intensive traversing of Pittsburgh and the broader Rust Belt region that the new (post)industrial human geographies required, Jerry Grcevich often compared his earlier experiences playing and composing with his near neighbor Miroslav Škoro. In the fall of 2008 and the spring of 2009, when I was conducting research in Pittsburgh, most Thursdays would find him playing with George Batyi, Bob Sestili, Peter Kosovec, David Kosovec, and a number of others who occasionally joined this core group at the Gypsy Café on Pittsburgh's South Side. The long commutes that most of them faced often resulted, however, in one or more of them arriving late or not at all, and Grcevich lamented the fact that they mostly met up in order to play there, rather than beforehand to practice the repertoire or to socialize (2009b). He, too, sometimes skipped this gig while providing little information to his bandmates, though often in order to seek out more musically, financially, and socially rewarding opportunities even farther away from his home in Homestead, Pennsylvania. Notably, when Zvonko Bogdan toured Canada with his band from Novi Sad, he would call Grcevich away to join them there.

Sincere camaraderie among male musicians evidently did not quite take hold in newer, public venues such as the Gypsy Café to the extent that performers nostalgically recalled from the ethnic clubs and households where they once socialized as neighbors. This, however, did not entirely dissuade tambura players from traveling in order to locate and engender intimacy. On the contrary, collaborations between musicians in the Pittsburgh and Toronto areas (who traveled much longer than forty-five minutes) have generated some of the most poignant moments of musical sincerity and affective intimacy in networks of performance marked by increasing geographic and ethnic diversity.

In February 2011 Miroslav Škoro performed a pair of concerts at the large Lithuanian Hall in Mississauga, Ontario, a city outside of Toronto with several tambura ensembles supported by sizable populations of Croatian and Serbian immigrants and their descendants.[27] The concerts drew audiences of a few thousand from throughout Ontario, neighboring states, and even US Rust Belt cities such as Pittsburgh. (Like many Croatian acts, Škoro, his band, and his guest tambura band Lyra had scheduled performances only in Canada, for which they could more readily obtain visas than for the United States.)

Jerry Grcevich and I met up inside the banquet hall, and he told me that he was hoping that I would be able to film parts of his performance using his digital camera. He found me an empty chair at one of the tables near the stage from which I would be able to record at close range. This table, it turned out, was otherwise in use by a number of Pittsburgh-area tamburaši whom I knew from my fieldwork almost a year and a half earlier: Megan Barišić, an alumna of the Duquesne University Tamburitzans and director of a Pittsburgh junior tambura ensemble; Dario Barišić, Megan's husband, the founder of Pittsburgh's

T. S. Barabe (Savages) and an alumnus of the Duquesne University Tamburit-zans, for which he auditioned while touring North America for the CFU with the tambura band Zvona (Bells); and Bob Sestili and his wife. They and many others had driven from Pittsburgh to attend the Saturday concert and to see friends there from the United States, Canada, and Croatia.

Škoro's performance that Saturday differed in size, length, and structure from concerts of his that I had attended in Croatia. Whereas his winter 2009 perfor-mances for sold-out stadia in Zagreb and Osijek had lasted approximately two hours with no intermission, in Mississauga he sang a two-hour set, took an intermission of more than an hour's duration, and then finished with a ninety-minute set. During the intermission, Škoro sat at a table signing CDs, T-shirts, and his new autobiography and took time to pose with fans for photographs and speak to them individually (in Croatian with some but in English with the majority). After the second set, he also welcomed backstage several Pittsburgh musicians and me. He spoke at length with Bob Sestili, though he turned his greatest attention to Jerry Grcevich, whom he suddenly and forcefully kissed on the cheek. As the somewhat more introverted tamburaš looked down with an embarrassed grin, Škoro exclaimed in English with evident earnestness yet delight at his friend's awkward response: "I love you Jerry Grcevich!"

Škoro developed his characteristic jokes at greater length than at other perfor-mances, garnering particularly lengthy audience indulgence and participation during "Moja Juliška," one of several songs for which Grcevich accompanied him onstage. In their original recording, Škoro follows the song's final chorus with a rendition of the verse melody sung to the vocable *laj*. At performances in Croatia, Škoro would joke about teaching the audience the words to this sec-tion of the song (which are simple enough not to require coaching): "Laj laj laj laj laj." He would follow this with a participatory performance of the verse and then a request that we allow him to teach us to sing the song in Hungarian—the joke here being that the lyrics were, again, "Laj laj laj laj laj." He would thereby humorously reverse the (non-)translation implicit in Bogdan's critique of the song's Hungarian lyrical content.

In Mississauga, in addition to the Hungarian rendition of the "laj" section, Škoro proposed to "teach" us to sing it in "German" and then "Chinese." These sections utilized the same melody and vocable but also mannerisms associated with these nationalities. For the "German" rendition, Škoro made his hands into fists and sang the syllables forcefully in imitation of stereotypical German severity. For the "Chinese" section, he pressed his flat palms together around the microphone and gave a small bow with his entire upper body on each of the *laj* syllables, alluding to clichés of formal, courteous Asian (if typically Japanese) mannerisms.

These latter "translations" invoked mannerisms common in much contemporary comedy in Europe and North America, in which Germans and Chinese are especially common targets. Yet Škoro's grouping of these verses with the "Hungarian" version also invites a consideration of how this song's layers of nontranslation once again fit within a particularly Croatian (or perhaps more broadly Yugoslavian) social and historical context. Not only Hungarian but also Germanic peoples (Austrians) dominated Croatian lands politically, economically, and to a large degree culturally throughout the eighteenth and nineteenth centuries, and Nazi Germany invaded Yugoslavia during World War II. In recent decades merchants and immigrants from China have brought a different form of economic competition and dominance over some portions of the Croatian market (especially the retail marketing of low-priced clothing). Thus the ethnic groups that Škoro targeted in this song have all occupied what some in Croatia consider positions of power, access, and advantage. Salient differences between them variously contradict and substantiate this commonality in the performance's treatment. On the one hand, as I argue here, the existence and gestural invoking of stereotypes for some but not others reveals deep intercultural power struggles. On the other, Škoro's selection suggests a certain equity of humorous objectification in its racialized span, from fellow "Hunkies" (Hungarians, who are also fellow "New Europeans") to both nonwhites (Chinese in this context are clearly a distant, racially distinct group and power) and those culturally "whiter" (Germans more fully assimilated into non-"ethnic" white America following the world wars[28] and are construed as more "European" within the EU).

The importance of translating "Moja Juliška" was all the more apparent in Mississauga for the many groups of Croats gathered there. Numerous audience members, particularly younger ones, spoke Croatian brokenly, if at all, and many from Pittsburgh spoke almost no Croatian. Škoro's physical gestures during his "translations" of "Moja Juliška" were thus key to the appreciation of the joke for many in the audience who could not understand all or much of his verbal introductions.

Škoro's multiplication of the song's meanings in his performances relied again on nontranslations. The fact that the vocable "laj" was exactly the same in each verse variant underscored the familiarity already in play in (non)translating between the versions as well as his relocation of the translated unfamiliar to his bodily gestures as he enacted stereotypical mannerisms. The translation of the translative act itself into the corporeal realm added another dimension to this song's play with the familiar and unfamiliar. In the process, the body became a site for experiencing differences between accustomed and foreign comportment and for the interplay and mutual blocking of affect and of conscious, essentializing discourse.

The bodies in Škoro's audiences were also important sites whose involvement allowed listeners to experience the pull toward these poles through what Arnie Cox calls "mimetic participation" (2016). This "avenue for affect," Cox argues, works through listeners engaging the skeletal-muscular system through affective desire for achieving musical-physical "goals" (178–182). In this respect, the German and Chinese versions of the "laj-laj-laj" verse worked very differently from the Croatian and Hungarian versions; the former elicited laughter but relatively little participation from the audience, who did not join in Škoro's singing or bodily gestures. The Hungarian version drew some initial chuckles but, like the Croatian version had much of the audience participating earnestly with their voices and gestures. As Grcevich (2018) communicated to me, Škoro's original idea for "Juliška" was to write a comedic song; from this perspective the melody that Grcevich supplied brought Škoro's idea and realization of the lyrics into a much more earnest set of potentials surrounding a conception of high-energy masculine nightlife (from which Škoro's "Chinese" and "German" renditions depart). Folklore tambura groups would sometimes distinguish Romani material with a similarly humorous release from the intensities invested in embodying South Slavic repertoire (MacMillen forthcoming). While it is impossible to speak to the internal feelings of all participants in response to these potentials, certainly the conditions of possibility for becoming differed between the embodiments of South Slavic/Hungarian musical performance and those of their geographic and racial Others.

Intensity is critical in (in)sincerely stepping into the gestures and corporeality of a racialized or ethnicized role. In his work on image reception, Brian Massumi distinguishes between the affect of an image's effects on the senses and body and the content of the image in "its indexing to conventional meanings in an intersubjective context, its socio-linguistic qualification [. . .]. This indexing fixes the *quality* of the image; the strength or duration of the image's effect could be called its *intensity*" (Massumi 1996, 218). This distinction is generalizable beyond image reception to other media and senses, and it isolates quality as a matter of form and content but intensity as a matter of effects and affect in the "immediately embodied" experience of sensorial practices such as musical performance (218). As Tomie Hahn has argued, "the senses reside in a unique position as the interface between body, self, and the world"; they thus "emerg[e] as the vehicles of transmission and the connection to embodied cultural expression" (2007, 3). Senses afford an essential pivoting point for performers and audience members between actions taken "to playact expressive modes not deemed appropriate outside [private spaces]" and the deeper, more intense "sensational knowledge" enacted in musically embodying such expressions with commitment (161). Škoro's adoption of the gestures of "Chinese" and "German" singers suggested the superficial form and content of the former, relying on the common forms (stereotypes) of gestures that he mobilized for his audience without leading them into a deeper embodied understanding of its senses, qualifying the song as translation.

Škoro's investment of affect (blocked in aggregation) or lack thereof (blocked off) via embodied musical intensity in interactions with audience members brings us back to questions of sincerity and race. "Racial sincerity," argues John Jackson, involves "a subject-subject interaction, not the subject-object model that authenticity presumes—and to which critiques of authenticity implicitly reduce every racial exchange" (2005, 15). Given the irreconcilable division along the axis of subjectivity and objectivity, he further suggests seeing sincerity as "authenticity's excess," its "inassimilable remainder" (13). Racial sincerity affords an alternative racialization of the real involving "social interlocutors who presume one another's humanity, interiority, and subjectivity" (15).

Singing, like speech, involves both vocalist(s) and listener(s) in reading a particular rendition as sincere or, alternatively, as a "disarticulation of sincere singing" from normative approaches to sincere performance (Jackson 2005, 187). As Jackson shows for African American emcees, these roles have to do with both masculinity and race. The two similarly intersect closely in tambura music; as a male tambura singer and the composer of "Ne dirajte mi ravnicu," Škoro took on the heavily gendered role of a musical and political defender of Croatia's sovereign nation (see chapter 1). In Škoro's case, as in that of hip-hop emcees, disarticulating vocalizing from sincere singing transgresses the racialized and gendered performance expected of him, and he "moves to increase the distance between those two forms by crossing that line in recognizably ironic and parodic ways" (187).

These forms of ironic singing are all the more effective for their distinction from Škoro's typical emphasis on sincerity and affective labor in his performances. "I can still make myself cry with my songs," he told me (Škoro 2011). Specifically, he may have had in mind a famous sold-out concert in Zagreb at which he cried while singing "Majko jedina" (Mother, one and only), a "simple, ferociously sincere [okrutno iskrena] and truthful song" dedicated to his then recently deceased mother (Škoro 2010, 223). Suddenly unable to sing, he turned to his fellow musicians for help, but they, too, were silent in sorrow, and then "my unmatched public, the like of which no one on this earth has, jumped to my aid. People cried with us and clapped for a long, long time, and I bowed to them the way that one bows to kings and to God Almighty" (223). Škoro's reliance on musicians whom music and personal circumstances still move to tears and on the thousands of unknown audience members suggests an investment in what Lauren Berlant calls an "intimate public"—an investment that has rewarded Škoro not only financially but also in the form of a fulfillment of the "expectation that the consumers of [his] particular stuff *already* share a worldview and emotional knowledge" with him (2008, viii). In his autobiography, captions beneath photographs of Škoro sobbing and yelling exuberantly onstage emphasize the importance of both his loved ones and his audience for the affect and sincerity that he engenders with valued musical collaborators such as Grcevich: "Škoro is sincere when he sings about everything: about [his] mother . . . about love toward his homeland and people . . . and when he revels together with his audience" (Škoro 2010, 220–221; my translation).

This sincerity, and its conditioning through gestures that undermine affectively intense reactions to those whose ethnicity places them outside this public, suggest a physical investment in an economy of affective labor. Hardt and Negri emphasize that "unlike emotions, which are mental phenomena, affects refer equally to body and mind" and "reveal the present state of life in the entire organism, expressing a certain state of the body along with a certain mode of thinking" (2004, 108). Thus affective labor both remains immaterial in terms of its economic production and retains a physical, corporeal base as it "produces or manipulates affects such as a feeling of ease, well-being, satisfaction, excitement, or passion" (108). Yet Škoro's labor to make himself cry requires affective work not only on the audience but also on the self, to produce within the body as well as in exchange with fans and other musicians an affective block. This aggregate of sorrowful yet at times also exquisite intensity wells up into its own selfhood as much as it hinders conscious work at rationalizing one's bodily comportment via narratives of economic value and exchange. Both he and Grcevich, whom he would compensate as a special guest accompanist at the Mississauga concert, emphasized to me that money is not their first concern and that they prioritize friendship and musicianship (cf. MacMillen 2011a).

The physical nature of such affective exertion ties Škoro's musical labor to concerns for the performer's positive work on audiences across broader networks of contemporary popular music. As Kelley Tatro demonstrates for the hard, affective work of vocalists in Mexico City's punk scene, singers may "not only arouse the intense feeling of their audiences, but [. . .] also try to demonstrate its channeling in ways that they believe to be good and potentially useful" (Tatro 2014, 447). Although producing passion and grief rather than rage, Škoro, like these punk singers, can "through the bodywork of extreme vocalizations [. . .] attempt to model an appropriate [affect to] friends and listeners, encouraging them to work to better themselves and to practice solidarity" (447).[29] No one affords a better target or collaborator for such modeling than the musician friends who join Škoro onstage in the work of moving their own bodies and those of the audience to sob and rejoice.

The sincerity and affective labor on which Škoro has long prided himself in his performances did register at the Mississauga concert, as an embodied interlocution between him and his audience. In this context we read one another's intensities as sincere as he taught and led us with humor and yet with restrained comportment in the Croatian and Hungarian refrains: strategically engendered affects that contrasted with the clearly pantomimed German and Chinese renditions. The crux of this distinction was not whether Škoro could authentically embody Croatian and Hungarian but not German or Chinese forms, but whether we could believe that he, as a male Croatian pop icon, was stepping into their gestures with sincerity (and whether he could, in turn, read this credibility in us).

Though discourse is surely one of sincerity's registers, it can merely fix the qualities of musical performance as representations of sincerity and is not the site of this music's intensities. Qualifications have their own embodiment, situated, as Massumi argues, in "depth reactions" but "also involv[ing] autonomic functions such as heartbeat and breathing," generating "a conscious-autonomic mix, a measure of their participation in one another" (1996, 219). Intensity, however, is yet another remainder, a block of affect beyond that afforded by any one discourse or conscious rationalization. In Massumi's words, "intensity is beside that loop [of conscious-autonomic participation], a nonconscious, never-to-be-conscious autonomic remainder" (219). The sincerely affective excess to race's discursive construction and embodied qualification is an inassimilable remainder in its own right, an affective block of intensity that, like other autonomic affects, is "most directly manifested in the skin" (219). This produces horripilation (goose bumps) and similar reactions with the right stimuli and under the right perceptual conditions. The alignment of such stimuli and conditions in musical performance results in what Lila Ellen Gray calls "the interanimation between different registers of feeling that [music] accrues—feeling as embodied, feeling as simultaneously of the social and of the subject, and feeling as discursive trope" (2014, 9). Given the liminality of embodied qualification between rationalist discourse as its conscious limit and affective intensity as its never-to-be-conscious excess, sonic stimuli and perceptual conditions hold great capacity for blocking musical affect (in the dual senses of engendering it in aggregate and delimiting it as excess) and this affect's potentially dangerous implications for racial becoming.

Such capacity is essential to understanding the work of racial sincerity and humor in Škoro's performances. Sincerity requires the participation of multiple subjects, and audience members were instrumental in clapping and singing along with evident earnestness during the Hungarian and Croatian verses. Their participation recognized and responded to the call for musical involvement and intersubjective reading typical of affectively engaged tambura performer-audience relations. In the other "versions," the musicians, particularly Škoro, strategically undercut the autonomic register in order to evince the insincerity of their embodiments. They qualified these gestures as racial distancing while reducing the risk of crossing into the intense embodiment of becoming (even as stereotypical gestures were the primary modality of this qualification). The joke in these latter iterations lay in the imitation of stereotypical, ethnic gestures as a form of paralinguistic translation—a meta-signification—rather than in the nontranslation of the syllable "laj." The joke cut the gestural embodiment from its potential affective remainder, blocking the affect of the Other.

Here we see the importance of imitation, not as a mode of likeness through recourse to "identity," but as becoming's inassimilable yet also indelible remainder. Similar to Deleuze and Guattari's analytical approach in *A Thousand Plateaus*, I have privileged intensity and affect over imitation. They base this distinction on simulation's incorporation of "a deeper zone of proximity or indiscernibility" rather than "a regulating or secondary imitation"; the latter, they suggest, serves only "to make people laugh" or "enters in only as an adjustment of the block, like a finishing touch, a wink, a signature" while "everything of importance happens elsewhere" ([1980] 1987, 305). Yet as I have shown in this section, making people laugh through secondary imitation was essential to Škoro's racial sincerity. This was so precisely because he led his audience in delimiting (not merely adjusting) sincerity through an embodied recognition and interlocutive reading of insincerity in the German and Chinese versions, stopping short of deep mimetic engagement.

With the Croatian and Hungarian versions, the vocable "laj" detached from its specificity as a Croatian syllable, transforming into a particle that multiplied meanings and becomings through mimetic engagement. While clearly delimiting the performed song's capacity for becomings whose terms (German, Chinese, etc.) belonged to more racially distant empires, Škoro opened up a smooth space of "Hunky" affect, a shared block (aggregation) of intensity.[30] Musical performances are particularly effective opportunities for this complicated juxtaposition of qualification and becoming, of sincerity's intense engendering and humorous denial. The affective diffusion that marks such Brechtian breaks from entrained engagement is mitigated here by the sonic continuity and the steady musical development across an ensemble's performance (the way it *keeps things humming*, to repurpose Berlant's term into a popular turn of phrase). As usual, Škoro, Grcevich, and the band finished the song at the Mississauga concert with a particularly fast performance of the "laj" chorus. They took no actions to qualify it as anything but an earnest, "Croatian" rendition, thus bringing the song around full circle to the serious affective work of becoming via the sustained *czardas* rhythms of the tambura band that, during Škoro's digressions, had prepared for the return of musical/racial intensity.

Commenting on matters of race, nation, and empire in the following month in Zagreb, Škoro (2011) told me that nationalism could not constitute a viable ideology in "the so-called melting pot" of the United States or Canada. In Croatia, 89 percent of whose population is Croats, nationalism is to be expected; unless taken to extremes, it is not necessarily harmful, as it arose in response to external imperial (Hungarian) adversity and allowed practices such as tambura music to unite regions of strong cultural differences (2011). In North American countries, however, the only thing that can work is *domoljublje*: "patriotism" (literally, "love of the home[land]"; 2011). Yet he also expressed amazement at the extent of interracial understanding in these countries (among "Japanese, Indians, Whites, Blacks"). He cited a particularly surprising experience of witnessing two Japanese men cheering on the Miami Heat basketball team in the Toronto Raptors' home stadium. In Croatia one would "kick his ass" for cheering on the away team (2011). The fact that cheers for a foreign squad (which had recently acquired one of Toronto's players) from two men of markedly foreign background drew no wrath from the fans of Canada's only National Basketball

Association team evidently challenged the capacity even of patriotism to redress such an offense. Škoro's performance in the Lithuanian Hall of the nearby city of Mississauga seems, in light of this, to have encouraged a somatic middle ground given neither to the singularity of ethnonationalism nor to the plurality of an inert and racially blind (or deaf) patriotism.

This middle ground of becomings-ethnic (but not racial Otherness) musically constituted its own "Hunky" melting pot. The zones of proximity for "Croat," "Hungarian," and the like are similar, even overlapping in performances such as Škoro's, in which audiences participate in multiple affective simulations. Their becomings may be minoritarian, but they are also multiple and assemble into a more general affective experience of ethnic whiteness: becoming-ethnic is becoming-white. Discursive construction is important to ethnic whiteness, but discourse is most significant here in its affective role, in its capacity to block certain affects, to delimit transgressive intensities at the limits of racial under-standing and embodiment and contain sincere intensity within white subjectivity.

MUSICAL WHITENESS AND BLACK MINORITARIANS

As Škoro's comments about racial diversity in North America suggest, however, Croatian Americans encounter far more than the Hungarians, Germans, and Chinese identified in his performance. The becomings-ethnic that musical affect facilitates among tamburaši in North America present a possible point of com-monality (a shared block of affect) with other minoritarian groups in the region. Olena Nesteruk and Loren Marks argue that Eastern European immigrants "are quite similar to populations with strong intergenerational relations and strong family ties such as immigrants from Latin America and Asia, or African Ameri-cans" (2009, 91). East Europeans, they argue, face challenges similar to those encountered by these other immigrants, to whom they "are probably closer (in terms of familiar values) [. . .] than to 'White' Americans, with whom they are often grouped due to a shared skin color" (91).

As anthropologist Karen Brodkin has argued, furthermore, ideas of white-ness itself have changed dramatically over the course of American capitalist industrialization's incorporation of Jews and other working-class European immigrants, "whose racial assignment in the last 150 years has gone from white to off-white and back to white" (Brodkin 2000, 240). Only around 1900, "when these immigrants took their places as the masses of unskilled and residentially ghettoized industrial workers [. . . ,] did Americans come to believe that Europe was made up of a variety of inferior and superior races" (242). Such "Euro-ethnic" (246) populations' racial pendulum swung back in the 1930s and 1940s when, as historian Matthew Jacobson writes, "'race politics' ceased to concern the white races of Europe and came to refer exclusively to black-white relations and the struggle over Negro civil rights" (1999, 247). Even "progressive coalition-building around the 'Negro Question,'" such as the work of Common Council for American Unity under Slovenian immigrant cofounder Louis Adamic (whose writings continue to influence American tamburaši and were well utilized at the Tamburitzans library), "contributed to the reforging of an undifferentiated racial whiteness" (247). These reclaimed white groups, and importantly the working-age women among them, are now often constructed as more "redeemable" than African Americans to white familial and labor organization "if they attempt to emulate ideals of middle-class white domesticity" (Brodkin 2000, 246). However, the inheritance of tambura performance and other traditions through several generations of practitioners and industrial laborers still qualifies their whiteness as "ethnic," "off-white," and "Hunky." This arguably separates them from the racialized majority in a way that sometimes parallels that of African Americans and Latinos/Latinas.

Yet as Brodkin's history suggests, whiteness, especially in cities long settled by East Europeans, is a space in flux within which such immigrants' descendants can mobilize.[31] The constant unraveling of the binary "between 'nation-races' and 'color-races'" created a "messiness" that needs to be taken seriously if we are to "encounter the harrowing and confusing aspects of how new immigrants learned of race" (Roediger 2005, 36–37). Such "trauma was not that of being made nonwhite but of being placed inbetween," yet because the construct of "Hunky" was strongly connected to hard labor, socioeconomic ascent enabled their transition out of this racial liminality (43–44). African American communities' possibilities for racial mobilization and their agency in negotiating whiteness are quite different from those whom this fluctuation sometimes incorporates. Ultimately, whiteness is, in Ruth Frankenberg's formulation, "more about the power to include and exclude groups and individuals than about the actual practices of those who are to be let in or kept out" (1997, 13). Slavic Americans' relations with these communities correspondingly are frequently tenser than those with differently white populations.

A great majority of Slavic club, lodge, and church members live in affluent (typically "white") suburbs well outside of the now diverse neighborhoods in which these institutions are situated and into whose proximities they still regularly draw. As Adam Krims notes, locales such as these afford a sense of place as "a matter of attachment, symbolism, memory, and constant cultural recreation"; yet place "is also one of the crucial cornerstones of the economic remaking of cities, conditioned by the movement and reproduction of global capital" (2007, 54). As such it is important to view music making within them not through the lens of "a folk resistance to the impersonality of space" but as part of the spatialization of an (often racialized) urban geography in which "the foregrounding of place and locality forms, to a great extent, the cutting edge of our current global economic regime" (55). Many of Pittsburgh's Croatian buildings proffer less a resistance to the loss of place or a territorialization in the face of encroaching racial Others than an architecture of sonic interiority that is key to understanding their users' spatial, economic, and racial mobility. Here my own ambiguously "ethnic" whiteness as a non-"Hunky" who could nonetheless readily enter these communities (facilitated by the many Gaelic-descended Americans who have married in) enabled a series of informative encounters with the architecture and urban geography of tambura performance.

That this sonic interiority's affect and intimacy could again depend on and sustain conceptions of racialized danger (beyond the architectural structures utilized for performance) became clear as I communicated with members at the thresholds of their organizations' physical structures. Driving me into the neighborhood of a Croatian establishment, a young man (I will call him Carson) who had performed and later volunteered in its affiliated Junior Tamburitzans ensemble told me as we neared the building that, unlike other organizations in the area, the Croatian establishment and its members had never had difficulties with nonaffiliated locals. "African American" residents always "left [them] alone" as they performed inside.[32]

In another instance, I visited a space in a Croatian social establishment that the owners had made available to a semiprofessional band that I will call Momci (The Boys), which was rehearsing for an upcoming gig at a Croatian wedding in Canada. The door to the outside remained open, and at one point that evening as we moved past it toward the quieter space beside the bar, the sound of shouting drifted in from the street. Affecting a high-pitched and heavily stylized southern accent, one of the band members exclaimed: "The negroes are fighting!"—thus seemingly parroting an effective appraisal of external violence by exteriorizing his vocality via the southern origin point of the Great Migration. These contrasting commentaries on black presence in the formerly largely Croatian neighborhoods outside marked sound—and specifically its propensity to cross these buildings' thresholds and its resistibility through drawing into architectural interiors—as a key dimension of racial spatialization. Reactions to such sounds as threat revealed interiorization to be a matter not simply of seclusion and security but of intimacy and intensity as well.

One exceptional experience from my fieldwork—which incidentally involved "Moja Juliška" again—highlighted particularly well the relationship among such interiority, the affective blocking of racialized sincerity and becoming, and tambura music's broader, urban socializing and spatializing forces in the region. In spring 2009 several tambura bands were performing at an indoor picnic at a Pittsburgh-area Hrvatski Dom (Croatian Home). Though unfamiliar with the Home itself, I already knew a number of its members, including Krunoslav, a man in his fifties. He had grown up in the Hrvatski Dom's neighborhood and long been involved in local Croatian institutions (although he was now living elsewhere and had only recently resumed playing there through an affiliated church tambura group).[33]

Krunoslav turned our conversation to the event's whiteness. We were down in the Croatian Home's bar area listening to a local tambura band composed of men from his generation who were playing English-language standards such as "I'm in the Mood for Love" and "Crazy" while older couples danced. We stayed there as they departed and were replaced on the floor by Momci, whose members were much younger and included a man from Croatia. They, too, would situate their relationship with me via *My Big Fat Greek Wedding*, shouting as I danced before them at a later picnic: "*Ajde* [Come on], Ian—*Eee-awn Mee-lehr!*" At this earlier picnic, however, I was just getting to know them, and I stood with Krunoslav and listened intently as they alternated sets of traditional instrumental pieces, which got the crowd up and participating in circular *kolo* dances, with selections from Croatian popular repertoire from the previous two decades. As they struck up "Moja Juliška," it occurred to me that their sets were quite different from those of the previous ensemble. Out of all their repertoire, Škoro and Grcevich's Pittsburgh-composed Croatian/Hungarian/Russian hybrid ironically came closest in its localness to the Anglo-American evergreen, country, and honky-tonk ballads of the older musicians' set list.

Despite the bands' differences, however, Krunoslav joked that the music was all "very white." He also complained that the event was "all white people" and laughed, explaining that he liked to provoke people at the Croatian Home with such comments. I nevertheless wondered initially whether racial discourses along these lines were arising around an anxiety over my presence—whether my interlocutors, of whom Krunoslav was merely the latest to make such a comment, were simply hedging their introductions of the music, lest it prove less interesting or exotic than I might have expected. But in these musicians' articulations of race, wasn't I, along with the other "Ian Millers" of the tambura world, on a whiter, non-"ethnic" side of the space in flux called whiteness, and thus positioned to hear tambura music as pure, exotic folk music? Similar comments made to larger publics at subsequent events suggested that these discourses were humorously channeling broader anxieties over incomplete assimilation into the area's white, postindustrial socioeconomic structures and over fraught interactions with growing African American communities in formerly largely Croatian neighborhoods: over becoming both "Hunkies" and "honkies."

Krunoslav had seen the Home's vicinity transition to a much more racially diverse and isolationist neighborhood. This isolation, however, was never fully exclusive on ethnic or even racial lines, and the Dom had welcomed a number of African American youths to its clubs. Upstairs on the main level, a picture of its basketball team from several decades earlier attested to the community's admission of non–East European children, including an African American boy, into its activities. More recently, as I learned from a member, another African American boy had joined and performed in the Home's Junior Tamburitzans ensemble alongside her children for a number of years. The acceptance of non-Slavic tambura enthusiasts had also been standard since the early 2000s.[34] The Croatian Home board's granting of membership to non-"ethnics" literally opened the organization's doors to a diverse array of participants by equipping them with keys to the side entrance, an important threshold of late-night comings and goings between the outside and the Home's basement-like bar area. The Home's official acceptance of diversity within as well as outside of its walls may have heightened perceptions of the continuously "white" nature of the musical performances there.

The experiences with racial tension that I detail in the following pages do not, however, represent a broader trend. Rather, they raise a number of important issues regarding race, sincerity, and musicians' responses to exceptional instances of racism. These experiences originated among visiting musicians (whose presence evidently reoriented the event's intimate performances to ethnic, rather than local, community) and transgressed the propriety afforded locally to strategic race-thinking.

Later that night the picture of the Rankin Home's youth basketball team featured prominently in a more troubling discussion of race. Momci had attracted the enthusiastic attention of the members of a Canadian tambura band, friends of Momci who had made the trip south from the Toronto area to perform at the picnic. It quickly became clear that this was a space and occasion at which the players and audience alike would vocally participate in generating a genuine exuberance boosted by tambura music and the consumption of alcohol. One of the Canadian musicians called out a request, shouting to the rest of us at the bar that if the band would oblige him, he was "gonna fucking lose [his] mind!" The band honored his request, and he and several of his bandmates lifted their hands in the air ecstatically. He shouted out over their performance: "Play *Miljenica*! Play *Mala*...! Hell, I don't care, play anything!" When the band obliged him with another of these requests, he shouted to a Pittsburgh-area tamburaš seated near me: "This is a bottle-smashing song!" To his Canadian friend's evident delight, this man replied: "This is a smash-anything song."

After Momci had played three sets of songs, the musicians moved with their instruments to a nearby section of the bar where a few other young tamburaši from the area, including Carson, had been sitting and listening. By this time, Krunoslav and most of the other older members had moved back upstairs. From the bellowing, fulfilling, and verbally violent ("bottle-smashing") celebration of song requests, the local musicians' vocal give and take with the Canadian band transitioned to competitive exchanges of jokes in which a number of others in the audience also participated. These are all hallmarks of the tamburanje ("tambur-ing") of young male *bećari* ("rakes") in Southeast Europe and its diasporas. Initially these jokes asserted ironically the musicians' heterosexual masculinity and friendships as they called one another homosexuals ("homos"). Eventually, however, one of the more outspoken members of the Canadian group began to dominate. He turned the focus of his witticisms to a variety of other targets (e.g., Jews, the handicapped) before settling on African Americans for a sustained series of racist jokes, the likes of which I had not previously and have not sub-sequently encountered during my fieldwork.

Most of the young men present reacted with loud, nervous laughter (one young woman was present, and she and I, it seemed to me at the time, stood out in our silence). Simultaneously, however, they made moves to express shock, seemingly shifting their reactions to the degree of the jokes' inappropriateness and away from a direct and sincere response to humor in the jokes' content. This purpose was most apparent in the reaction of one local tamburaš (one not affiliated with the Home) to a particularly abhorrent remark concerning facial features. This man laughed at the lead joke teller's remarks but then clutched his stomach and added: "I think I just threw up in my mouth." His disgust emphatically located his reaction in a solid awareness of the remark's indecency.

Another of the young male tamburaši who were gathered around the man telling the jokes smiled and commented that we were right "in the heart of the black area," pointing out the increased impropriety, potential danger, and daringness of joking about race in the Croatian Home due to its situation in a largely African American neighborhood. The joke teller responded, "Yeah, I saw that picture upstairs with the *crnac* in the middle." *Crnac* is a noun that comes from the Croatian word for "black" (*crni*) and is the equivalent of "black" as it is used, often derogatively, as a noun in English. He then turned to me and said, "You know, you didn't laugh at one joke," and asked, "we're still friends, right?" Not knowing what to say without compromising my offense at the jokes, my persistent thoughts about African American members of my own family, or my indebtedness to Carson and my other hosts at the Croatian Home who took no part in these jokes, I gestured with my head as noncommittally as I could. As promptly yet subtly as I felt was possible, I then made my excuses and left.[35]

I stepped out of the Home's doors and onto the street at about 11:00 p.m., only to discover that I had missed by a few minutes the last bus back from this neighborhood to my own area of residence several miles away. Wary of a long walk home through an unfamiliar area that members had warned me was dangerous after dark, I called Carson on my cellular phone to ask for a ride. He himself was getting into the car of the lead joke teller from Canada, so I found myself, at Carson's recommendation, accepting a ride from the very person whose comments had prompted me to leave early. Motivated by divergent concerns based on vastly differing degrees of experience with the neighborhood and its residents (this band had played at the Home before), we nonetheless found ourselves interiorizing in our transport in like manner, drawing inside the automobile's recesses as anxious "honkies" and gazing at the night outside from the thresholds of its windows. This, I later found, was an experience of the threshold between the Home's interior and exterior that was common among its members.[36] Before departing, as I hesitantly stepped into the car, the joke teller noted that this was a dangerous neighborhood and that it was "a good thing" that I had asked them for a ride.

As we drove off we passed a black man who was walking on the sidewalk. This seemed to provide our driver with both confirmation of this remark, for he pointed to the pedestrian, and fodder for an additional series of jokes. When I told him that I did not appreciate such humor, he asked rhetorically what sort of jokes I did like and launched into a series of cracks about rather mundane topics (fish, for example) whose humor depended on simple puns. His point seemed to be that he enjoyed telling jokes and the attention it garnered him, that he intended no sincerity in his biocultural racializations, and that he would easily and unconcernedly switch topics if his audience so desired.

Thus both he and the other male tambura players who had been in his audience (local Croatian Americans as well as those who had driven down from the Toronto area, another important intimate of Croatia) made deliberate attempts to demonstrate their insincerity: to block their affect, to dissociate themselves from any real intent or intensity behind the jokes and the humor in which they were engaged continuously for nearly an hour. The lead joke teller's ease in switching comedic topics and the disgust that the local tamburaši expressed (though again with humorous inflection and likely intent, given their continuing laughter) served to position their enjoyment in provocation and humorous performance rather than in serious denigration of a specific people. This performance of intent may have been partly for my benefit, but it was also for theirs. This parallels a trend that one can recognize in racially and ethnically charged jokes in North American society more generally. Ideologies of political correctness and the pluralism of views that comedians encounter often privilege their locating of humor in the transgression of that very political correctness through the use of profoundly racist jokes.

There is a certain pleasure in disgust, too—even in disgust emitted as much (or more) as a performance concerned with correctness as internalized through any physical sensation. As Winfried Menninghaus, consulting Sigmund Freud's theories, writes: "Expeditions into the underside of disgust breathe an unmistakable sympathy with their object—an affect for the uncivilized, which habitually infuses even the most striking 'perversions' as proof of the power of the abandoned positions of libido" (2003, 191). These jokes, however, did not transpire in North American society more generally, but in the context of an event incorporating members of two of Croatia's intimates in a building situated in a now largely African American neighborhood. Their intent was provocation and through it the fostering of intimacy between ethnically varied white subjects (if Croatia-oriented, we were not all "Croats"). Ethnic jokes are a common part of interethnic (heterosexual male) camaraderie in South Slavic communities in Southeast Europe and its diasporas. In a speech targeting "political correctness," Slavoj Žižek (2015) has provocatively argued that "progressive racism" in the form of "friendly obscenities" was what preserved good interethnic relations in

Yugoslavia. The "cold respect" that replaced this humorous form of "real contact" was, he claims, complicit with the genocidal acts of Yugoslavia's dissolution (2015). (In the Hrvatski Dom that evening, however, there was no contact—"friendly" *or* "cold"—with the neighborhood's African American residents.) These factors heavily conditioned and facilitated the enjoyment of disgust and provocation even as those involved performed their own dissociation from the racist content of the jokes and from the block of affect (for the uncivilized) that cogenerated with them.

The session of jokes that followed the tambura performances at the Home's picnic was also a ripe context for becomings-Croatian through a linguistic particulation that mirrored that of Škoro and Grcevich twenty years earlier. The translation "crnac" was an effective "something else" for the becoming-Croatian of the lead joke teller precisely because it was a translation with no appropriate original text. To infer that he translated from a one-word English noun such as "negro" or an even more offensive alternative would be to discount the greater cultural acceptability of "crnac" in Croatia vis-à-vis the English terms in present-day English-speaking North America. Alternatively, to infer that he translated from the word "black," which is far more commonly acceptable in North America as an adjective than as a noun, would be to lose the fixity of the single-word noun form. The lead joke teller's translation was part of his becoming-Croatian[37] and simultaneously of his becoming-ethnic, becoming-"honky." Context was crucial here; he and his fellow tamburaši were Croatian not in distinction to Serbs, Slovenes, or even Roma, but to the African Americans who (they perceived) were racially isolating the Croatian Home where they had assembled in the basement interior to play tamburas and to enjoy each other's music, company, and humor.

The "affect for the uncivilized" that marks the expressions of disgust at such jokes is the very site of this becoming. Insincerity affords a strategic positioning and affective blocking in relation to these jokes' sociolinguistic content. Yet underlying it is an attachment to an intense, embodied feeling (the block itself) of estrangement with an irreconcilable term: in this case, the black body as the locus of an impossible becoming, a not-to-become. This instance of insincerity differed from Škoro's, for here racializing humor was not the agent but the object of disruption. Countering racial stereotypes could have taken the form of breaking out of the racial distancing employed within the humor, but two insincerities do not a genuine engagement make. Instead, it once again blocked the affect of becoming-Other, leaving a resilient affective block, but of a becoming-Ethnic (not becoming-Other): what Massumi terms "limitative becoming" (1987). In such instances, the significatory (discursive and gestural) cutting of sincerity blocks off the more immediate form of affective enjoyment that might emerge among such musicians but for the excessive, transgressive nature of the jokes' racial content, which requires laughter's diffusion of intensity (see MacMillen forthcoming). Yet it also blocks as an aggregate the pleasure of disgust, leaving a residual affect beyond the limitative becoming that also bolsters the becomings-ethnic straddling the boundaries of intimate interiors and dangerous exteriors. Affect is blocked, but also blocked (and discourse blocks off, but what it aggregates is not discursive but yet again a block of affect).

CONCLUSION

The zones of proximity of ideas, bodies, affects, and particulate language that facilitate becomings-Croat also in such instances are constituted by distances from Others-becoming-race, by individuals comprising a "something else." Translation through accent and language particles elevates such estrangement to the greatest intensity when the translation's object is this irreconcilable term that demands a distance: a Croatian word to identify a black presence on the sports teams housed within the architectural interior; a southern accent to project black violence outside such architecture's threshold; a German or Chinese gesture to qualify participation as humorous imitation moving beyond the intimate "Hunky" space of the Lithuanian banquet hall; or a Greek accent to identify a non-"ethnic" ethnographer who regularly crossed into such interiors. But on these particular evenings most of the musicians (those from Canada and Croatia) did not yet know me and likely did not identify me as such before our car ride or backstage meeting. Thus the intimacy of the buildings' interiors was seemingly left untransgressed.[38] The affective spaces of these jokes may not have extended in anyone's mind but my own to the broader civil society, white America, or even the local neighborhoods in which such remarks would have been truly uncivil and political (as opposed to the quips of one marginalized group at the expense of others).

Such affective interiorization is part of tambura music's "deterritorialization" (Deleuze and Guattari [1980] 1987, 291). Anthropologist Alexei Yurchak has linked this process to what he describes as "an intense and intimate commonality and intersubjectivity" (in Russian, *obshchenie*; 2005, 148) and "a condition of being simultaneously inside and outside of some context" (i.e., "being *vnye*"; 127–128). Examining late-Soviet confluences of labor, socializing, and interior spatialization of music listenership, he warns that the times and activities of *obshchenie* and being *vnye* within various milieus should not be seen as spaces of authenticity and freedom that were clandestinely "carved out" from the spatial and temporal regimes imposed [. . .]. They were not exceptions to the system's dominant spatial and temporal regimes but, on the contrary, were paradigmatic manifestations of how these regimes functioned. (156)

Boiler rooms, walled courtyards, and freight train compartments afforded many Soviet rock musicians official employment opportunities in which they could work within but simultaneously pursue (musical) interests moving outside of the prescriptions of the official economy (152–153). Similarly, the basements, bar areas, and other architectural interiors where people partake in tambura music in the postindustrial Rust Belt do not provide escape from but in fact functionally constitute the (racialized and gendered) system of spatialization across the region's urban geographies, which has resulted in these Croatian Homes' perceived isolation. Territorialization and the defense of place do at times play a role in the sonic constitution of these spaces (particularly in relations between Croats and Serbs, which I analyze in chapter 3). Their usages within networks of mobility that mostly depend on the interiority of car travel rather than on walking outside, however, open up spaces in which both greater physical distances and greater ethnic differences find their zones brought into one another's proximities (if sometimes strategically resisted through interiorization in basements and cars).

The zones of physical proximity of Croats, Hungarians, Serbs, and others change with the continual flux and spatialization of the urban geography of Pittsburgh, Chicago, Mississauga, and the routes in between these and other such cities. Tambura players' affective experiences of minoritarian whiteness correspondingly shift in relation to both friendly and threatening entities within and outside of racialized communities. Musical affect and its strategic employment at the limit of a racial sincerity in performance contexts throughout these (post)industrial geographies enable a mobility between "honky" and "Hunky" sensibilities, a capacity to aggregate as a block of affect with respect to one while simultaneously blocking off the other. The important corollary is that when one potential affective engagement is blocked discursively (or through other significatory processes such as gestural stereotyping), blocking in aggregation still transpires, but this block is again affective. It leaves a resilient remainder of feeling that can be called upon again for ambivalent solicitations of the strangeness and danger of Others. Music's particular claim to affective work, then, lies in its capacity for holding attention (through rhythmic entrainment, phrasing, progression, etc.) and sustaining its stimulation in ways that keep this resilient embodiment present. As I show in chapter 3, such mobilities and resilience bear significantly on relations between ex-Yugoslav groups (Croats, Roma, and Serbs in particular) in the post–Yugoslav conflict era.

THREE

Feeling and Knowing Race in
Postwar Croatian Music

August 2008: I met for the first time with Antun and Vesna, leaders of Osijek's STD "Pajo Kolarić," whom I had contacted from the United States beforehand via email. They hosted me at two events with live music, the first being a dinner that they had organized at the Krčma kod Ruže (Tavern at the Rose) in the part of Osijek known as Tvrđa after the eighteenth-century Austro-Hungarian fortress whose remains enclose it. There, Dule Bend, a group consisting of three tambura players, a violinist, and Dušan "Dule" Đurđević, the group's leader, accordionist, and singer, gathered around one table after the next to play (as they do on nearly every weekend night). When they approached our table, Antun told them that I had come from America to study tambura music, and the band elected to play "Ne dirajte mi ravnicu," by Osijek's Miroslav Škoro, in my honor. We gazed across the table at one another as we sang along with the musicians, our intimacy and expressions of joy deepening, it seemed to me, as we came to recognize our mutual familiarity and contentment with the song.

The following day we drove to Bački Monoštor, a town with a sizable Croatian population located approximately forty kilometers northeast of Osijek and just across the Croatian/Serbian border formed by the Danube River. In between the children's choir's performances and discussions with local tambura leaders, which were our ostensible reasons for the trip (see chapter 1), we were entertained by a similar band of tamburas, violin, and accordion. Like Dule Bend at the Krčma kod Ruže, this ensemble featured a majority of tambura players but was comprised of Roma and marketed simply as Cigani. Institutions of tambura performance in Croatia and in its intimates across the border in Serbia structured Croatian musical relations through official meetings and events. Yet Romani musicians, with what I came to understand was a disputed claim to tambura music, provided a vital if often informal part of this musical system.

In this chapter I consider the sonic emergence of racial boundaries, of practices of inclusion and exclusion that mobilize affect and faculties of musical understanding in the shared and contested spaces of tambura performance. If the ethnic performances in the American Rust Belt discussed in the previous chapter afford a telling perspective on affect's mutable role in situating communities of listeners between whiteness and Otherness, Croatia's contemporary tambura scene reveals how musical sensibilities and the affective and discursive responses that comprise them can racialize even at the level of a majoritarian population. While Croatia's autonomy long postdates that of the United States, its tambura players, most of whom identify as Croats, assert deep and primary territorial belonging to Slavonia, staking their claims through feelings of love and loss and through discursive tropes of material connection in their DNA. The inconsistent discursive and physical inclusion of Romani and even Serbian musicians that characterizes the East Croatian tambura scene fluctuates as multiple actors navigate limited capacities for shared musical affect and for understanding the musical *melos* of Others. What results is at times a deep and diverse musical intimacy; at other times it is a drive of musical aggression and territoriality that channels sentiments most intensely embodied during Croatia's war for independence.

Becoming, as Deleuze and Guattari argue, is a minoritarian process—to become-Croat or -Roma wrests one from a majoritarian positionality—yet it is also a process that impinges on majoritarian subjects ([1980] 1987, 291). The musical affects and melos that diverse tambura musicians share and contest with one another contributed to the emergence of an imagined Croatian community and the intimate mobilization of a tradition well recognized for its inventedness but nonetheless intensely embraced as national heritage. As Croatia's waxing territorial sovereignty increasingly assured its inhabitants of their majoritarian status over the course of the 1990s, they began once again to partake of non-Croatian musics in public (an indulgence that in some cases had ceased even in private following the split with Yugoslavia). The renewed popularity of ensembles such as those that performed for Antun, Vesna, and me at the Krčma kod Ruže and in Bački Monoštor rests on an affective experience of Otherness. It involves a flirting with becoming-Other, but also its simultaneous dissociation from the paradigms of national sentiment and referentiality employed in forging the musical networks between Croatia and its intimates.

For all of postwar Croatia's presumed ethnic homogeneity, the country's tambura performance scape is today nearly as varied and as spatialized via racialized economic dynamics as that of the American Midwest discussed in the previous chapter. Its loss of industry, however, while certainly heavily affected by global changes in economies and production processes and by the transition from Yugoslavia's own particular form of socialism, is largely associated with local factories' physical (wartime) as opposed to fiscal devastation. The identification of the Yugoslav Army as both faulted enemy and Serbian Other marks the uncertainties of the region's music market as the disturbances of minority interests infiltrating into a majoritarian space. Correspondingly, it is racial authenticity (rather than sincerity) that takes pride of place in musical encounters among the region's diverse populations.

This chapter refocuses the concern for musical affect and the materialities of spatializing performance on authenticity. "Aggressive" (*agresivna*) music is a strategic response to the potential territorialization of Romani and Serbian tambura spaces within Croatia's borders; it plays out in ambivalent encounters through which divergent *meloi* (in Croatian, *melosi*) are technically and conceptually parsed as "clean" and "dirty." I show that non-Romani perceptions of the "dirty" quality of Romani tambura musicianship connect on technical and affective levels to differences in the rhythmic organization of ensembles. These perceptions relate back to concerns over "clean/pure" Croatian traditions that the emergent Croatian state bolstered during the war. I argue that Serbian musicians also challenge the purity of musical culture in Eastern Croatia, but not through their Otherness, rather through the ability to *pass* musically and racially.

Romani musical practice, however, can feel exotic and enticingly dangerous in its virtuosity. It rhythmically disorients South Slavic listeners, contributing to their ability to understand Roma as safely nomadic and thus dissociate them from fears of aggression. This understanding, however, comes through the *affective blocking* of discourses of shared musical sensibilities: the capacity of feelings of musical strangeness to delimit conscious attempts to make diversity meaningfully inclusive. I begin the next section with an instance of aggressive territoriality that contrasts sharply with the tavern scene and the examples of inclusive interpretations of "tambura music" that opened this chapter. I ultimately demonstrate, however, how the taverns where Romani bands typically play can function as what Deleuze and Guattari called "deterritorialized milieus": they remain flexibly outside of concerns over territory and representation ([1980] 1987, 61).

MUSICAL CLEANLINESS AND TAUTOLOGIES OF NATIONAL INCLUSION

November 2009: The house band Biće Skoro Propast Sveta (It Will Soon Be the Downfall of the World) was playing around tables in the City Basement restaurant at the Waldinger Hotel in Osijek, a city in the East Croatian region of Slavonia. The band consisted of five tambura players, an accordionist, and a violinist, all of whom were Roma. The band played frequently in Osijek, Zagreb, and other Croatian cities but hailed from Deronje, another town approximately forty kilometers from Osijek in Serbia's Vojvodina province (and ten kilometers beyond the Croatian/Serbian border). To an enthusiastic Croat clientele, the band was playing sets of Slavonian folk dances, newly composed Croatian tambura ballads, old city songs, and favorites from what is known as the "*ciganska*" genre; I had come to interview the band members and to record their performance.

On my way out, a woman who was also dining at the Waldinger Hotel stopped me to ask my nationality and whether I was studying music. When I replied that I was writing about music in the area, her husband told me with evident concern that "the music isn't really ours" and explained that the band had come from Novi Sad (a Serbian city much farther from Osijek). He added that the music that the group plays is not "Slavonian" and that Roma play "from birth," implying that their musicianship was the result of a natural talent rather than the training that local Croat tamburaši receive in Slavonian music.

His dismissal of the band's mostly Slavonian repertoire and its members' origins in the much closer town of Deronje (which many include in a projected Greater Croatia that also encompasses Bački Monoštor and most of the rest of Vojvodina) echoed sentiments that other patrons and wait staff in Osijek conveyed to me: bands such as this (even popular groups from Slavonia itself, such as Dule Bend at the Krčma kod Ruže) were ethnically and musically foreign to the local tambura scene. When I called to ask in advance about a venue's live music lineup, restaurant staff repeatedly distinguished between their offerings of *ciganska glazba* ("gypsy music") and *tamburaška glazba* ("tambura music"), despite the fact that Romani musicians predominantly played fretted tambura chordophones. Advertised to patrons simply as Cigani or, rarely, as Roma, these bands were racially marked.

The couple's comments seemed at odds with the City Basement clients' patronage of the band as well as my frequent exposure to Romani tambura performance through promoters of Slavonian tambura music. They constitute, however, part of a tautology that has proliferated publicly for decades and that concerns the relationship among the players, the instruments, and (especially since the war) the territories of tambura music. One side of the tautology asserts that tambura instruments and music are the national legacy of Croats (not of other ethnic groups or races); the other side states that Croats who play these instruments are "tamburaši" playing tambura music (but Serbs and Roma are foreigners playing "Serbian" and "Gypsy" music from Serbia). In promoting such circular logic about who constitutes tamburaši, clientele and staff at Slavonian establishments ignore or dismiss the use of the same instruments, repertoire, and venues by Roma and Serbs who have been situated or at least professionally active in Croatia for generations. They also commonly overlook the fact that the Ottoman Empire introduced the tambura to the region and that Croats only began to view it as their national instrument in the nineteenth century, by which point it was also popular among many other ethnicities.

I spoke about this with Đura Jovanović, the kontra (rhythm tambura) player of Biće Skoro Propast Sveta. He told me that he could talk about tamburas for two days straight, but hesitated when I inquired how he would describe his ensemble's style. I pushed further, asking whether it could be considered "Vojvodinan." He told me (not in disagreement) that the band plays in the style of Zvonko Bogdan (2009). This reply was nearly identical to one that I had received upon asking the members of Dule Bend how they would describe their music. Jovanović added that members do not hold rehearsals but play songs as they hear them, affirming the widely held conception of the region's Romani tambura players as musicians who learn by rote. This notion recognizes the disenfranchisement of many such musicians from institutions of musical pedagogy but also overlooks the conservatory training of a number of musicians, including members of these two bands.

Jovanović's reference to Bogdan strategically aligned the band's performance practice with a famous Croat singer from Vojvodina whom Croatian audiences eagerly accepted. His response, moreover, avoided specifically addressing the question of whether its music was "tambura music," indicating a seeming willingness to let me call it what I liked so long as I accepted it. It nonetheless carved out a space for the group within the broader popular tambura scene by virtue of Bogdan's association with tambura bands and the specific mention of tamburaši in many of his songs. In fact, one of Bogdan's most famous songs is entitled "Osam Tamburaša" (Eight tambura players), and in many performances of the song he references by name the late Janika Balaž, the most famous Rom tambura player of the second half of the twentieth century and the leader of the tambura band that accompanied Bogdan in Vojvodina for many years. Jovanović framed the players' practice stylistically, referencing its ethnic marking as Romani only indirectly (via allusions to Bogdan, a Bunjevac/Croat who performs with many Roma). While acknowledging the stylistic distinction stemming from playing how they hear the music, he eschewed labels (territorial, ethnic, etc.) that would erect discursive barriers across diversely shared practices of instrumentation, repertoire, and professional networking.

Many Croat tambura players similarly propagate the instrument's more diverse and nuanced history among Roma and other groups, conceiving of their people's own contribution to the music on the scale of a regional "melos" or national style rather than of an entire genre or instrument tradition. The public conviction that the tambura is Croatian has intensified since Croatia's independence, however, particularly through the media narratives discussed in chapter 1. Yet these in turn were successful in the face of contradictory information and discourses because, as I argue, the tautology conflating tamburaši with Croats often relies as much on affective responses as on discursive rationalizations; tambura music is Croatian because playing and listening to it *feel* Croatian (while *feeling* Cigan transpires through a different set of musical relations). The resultant affective intensification surrounding the terms "Croat" and "tambura," while not absolutely affirmative of such strategic discursive tropes, has bolstered the Slavonian melos's proffering of a sense of comfort to Croatian communities still recovering psychologically and economically from the war. It also inhibits the musical and cultural integration of minorities, who in some cases also emphasize their musical and ethnic distinction to potential clients. This "wall to diversity" (Ahmed 2012, 129) persists in spite of many local Croat tamburaši's *will* (and work) to embrace them and in spite of the affective indulgences and diverse becomings that characterize nights at the City Basement and the Tavern at the Rose.

It is on the affect of tambura performance and its work in stabilizing or subverting essentializing, tautological discourses of racial difference that I focus in this section. In doing so I concentrate on tambura usage in an East Croatian geography of musical performance, making this, rather than any particular people or even the notion of race, the object of my study. Such an approach, I suggest, better eschews scholarly complicity in racial tautologies and essentialisms. Shedding light on race's continual emergence as an affective relation and not solely a biocultural construct helps to explain how a "will to diversity" may contend with yet remain susceptible to institutionalized "walls" (Ahmed 2012, 129). I develop this approach to understanding and countering such blockages to will in a section that traces race's simultaneous emergence and reification through discourses and aesthetic practices of the musically "clean."

The Socializing and Discoursing of Musically "Clean" Milieus

In the context of performance, the degree to which aesthetic concerns register consciously may vary greatly from one audience member to the next. Significant in this respect is that tambura musicians are some of the most common and enthusiastic fans of tambura performance, for they constitute a considerable and knowledgeable listenership that actively contributes to the reception of the ensembles on stage. At nearly every performance that I have attended, from folklore ensemble concerts to private parties for which patrons have hired small tambura bands as entertainment, I have met significant numbers of tambura musicians among the guests. In Osijek, tamburaši would often attend performances at restaurants by Romani bands such as Biće Skoro Propast Sveta and Dule Bend when they and their families organized dinners at such locations. More frequently, they actively seek out and attend performances at bars, concert halls, and city festivals by other professional and amateur Croat ensembles. Nearly every Thursday after rehearsing with the HKUD "Osijek 1862", for example, I went with other members of the group to Osijek's Old Bridge Pub to listen to a band. Most of these members were women from the group of male and female singers/dancers in which I was performing, but one of them, Josipa, was often accompanied by her boyfriend Mario, a musician in the HKUD's tambura group and also in the semiprofessional tambura band Sitan Vez. Other members of Mario's band frequently found us at Old Bridge Pub and would usually move back and forth between our table and the stage, where they would interact with the particular band playing that evening (usually a different group each week) and sometimes join the musicians onstage. I frequently ran into musicians from one or another of the tambura schools with which I was affiliated, as well as members of other semiprofessional tambura bands in the area. Thus at these performances, a large portion of the men, and often some of the women as well, either were tambura musicians themselves or were involved in folklore performance to tambura accompaniment.

As a whole, however, the clientele at Old Bridge Pub and the other taverns and restaurants that house much of the East Croatian tambura performance scene represent a wide range of musical backgrounds. A good number of patrons have never performed tambura music or learned to play an instrument, and while some of them are familiar with a wide range of tambura music styles, many others have listened to and/or supported primarily local Croat bands and their particular performance aesthetic. The mixing of these with patrons of greater experience and/or openness has given rise to a plethora of views on and interests in appropriate tambura style. Yet what is true of nearly all patrons of tambura music in Slavonia and other parts of the country, including tamburaši themselves, is that their experience with Romani musicianship consists of listening to rather than playing with such musicians (there were almost never Romani tambura players or other Roma in such audiences, and mixed Croat-Roma performance has become exceptionally rare in post-Yugoslav Croatia). This contrasts sharply with their experience with Croat musicians; at any given local performance (as opposed to concerts such as Škoro's that draw thousands from the surrounding area), many in attendance have performed in some sort of folklore, orchestral, or popular ensemble involving tamburas at some point in their lives. Moreover, they have often played with one or more of those currently performing onstage, whether in informal gigs or jams, in other bands, or in larger folklore groups or city orchestras.

Ensemble memberships frequently overlap, and active professional Croat tamburaši experience one another's styles from playing with as well as patronizing each other. The creation of a tambura melos particular to Slavonia, where most Croatian tamburaši live, is therefore the product of intimate knowledge of and sharing among the practices of the region's various ensembles. This melos is characterized not only by the songwriting structures, close tertian baritone vocal harmonies, and chromatic passages on the lead prim tambura discussed in chapter 1, but also by an aspect of musical style that requires intimate musical coordination of "aggressive" plectrum technique across an entire ensemble: the realization of uniform rhythm. This consists of quicker tremolos, stricter duple division, and harder attacks than in northern Serbia and Bosnia or in the mandolin tradition of Croatia's coast (where, I was assured, even non-Slavonian Croats find "aggressive" tambura music more compelling than mandolins and therefore hire Slavonian bands). While such intimate coordination is emphasized in many types of large music ensembles, its implementation has been particularly overt in Croatian tambura music. This music's ample use of tremolo, with its unspecified rhythmic divisions of the pulse, has combined with a surge in musically unschooled professional musicians (due to the music's wartime economic and social capital) to generate frequent rhythmic discrepancies. As I show in this section, tambura pedagogues have worked hard to correct the latter by instituting training programs for youth. Orchestra directors also frequently spend significant amounts of time working closely with orchestral sections to coordinate a precisely metric manifestation of the Croatian tambura melos through an "aggressive" approach to rhythmic articulation.

The insular aesthetic that has resulted from musicians working together in bands and in city, regional, and national orchestras proffers an important window into the relations of musical affect and essentializing discourse through which acceptance into the tambura music scene is negotiated. Among tambura musicians themselves, this aesthetic is as much (if not more) the product of intimate in-group musical socialization as it is a matter of othering or exclusion. The spatial and social conditions for sharing musical aesthetics that extend beyond state and private media to other venues of performance in Osijek and the surrounding region help to explain the mobilization of both territorial representation and racial affect in postwar Croatia. Geography and genetics, with their ties to wartime discourses on Croats' territorial claims to occupied Eastern Slavonia, are common explanations for the special ability to perform tambura music of the people of the Slavonian plains and the broader musical sensibility that allows the Croatian nation commonly to appreciate aggressive Slavonian playing (even if it is also clear that this is something that the former carefully cultivate in rehearsals). As I argue later in this chapter, the concern for musical territoriality intersects with the connotations of the term *agresivna*, whose usage during the war was highly fraught. This is due to its association (in music as in military tactics) with territorial incursions and to Croatian media's efforts to highlight the Yugoslav Army's fault in this while downplaying and discouraging aggressive domestic actions.

In describing their ideal performance aesthetic, Croat tamburaši and tambura pedagogues also consistently employed another word closely related to ethnicity and genetics: the adjective čist, meaning "pure" or "clean." Individuals should produce "aggressive" but "clean" tones with their plectra rather than ones that buzz; the coordination of instruments should be čist, with precise and uniform articulation of rhythms (this was a particular concern for those directing self-taught amateurs who had turned professional); the general aesthetic for ensembles should be *čiste tambure*, or pure tamburas (excluding other instruments or featuring them only rarely for guest solos—Serb musicians in the area also affirmed that "pure tamburas" constituted the Croatian aesthetic, whereas Serbs and Roma often incorporated accordion and/or violin); and finally, in a less common but still extant nationalistic deployment of the term, tambura music is the legacy of *čisti Hrvati*: "pure Croats."

Dubravka Ugrešić has demonstrated that discourses on cleanliness in 1990s Croatia connected a number of public concerns over the "dirty war" waged by the Yugoslav army (1998, 60). These ranged from the symbolic bottling and marketing of clean Croatian air and pronouncements about the clean conscience and unsoiled liberty of the Croatian people to the public lauding of clean Croatian women and bloodlines untainted by "an undesirable blot" (59–63). Ugrešić writes: "In the new system of values (clean–dirty), 'Byzantine blood' is the most dangerous polluter. 'Byzantine' is simply another (more refined) word for Serb, Orthodox, which, in the same linguistic and ideological system, means: sly, dirty, deceitful, in other words whoever is different from us" (61). Other minorities and people of color were potential polluters as well (60–61), and it became clear in my research that their musical influence similarly posed a challenge for the preservation of pure or clean rhythmic practice. That local Serbs, too, practice a relatively "clean" style of tambura performance actually makes them all the more dangerous in clean Croatia, perhaps even more so than Roma. As Mary Douglas argued in *Purity and Danger*, "All margins are dangerous" ([1966] 2005, 122). In societies that structure "work" and "status in terms of purity and impurity as these ideas are applied throughout the regime of castes" (124)—or in this instance, the regime of ethnic groups, nationalities, and nations—it is perhaps not surprising that those who can pass as clean (while harboring or creating impurities) should be more dangerous than those of clearly lower status who perform the dirty work of musical labor that is expected of them.

Pedagogies of Musical Cleanliness

Ensembles in Osijek and other Slavonian cities took considerable time to "clean up" their rhythmic articulations and often framed the issue in overtly ethnic terms. At an October 2009 rehearsal of the "Pajo Kolarić" orchestra, the director paid particular attention to the straight pulses of a waltz, and he stopped the group in the middle and shouted in rhythm (see figure 3.1). He added that

Je'n dva tri,   je'n dva tri,   ne: je'n dva___ tri,___ je'n dva___ tri.___
One two three,   one two three,   not: one two___ three,___ one two___ three.___

FIGURE 3.1 Waltz rhythms

FIGURE 3.2 "Hopa, Cupa Skoči" and "Zaplet". *Source:* Bartók (1978, 459).

rushing the offbeats of the waltz meant playing *kao Mađari*—"like Hungarians"—and demanded greater concentration on the cleaner Croatian manner of performing these rhythms.

The "clean," "Croatian" tambura aesthetic developed in opposition not only to Hungarian styles but also to those of neighboring Vojvodina. This Serbian region's Romani and Serbian tambura musicians have long been known for offbeat articulations that fall outside of Croatian conventions of strict, symmetrical division. In 2009, as a member of HKUD "Osijek 1862," I learned and performed a song called "Hopa Cupa Skoči," in which we articulated the eighth-note runs, such as in mm. 4–7, with strictly duple and symmetrical durational divisions (see figure 3.2, upper voice). In 1912, however, Bela Bartók recorded a Serb tamburaš in Western Vojvodina performing "Zaplet," a nearly identical dance, and in his collections of Yugoslavian folk music (1978, 453–471), Bartók analyzed many of the dance's rhythms as quintuplet sixteenth notes grouped in 2 + 3 (figure 3.2, lower voice).[1]

In 1980s Vojvodina, Mark Forry similarly found certain figures sounding like triplet eighth notes and others more like two sixteenth notes followed by an eighth note; his instructor, from Novi Sad's tambura orchestra, explained that it was entirely "something else" (1990, 1). Uneven divisions still persist in Vojvodina, and Slavonian tamburaši compared the style to jazz in that it requires asymmetrical durations not specified by the conventions of classical Western rhythmic notation, which many Slavonian musicians learn from a very early age (though the "swinging" of rhythms is reversed in comparison to jazz, with offbeat articulations coming early rather than late with respect to Western classical conventions of symmetrical division). While many Croat musicians like the Vojvodina style, they distinguish it from their own dominant musical practice, which is characterized by symmetrical, recursively duple (or, in less common cases, triple) division of the beat. This practice developed in part from the pedagogical reaction against the professionalization of untrained, formerly amateur musicians in the 1990s.

The exception to the Croatian aesthetic for clean, evenly duple division in tambura performance is the kontra (or *bugarija*) tambura, which plays chords on the offbeats in a pattern known as *estam*. This is a term borrowed from the Hungarian concept of *esztam*, which David Schneider notes is of unclear etymology: "It may have roots in the Romany language or be derived from the Medieval *Provençal* dance the *estampida*," while "the two short vowels of *esztam* imitate the quick interchange between the two accompanying instruments" (2006, 25). It was the latter explanation that tambura players repeatedly offered me. Kontra players articulate their rhythms (the "-tam" beats) in relation to the strokes (the "es-" beats) of the berda (bass) tambura, and it is common throughout Slavonia and Vojvodina for them to *rush* the offbeats a little, that is, to articulate them slightly before the halfway point of the pulse. In this way they propel the pulse of the ensemble forward, generating a sense of energy and momentum within their ensembles without losing the central pulse.[2] For the most part, however, the aesthetic for "clean" tambura performance, marked predominantly by even duple division of the pulse, dominated among both amateur and professional Croat musicians and set their practice apart from musicians in Vojvodina and from local Romani groups.

The dominant, "clean" style is particularly audible in Croatian orchestral playing, such as the Croatian Tambura Orchestra's performances for the annual event known affectionately as Sto Tamburaša (100 Tambura Players). Concerts such as this that bring together professional musicians from all over the country (though predominantly from Slavonia) solidify the concept of a national playing style through which one hundred musicians can join in playing the national instrument. They typically travel widely throughout Slavonia for the performances before setting out together in buses for the events in Zagreb and in Croatia's intimates (such as Budapest, where many in the audience were Hungarian Croats). In this way the familiarity with each other's repertoires and styles that musicians share at the local level also develops regionally. Although they typically earn at least meager compensation for performing in the Sto Tamburaša concerts, musicians also travel at their own expense to hear bands play around the region. Economic motivations for performing (see MacMillen 2011a) are further attenuated by these musicians' expenditures on gasoline, food, and beverages as they participate (typically with great passion) as both listeners and performers in the larger Slavonian tambura music scene. Tambura music's spatializing force in the region is that of the economic drive of affective consumption and labor. The economy of musical affect crosses into other spatializing economies: those of Slavonia's reviving but still comparatively curtailed (with respect to prewar figures) industries, of food and alcohol consumption, and of transportation. In 2010, while I was living in Osijek (Slavonia's largest city), a Dalmatian taxi company opened a location there and significantly undercut all competitors, effecting a dramatic change in the city's nightlife by enabling quick and affordable transportation to tambura music venues with limited parking. Some young tambura musicians even took jobs as drivers for the company, and the contacts between fellow tamburaši and between musicians and fans enjoyed a surge in speed and frequency, with groups of friends suddenly able to visit multiple establishments on a single night. The economic growth of affective labor and consumption very quickly resulted in audiences and tambura players hearing multiple approaches to clean performance over the span of an evening or entire day.

The affective dimension of this music's appeal—to them as well as to their listeners—is not lost on the area's tambura musicians. As the musical director of HKUD "Osijek 1862" extolled the merits of the national orchestra to me, he added that the sound of so many tambura players performing together gives him goosebumps. Known physiologically as horripilation, this visceral, affective response to clean playing at great volume is something that many tamburaši recognize and take advantage of, even in smaller performance contexts. For example, the tambura bassist of an Osijek band that I will call Croatian Ducats told me in summer 2015 that in order to elicit horripilation in patrons who could potentially tip the musicians, his ensemble deliberately juxtaposes soft, pizzicato verses of the instrumental number "Pjesma rastanka" (Song of farewell) with renditions of the melody featuring full volume and fast tremolos, yet neat rhythmic alignment. The clean, aggressive aesthetic that Croats such as the director and the tambura bassist lauded, and the associations of this aesthetic with an independent and ethnically pure nation, serve especially in large orchestral performances to evince and reinforce the monolithic tambura music culture that has been suggested by the nickname 100 Tambura Players since its founding in 2006 and that the state, audiences, and musicians alike have fostered since Croatia's independence.

MUSICAL DIRTINESS AND DIVERSE ENCOUNTERS IN EASTERN CROATIA

It is the clean, secure, and comforting monolithic tambura music culture that the tautology of the relationship between Croats and tamburas substantiates. Yet the importance of this tautology is most salient precisely in those instances in which the monolithic musical culture exposes its own faults and inconsistencies. It has become common for Roma and even some Serbs to perform in restaurants and taverns in Slavonian cities. On the discursive level and also, if less commonly, through actual collaborative practice, many Croat tambura players have similarly made strides to make the tambura scene more inclusive and diverse. I turn now to musical encounters in Eastern Croatia among Croats, Roma, and Serbs to examine the role of musical affect and experience in shaping these ideas and practices.

By and large, the tautology excluded Serbs as well, though often implicitly, as the general assumption was that as of the early 1990s there were no Serbs playing tamburas in Croatia. Yet a few musicians remained active, and I found my research acting as a point of encounter among various ethnic groups. When I told the members of the band Croatian Ducats that I would attend a performance for the Orthodox holiday of St. Trifun's Day in Vukovar, they responded by joking snidely about accordions and new Serbian folk music. They expressed surprise when I added that the band I was going to hear, Vučedolski Zvuci, was a group of Serb tamburaši. In the marketing of Croatian popular music during the war, when these musicians were children and just starting to play, the accordion had become an index of Serbian music and virtually vanished from official musical practices as the tambura was propagated as Croatia's national instrument (Pettan 1998, 16–18). Croatian Ducats, whose members ironically were then considering featuring accordion on their first album, affirmed a social imaginary of a Croatia in which Serbs, if heard at all, always sounded foreign.

Present at the actual St. Trifun celebration, however, were a number of prominent Croat tamburaši of an older generation who have maintained prewar friendships with Serbs. Their specific ties to Vučedolski Zvuci and its parent organization in Vukovar include long, shared histories of participation in tambura music. For example, Marko Benić, the founder of the important wartime and postwar Croatian group Berde Band, was there to drink with and listen to Mirko Delibašić and the latter's ensemble. They related how the older tamburaš had endeavored to convince Mirko's parents to let him join Marko in the Radio Tambura Orchestra of Novi Sad several decades earlier.

Although not present at this event, the director of HKUD "Osijek 1862" is a close colleague and friend of an older čelo tambura player in Vučedolski Zvuci (it was in fact the latter's introduction to the director that made it possible for me to join HKUD "Osijek 1862"). The director also consults and instructs regularly at the Serbian Cultural Artistic Society near Osijek in which the čelo tambura player and his wife, a vocalist, perform. In 2003 this society's folklore group became the first Serbian ensemble since the war to perform in Zagreb's annual International Folklore Festival. According to its directors, the group's members felt quite nervous about this performance at a prominent public event whose domestic performers had been predominantly Croats for several years, and they particularly felt exposed as they walked onto the stage bearing the "Serbs in Croatia" banner given to them at the festival. They were pleasantly surprised at the audience's positive reaction, however, and the performance went smoothly and bolstered their trust of both local and national Croatian folklore organizations. Although such relationships typically do not lead to collaborations and mixing of ethnic groups within public musical performance itself, they do at times place certain individuals in the "shoes," sometimes quite literally, of other ethnic groups' musicians, such as when the director of HKUD "Osijek 1862" visits to teach local Serbian or more broadly Slavonian repertoire. Similarly, the vocalist (the čelo player's wife) often sings Croatian or Romani songs, for example with her town's Romani Cultural Artistic Society, with which she has appeared as a soloist.

Such practices parallel in important ways a limited number of narratives and discourses countering the prominent tautology of the tambura as Croatia's national instrument. Again, tamburaši themselves are often those most willing to recognize and, collaboratively, to engender continuity across supposedly fixed ethnic, racial, and geographic boundaries. Some Croats, and members of a number of minority groups, suggested that those who claimed the tambura as exclusively Croatian did so for simple, often interrelated reasons. These ranged from xenophobia and nationalism to ignorance, jealousy, and economic competition. Another competing discourse pertained to the biological basis of musical ability. As Tomislav Longinović has noted, South Slavic cultures have long associated racial character and musicality with "blood" (2000, 622). Musicians of various ethnic backgrounds volunteered blood or genetics as the origin of their musical sensibilities, and Croat tamburaši in particular emphasized that their claims to tambura music and their ability to play and understand the Slavonian melos were rooted in biological heritage.

What was oppositional about this idea was their inclusion of Roma. "They really have it in their blood," one Croat tamburaš told me. Others claimed that Roma were born musicians and saw this as a justification of Roma's importance in the region's tambura music (a striking difference from the hotel guest I mentioned previously who connected playing from birth to the Romani band Biće Skoro Propast Sveta's foreignness). The downplaying of tradition and upholding of biological determinants fits a broader pattern of what Mattijs Van de Port has described as a racialized tendency of South Slavic communities in Vojvodina and in the former Yugoslavia more generally to view Roma as "endowed with 'a natural talent'" for music (1999, 296). Slavonian Serbs and Croats lauded the Roma's ability to feel and hear lively, energetic rhythms as based in a natural predisposition (owing, again, to geography and genetics) for nervous, nomadic wandering.

The Serb couple who performed in the local Romani Cultural Artistic Society, for example, told me that Roma "have an awesome ear [*sluh*] for rhythm" as well as a remarkable ability to "feel" rhythm. The vocalist noted that Roma play much more "lively" (*živo*) than Serbs and Croats, and her husband, the čelo tambura player, added that they either play lively or *jako, jako teško i tužno* — "very, very heavily and sadly." The vocalist explained to me that the difference in liveliness is attributable to the fact that Roma constantly move around, a reference to their mythical nomadic existence (which most Roma musicians active in and around Osijek had never actually adopted, though some did commute to work). Serb and Croat musicians, she continued, are rooted in the Slavonian plains and therefore play *lagano* ("leisurely," "lightly"). Only those Slavs who eke out a wilder living in Serbia's mountains or Dalmatia's coastal Dinaric Alps play comparably lively music.

While this couple's comments should not be taken as representative of the opinions of all Serbs in the region, and it is possible that they did not voice such views to local Croats, they do usefully throw into relief the dominant Croatian discourse on musical cleanliness and aggression. Their comments served to stake out a musical and geographical commonality between their own population and the region's dominant Slavic group (which one local tamburaš of mixed Croatian and Serbian parentage described to me as related to the Serbs the way that the "children of two brothers" are related). Locals' lauding of their own music as clean and aggressive, on the other hand, strategically emphasized both their ability to compete with famous Romani and Dalmatian performers and their purity and distinction from local Serbs, with whom they theoretically have much in common ethnically and musically.

Though couched in positive terms, such comments about the Roma's musical disposition being endowed through their blood and nomadic wandering also constitute a process of othering, one that has parallels in "white" discourses on the innate, irrational rhythmicity of people of "color" around the world. Ample literature has documented discourses (in many cases those of Roma themselves) on the supposedly innate ability of Romani musicians in European musical practices ranging from tambura groups in Serbian bars (Van de Port 1998) and wedding bands in Macedonia (Silverman 2012) to Czech music pedagogy (Gelbart 2010) and Spanish flamenco performances (Leblon [1994] 2003). Occasionally such discourses juxtapose their music with the "clean" or "pure" musical endeavors of majority populations (Washabaugh 1998), though typically claims of impurity compete with conceptions of Roma as naturally endowed (Malvinni 2004). Looking at the considerably larger geography of African music's construction and representation, Kofi Agawu has dated to the eleventh-century Christian world "the racialist conferral of particular sensibilities on particular groups of people, and the construction of African rhythms as complex, superior, yet ultimately incomprehensible" (2003, 55). He and other scholars have documented the detriments of what Ronald Radano calls "the idea of Black rhythm" for racial understanding in contemporary Europe and North America (2000, 459). This idea is certainly borne out in the context of Romani practice by comparisons of their rhythms to swing in jazz.

Though praise from non-Roma musicians helps to solidify Roma's musical status, it similarly reifies their exoticness; like African American musicians, Vojvodina's Roma and even sometimes its Serbs produced the enticingly different rhythms of people of color. These both pleased some Croatian musicians and reassured them of their own style's musical and racial distinction. It is the triangulatory positioning of Croatian tambura music in relation to both Serbian and Romani performance that makes this a matter of race (a varying notion of European whiteness that I discuss later in this chapter). Since the Roma's tambura musicianship may be elided with Serbian culture, their exclusion from tambura music as a genre is not merely a case of ethnic discrimination. Because Serbian and Croatian relations—affective, discursive, and ideological—to Romani performance overlap significantly, claims to Croatian ownership of tambura music are not merely a case of nationalism.

Horripilation (Goose Bumps) and the Musically Dirty

November 2009: Driving back from the workshop of tambura luthier Drago Knobloch in Orahovica, where I had spent the day with members of Croatian Ducats watching the master at work and drinking beer in the town's shaded establishments at the base of Mount Papuk, the driver (the band's *brač* tambura player) played me a recording of a Romani band that he liked. He had been comparing the scene in Croatia to those of Hungary (where bands are "weaker") and Serbia (where there are simply fewer groups left) and put the CD in to demonstrate the Serbian Romani sound. He asked me whether I liked such *ciganski stil* ("Gypsy style"), and when I confirmed that I did he added with a smile: *da, malo je prljavo*—"yes, it's a little dirty." This description drew on a common discourse on musical dirtiness (one related closely to that of musical and ethnic cleanliness/purity) that numerous non-Romani tamburaši voiced to me. He went on to comment that he didn't understand how they played it but that he loved the "interesting" sound and the way it made him feel. This style, he surmised, likely resulted from each musician playing a musical line "on his own" rather than from an arrangement worked out in rehearsal or written down on paper. His reasoning about this style's dirtiness, however, evidently made it no less foreign or irreconcilable to his own tambura practice; his experience with the clean rhythmic coordination and careful arrangements that Croatian Ducats' rehearsals emphasized offered no ready way of realizing or even imagining such individualistic, improvisatory passages in a group performance setting.

One could imagine oppositional ideas and discourses regarding diverse tambura performance in Slavonia giving rise to interpersonal tensions between competing bands or alternatively being quashed through Slavonia's postwar socioeconomic relations of musical patronage and institutional support. Yet I only rarely found evidence of this. In our discussions, many Croat tamburaši expressed similar reverence for Romani musicianship, which they tied to close personal experience with it and to their own perceived inability to understand it. The common musical ground that the Serbian musician couple described to me did bear out at least in the visceral nature of their reactions to Romani tambura performance. The čelo player and the director/bass player from Vučedolski Zvuci similarly commented that they did not understand how or why the Roma played the way they did, and that it inexplicably made the hairs on their arms stand on end. Croat musicians also acknowledged horripilation in response to a music that they could understand neither ontologically nor epistemologically. In other contexts, such responses might have worked against the oppositional discourses that include Roma in the tambura tradition, or such discourses, along with economic competition, might have generated tensions precluding such positive if seemingly irrational reactions to Romani tambura music. Instead, competing ideas of musical belonging and ownership as interpreted through musical style existed in tandem in a dissonance that was not purely cognitive but in fact largely musical and affective.

These tambura musicians' responses are physiologically similar to their reactions to clean and aggressive playing by skilled Croatian groups ranging from small professional bands to the national one-hundred-piece orchestra. This affective commonality affords a crucial window into the dissonantly mutual inclusion of conceptions and feelings of both commonality and distinction that have given rise to emergent understandings of race in postwar Croatia. There is, however, an important difference: here horripilation does not occur in recognizing a sonic symbol of a nation but in a nonrecognition, an intense disorientation that I argue is largely rhythmic and that, in its affective block, still reinscribes essentializing discourses. I begin this section with an analysis of this disorientation's general conception and specific occurrences before returning to the importance of affective responses for these reinscriptions as well as the potential for resilience in countering them.

The attribution of dirtiness and chaos to Romani music is part of a broader construction that has been well documented throughout the former Yugoslavia as well as across Europe and North America: that of Roma as "dirty gypsies" who live "chaotic" lives. Yugoslavian filmmakers particularly celebrated these attributes, portraying Romani bands playing tamburas among violent tavern crowds and in the dust and mire of fantastically squalid villages. Films exemplifying this include Aleksandar Petrović's *Skupljači Perja* (The feather gathers, distributed with the English title *I Even Met Happy Gypsies*, 1967) and *Biće skoro propast sveta* (known as *It Rains in My Village*, 1968) and Emir Kusturica's *Crna mačka, beli mačor* (*Black Cat, White Cat,* 1998). These films tie depictions of excited musical performance directly to the chaos and dirt that are raised by the musicians' feet. While celebration and excitement often register in the performances of bands such as Croatian Ducats as they communicate with audiences via whistles, shouts, and clapping, these Croat musicians endeavor to maintain their clean rhythmic coordination and tones throughout. They enjoy Romani tambura style, but to many of them it remains a dirty, irrational, foreign, and naturally inherited practice by which they delimit their own clean, Croatian performance aesthetic.

Osijek's Roma are not entirely passive in constructions such as those propagated by the musicians of Croatian Ducats. The Waldinger Hotel band's use of the name Biće Skoro Propast Sveta, which translates literally as It Will Soon Be the Downfall of the World, capitalizes on fantasies of chaotic existence sensationalized in the eponymous 1968 film. This band from Deronje and Osijek's resident Romani ensembles, such as Dule Bend, often advertise their music as "Romani" or "*ciganska.*" Thus they themselves sometimes associate it with ethnicity rather than instruments, and they play popular songs with texts glorifying the roles of Roma musicians and women in the wild, frenzied tavern nightlife. Moreover, in the conceptualizations of Romani tambura performance that non-Roma musicians presented to me, Roma musicians were the active creators of an inexplicable musical practice. Many Croats' expressed inability to comprehend how Roma musicians play what they do draws upon conscious evaluation but also embodied and affective experiences of performance. I argue that these different forms of understanding stand in a dialectical relationship that blocks affective understandings in the dual sense of aggregation and delimitation.

What distinguishes Romani tambura style—that which others hear as "dirty"—is not merely the rhythmic character but its organization. Essentially, there is no rhythm section, as no one instrument asserts a pulse so hegemonic that others align with it precisely and uniformly (this includes the bass and harmony tamburas, which in Croat and Serb bands typically constitute a rhythmic section to which the other musicians listen for the pulse). Instead, in Romani bands, musicians typically participate in a rhythmic give and take, with first one and then another pushing ahead of a collectively slurred pulse. It is this give and take that is both affectively moving and musically incomprehensible to most Slavic musicians in the area.

Dirty Rhythm

While listening to Biće Skoro Propast Sveta at the Waldinger Hotel the same night that the local couple warned me about not taking this group as representative of Slavonian music, I was struck by how much local repertoire the ensemble played. Its groupings of songs were nearly identical to those that local Croat bands played: sets of new Croatian tambura ballads, traditional Slavonian folk dances, *starogradske pjesme* (old city songs), and hits from Dalmatian *klapa* (a men's a cappella vocal tradition) and new Bosnian folk musicians such as Halid Bešlić. I recorded the band's performance of several famous Croatian songs, and I discuss one of these here in order to analyze the differences in style as opposed to genre that actually seem to elicit the strongest reactions by other musicians in the area. The transcription in figure 3.3 shows the beginning of the band's performance of Škoro and Grcevich's song "Moja Juliška" and demonstrates minor discrepancies between the players' attacks on particular beats. The tip of each vertical wedge *points* to the note articulated first, while the width of the opposite end indicates the relative length of the time interval between attacks. Vertical dotted lines connecting notes emphasize that different instruments attacked them simultaneously. Of note here (on the two bottom staves) are the late and separate arrivals of first the rhythm (*bugarija*) tambura on the offbeats and then the tambura bas. The players of these two instruments neither established the typical rhythmic ground used by Croatian and Serbian bands (in which the *bugarija* player responds to the bass player, who establishes the main pulse) nor entirely followed the melody instruments. Rather, all the musicians were constantly shifting their relations with one another (this included slight variations in the relationship of *bas* and *kontra*).

I posit that each player performed to his own sense of the pulse and therefore, whenever he entered earlier than another instrument, was not playing in a syncopated manner but merely relationally ahead. This is a corollary to the conclusion that no one instrument asserted a hegemonic articulation of the pulse. Each player's musical expression of the pulse, however, changed over time in response to the others', as evinced by the realignment of certain instruments after moments of disparate articulations. It is this manner of multirelational responsiveness and communal slurring and shifting of the pulse, in combination with sometimes dissonant heterophonic doubling of lines, that registers as dirty and chaotic to Slavic groups in the area.[3]

The constant nonalignment of attacks in performances by Biće Skoro Propast

FIGURE 3.3 "Moja Juliška," as performed
by Biće Skoro Propast Sveta

Sveta and by similar Romani bands active in Croatia constitutes what Charles Keil has called "participatory discrepancies" (1994, 96–99). This phrase refers not merely to the location of such discrepancies in participatory musical practices, but also to the active participation in producing discrepancies that characterizes such music's sounds. Each member of Biće Skoro Propast Sveta, in fact, participated actively in generating discrepancies by variously pushing ahead of some of the others and then realigning with them. It is this participation that affectively moves yet technically eludes many non-Roma musicians, especially Croatian tamburaši trained in the so-called clean performance practice. It is true that rhythmic articulation outside of strict duple or triple division has long marked the performance of some Slavs as well as Roma, particularly in Vojvodina (Forry 1990, 1), and that "varying and individualising the patterns used" emerged as a new ideal in the folklore festivals of independent Croatia (Ceribašić 1998, 37). Yet it is largely among Romani ensembles, and a few South Slavic bands famous for emulating them (such as Zlatni Dukati and Jerry Grcevich's ensembles), that nearly complete participation in individualizing rhythmic feeling and spacing at the level of the beat (*takt*) not only produces musically meaningful discrepancies but also makes them the metric basis of the performance.

Of Romungro (Hungarian-speaking Romani) performers across the border in Hungary, Barbara Lange similarly writes: "The irregularities in Gypsy nóta style are excellent examples of how 'participatory discrepancy' can generate musical power," and the resulting "intentional discontinuity is so pervasive, in fact, that it seems to go beyond increasing participatory momentum to generate a peculiar affective power" (1997, 528). *Esztam* rhythm, often devoid of the grounding bass articulation of the downbeat, is one particularly salient element of this (526). The affective power of both *nóta* and tambura bands seems, however, to derive from the experience (as opposed to the cognitive processing) of the phenomena of discrepancies and discontinuities on the parts of both musicians and audience.

Rhythmic Precision and Lines of Flight

For non-Roma musicians in Eastern Croatia, this experience eludes not only cognitive processing but also "sensational knowledge" of the technique of performance (Hahn 2007). One night, for instance, when Croatian Ducats was filling in for Biće Skoro Propast Sveta at an Osijek restaurant, I witnessed the band accelerating a song for a table of enthusiastic guests. A few of the musicians got ahead of the pulse maintained by the rest, and I saw exchanges of concerned facial expressions between the tambura bass and *bugarija* (harmony) tambura players. These two eventually reasserted themselves as a distinct rhythm section with a clean, slower pulse to which the other musicians adjusted, but afterward they walked back to their table shaking their heads, laughing, and sending me sheepish smiles. While decidedly not trying to imitate the style of Romani bands, Croatian Ducats had arrived at a moment of metric tension that clearly made the musicians uncomfortable. The effect was not that of pushing forward against the pulse multirelationally but of coming dangerously close to having to stop and restart. The band avoided a complete metric disjuncture only when the *rhythm section* consciously asserted a hegemonic pulse.

Earlier that same year the group had appeared on Croatian television playing "Moja Juliška" for an enthusiastic young audience, and the musicians approached that performance with the deliberate, even articulation of the rhythms that is more typical of their musical execution (see figure 3.4). They played it quite slowly, at approximately ♩ = 121 beats per minute (in contrast, Škoro and Grcevich recorded their original version at approximately ♩ = 130, and my field recording of Biće Skoro Propast Sveta's performance clocks in at an impressive clip: ♩ = 158). While there are certainly many ensembles capable of playing both quickly and "cleanly," as Croatian Ducats does on many pieces, this slower tempo allowed the players to coordinate the melody instruments particularly closely at the beginning (see mm. 1–8). The entrance of the vocals (m. 10) brought slight departures from the straight, recursively duple division of the pulse audible in the introduction, but the players shifted the accompaniment in the melody instruments to match and, more significant, kept their articulations of these rhythms uniform. Note that the refrain in this song (mm. 27–41) utilizes the same type of descending linear motion between scale degrees 6 and 1 that I examined as typical of new Croatian tambura ballads in chapter 1. One can also identify an exemplary Schenkerian 5–1 *linie* in the introduction (mm. 1–8). The band's clean playing, in contrast to the rhythmic give and take, heterophonic doubling, and improvised turns around or even in lieu of the tonic that Biće Skoro Propast Sveta employed, clearly emphasized these melodic lines' progressions down to the tonic.

Drawing on Gilles Deleuze and Felix Guattari ([1980] 1987), Ildar Khannanov has suggested, however, that "there are no lines in music in the Euclidian sense of a line. [...] *Music has a distinct nomadic quality and a weak sedentary tendency. Music is like the nomadic war machine: it follows the lines of flight and travels across the channels of communication at the speeds immeasurable in units*"

FIGURE 3.4 "Moja Juliška," as performed by Croatian Ducats

(2010, 250). His critique here is of Schenker's *urlinie*, which emerges through analysis on a much larger temporal scale than the sequential lines I highlight here. Without engaging in the larger analytical and epistemological debates that Khannanov's writing raises, I take his point for its more immediate significance with respect to the performances by Biće Skoro Propast Sveta and Croatian Ducats: musical performances can be particularly compelling for their lines of flight (their participatory discrepancies) away from dogmatic order. One can easily recognize the relative liberties that Biće Skoro Propast Sveta takes from the linear progressions that Croatian Ducats and other Croat bands so clearly delineate. It is in this respect, most likely, that Roma in Croatia are sensed (heard, felt, imagined) to be nomads: not literally moving (though that capacity, too, is sustained in myth) but part of the nomadic machine, an assemblage of greater speed than rest that non-Roma hear in their playing and from which they deduce an inclination for nonsedentary lifestyles. What David Malvinni calls the "nomadic logic of improvisation" breaks from the territorial lines of music as meaning and deterritorializes refrains in order to "open [the] music up to new sonorities, new combinations of sound, indeed, to the cosmos" (2004, 69). It is in this respect that Romani tamburaši are considered "dangerous" musicians; theirs is a danger that entices its listeners even as it threatens other musicians, not in terms of musical or racial pollution or even of economic competition, but for their virtuosic sonic and affective allure. The incomprehensibility of this allure on the part of institutionally trained Croatian and Serbian musicians seemingly dooms to technical failure any attempt to replicate the rhythmic give and take of a band collectively distributing the metric center.

THE QUALIFICATION OF RACE, OR THE BLOCKING AND BLOCKING OF MUSICAL AFFECT

In confronting the limits of their own ready understanding of such musical lines of flight, tambura players reinforce discursive explanations of racial and musical distinction that belie commonalities in affective responses to Romani and non-Romani tambura musicianship (commonalities that extend to their physiological states but not to the referentiality of their horripilation to known and therefore meaningful traditions). At the point at which it is more comfortable and feasible to *know* an ethnic group than aspects of musical practices associated with it, tambura players defer examination of the technique and experience of this practice from the affective to the discursive realm. These two ways of knowing and forms of relation are deeply connected to one another. They nonetheless veer toward distinct planes of awareness: one plane given to qualities and emotion, the other to intensities and affect. This is evident in the dynamic of articulation by which understandings objectify into discourse (into pronouncements of difference, such as the construction of "dirtiness" and "cleanliness").

Internalization remains elusive and through its very unattainability assumes the role of an affective supplement to discourse. Bourdieu argued that social practices emerge not merely via discursive objectification but in an oscillation between "objectification and embodiment" in which people ultimately internalize objectified structures as habitus (1977, 87–95). This dialectic does not internalize conscious thought unilaterally, as it may be affectively blocked (see figure 3.5A, in which the dotted line represents the blocking of affect on the nonconscious side of embodiment beyond the internalization process). To restate the tenet detailed in this book's introduction, the affective block, as supplement or remainder, connotes both processes referenced by the term: it blocks, or aggregates as a block of intensity, and it blocks, or keeps at a remove.

On the dialectical, supplementary relationship of discourse and affective embodiment much light is shed in considering the phenomenon of horripilation. Silvan Tomkins argued for "a central role for the skin and its specific receptors" to account for motivational properties of stimulation and the peri-cognitive processes of such phenomena as "'goose bumps' in excitement and fear" (1995,

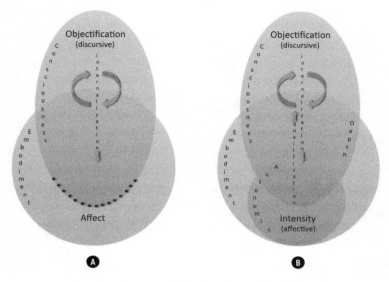

FIGURE 3.5 (A) Affect's blocking in embodiment and
(B) autonomic intensity and qualification

42–43). This affords an important point of return to the issues of affective aggregation and delimitation raised in the previous chapter and an opportunity to reevaluate the contributions of Brian Massumi. In his work on affect and image reception, Massumi redirects this concern for the connection of emotionally distinct but affectively similar states such as fear and excitement by distinguishing between the embodiments of a stimulus's affective intensity, which register in "purely autonomic reactions most directly manifested in the skin," and of its "qualification." The latter's sociolinguistic indexing of content to conventional meanings and emotions mostly involves bodily depth reactions and moves the sensory reactions toward the fully cognitive meaning making of objectification, though at times it also accesses deeper autonomic functions (see figure 3.5B) (Massumi 1996, 219).

Massumi is most concerned with isolating intensity as a distinct process, an autonomic remainder outside of the "conscious-autonomic mix" of qualification (1996, 219). Yet it is the autonomic system's very flexibility *across* the conscious/unconscious boundary (see figure 3.6A) that enables the dynamic of reification and internalization, the blocking and blocking of affect in musicians' horripilation in response to music. Indexing excitement to knowledge of a cleanly coor-

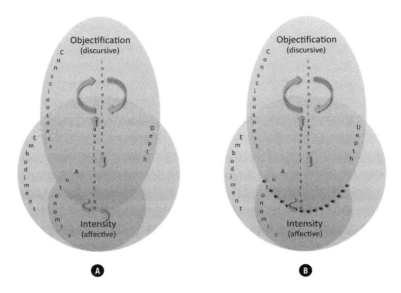

FIGURE 3.6 (A) Flexibility across limits of the conscious and
(B) affect blocked from qualification

dinated practice symbolic of national unity internalizes these structures within
the conscious-autonomic mix of satisfying horripilation. Conversely, the inability
to define Romani playing or responses to it operates at the level of autonomic
intensity in which fear and excitement remain an unqualified block of affect. It
is just this nondistinction between fear and excitement that the acclamation that
a musician plays dangerously recognizes; it involves a transgression of musical
sensibility and bodily comportment that few non-Roma claim to comprehend or
are willing fully to embody in their musical assemblages. Affective engagement
via what Arnie Cox (2016) terms "mimetic participation," which may transpire
even in listening to music, risks a participatory transgression that is thrilling in
its fearsomeness. The participation for the two instances identified here is quite
different; sensational knowledge of "clean," satisfying coordination marks the
one, while a lack of understanding of "dirty" and fearsome-exciting discrepancies guides the other.

Experience in musical listening and performance and the process of rationalizing these crucially impact the autonomic-conscious loop; engagement in
what one considers one's own transparent practice embodies a crossing over
of the autonomic and the conscious, and affect thus serves as an assimilable

remainder to rationalizing discourse. Yet in unsuccessful mimetic engagement with different practices, embodiment remains mostly at the level of intensity and thus constitutes an inassimilable remainder to a discourse that affectively blocks and reobjectifies as a sense of foreignness. Unlike in the concerts analyzed in chapter 2, embodied intensity in these cases is not only blocked (delimited) but also blocked (it aggregates; it is not fully prevented), giving rise to a seemingly impossible becoming. Its object, however, has again been captured in distinction from its source: Romani musicians offer "something else" (Deleuze and Guattari [1980] 1987, 274), relations to which enable a becoming-Croat (to the extent that Croats become clean music). If the resultant privileging of the sociolinguistic qualification of an Other's musicianship as dirty (in opposition to the clean Croatian object of such becoming) bolsters tautological constructs and racializations (see figure 3.6B), then participating in the discrepancies of musico-affective intensity is an imperative of research. Ethnomusicologists have often maintained as much, if under the differently worded banners of bimusicality and participant observation. But it demands alongside it what could too easily be overlooked in the donning of strict discourse-analytical, affect-theoretical, or participatory and phenomenological blinders: a critical attention to the mutual inclusions and impingements of affect and discourse in which the latter's objectifying conquests do not dissociate from but connect to seemingly impossible intensities through processes in which musical affect is blocked (but also blocked).

RHYTHMS OF TERRITORIALITY
(A RETURN IN LIEU OF A CONCLUSION)

The argument for scholarly attention to the interactive, dialectical relationship of affective and discursive understandings of race brings me back to my premise that approaching tambura music as a geography of practice through which race constantly emerges fosters a more critical and less complicit examination of racial essentialization. This is not to say that ethnic and racial categories do not matter. I reference them frequently in this chapter and throughout this book. Ethnicity in Croatia is typically understood to exist a priori, justifying various forms of nationalism. As Anikó Imre writes, citing "Zillah Eisenstein [. . .] in relation to recent events in Bosnia, nationalism in Eastern Europe functions as a form of racism" (Imre 2005, 84; Eisenstein 1996, 48). The terms "race" and "racism" do not themselves frequently appear in discourse on tambura music. "[T]he category of 'race' has remained embedded within that of 'ethnicity,'" yet, as Imre also argues,

"East European nations" maintain an "unspoken insistence on their whiteness," which "is one of the most effective and least recognized means of asserting their Europeanness" (2005, 83, 82). I have attempted neither to assert the importance of race over local understandings of ethnicity nor to reinscribe ethnic categories at the expense of processes of racialization and new forms of becoming. I have thus framed my fieldwork (to myself as well as to my interlocutors) in terms of geographical coverage and found that understandings of rhythmicality stood in, both discursively and in embodied practice, for the concept of race and enabled the blocking and blocking of musical faculties in the delineation of whiteness and Europeanness. Such a discursive intervention (both spoken in fieldwork and ethnographically written) aims at an alterity of representation, its othering from the central status it typically holds (within logics of inclusion) to a plural periphery that also admits affective and other material experiences.

Rhythm, as a sonic material agent capable of eliciting strong qualitative and affective responses, holds great potential for the marking of territory as well. In their seminal work on the refrain, Deleuze and Guattari argued that

> there is a territory when the rhythm has expressiveness. What defines the territory is the emergence of matters of expression (qualities). [A component such as rhythm] remains functional and transitory as long as it is tied to a type of action [. . .]. It becomes expressive, on the other hand, when it acquires a temporal constancy and a spatial range that make it a territorial, or rather territorializing, mark: a signature. ([1980] 1987, 315)

Here, Deleuze and Guattari's description of rhythm gaining a temporal constancy can refer both to musical processes such as the organization of recurring patterns into what we can recognize as meter and also to social processes such as the regular, recurring use of music or other practices in culture unified through territorial belonging. I evoke both of these meanings as I return (again) to the performances with which I opened this chapter.

The concern over "clean" and "dirty" tambura performance styles is a matter of territory. The "clean" or "pure" delivery of strict, dogmatic meter in the performance of Croatian melodies became expressive of the domain of the homeland when it acquired a temporal constancy—a rhythm of recurring performance and discourse, of programming in radio and television, of circulation in packaged materials and in the cars and buses of traveling musicians—over a span of many years. The promotion of "clean," "aggressive" tambura music was successful because of the capacity for hard metric articulation to territorialize the performances of musicians playing in resistance to invasion and in support of establishing a religiously and ethnically homogeneous nation-state. The similarity in style of Croatia's Serb musicians marked them as equally aggressive, territorializing, and therefore threatening. It necessitated, for the realization of the new national narrative, that their music be removed from public consciousness and from the spaces that the Croatian state had recently established as its own (though in practice, of course, and especially in semiprivate spaces such as the St. Trifun celebration mentioned previously, musicians and audience members of various backgrounds worked to create more inclusive milieus).

Conversely, the performances of Romani bands deterritorialize the melodies of the Croatian songs through the rhythm of their playing. To non-Roma in the area, Romani music is not a cleanly rhythmic tradition capable of expressing qualities of a folk rooted to territory through its musical, religious, and governmental institutions. Rather, the music's chaotic rhythmicity suggests the natural restlessness of a nonaggressive people; the Roma are the deterritorialized, nomadic musicians par excellence in Croatian and Serbian imaginaries. Performance spaces such as the Waldinger Hotel's City Basement, where Romani bands play *ciganska* as well as *tamburaška* music, and medleys of local as well as foreign songs, thus function primarily as deterritorialized milieus. As Alexei Yurchak argues, in such spaces citizens need not act either in opposition to or in support of dominant national narratives and authoritative discourse, but rather enter into a relation he terms "being *vnye*": a deterritorialized state of being both inside and outside the dominant regime (2005, 128–130). In the Waldinger Hotel, Croatian audiences do not typically assert tautologies of national music against the Romani musicians and international repertoire they hear there, nor do they resist them; instead, audiences suspend concerns over territory and national symbols.

This is possible because Roma's purported nomadism makes them unthreatening musical laborers, attractive loci of affective indulgence and racial becoming, even if the couple's reaction at the Waldinger Hotel to my inclusion of Romani bands in the area's music makes it clear just how easily the matter could turn territorial. In an instant, through my assertion of the very nonethnic and non-racialized scope of research that I had deliberately framed so as not to delimit or essentialize population categories, these musicians' societal roles, as expressed in the discursive imaginaries of the customers, transformed from unproblematic, wandering musicians to invading asserters of Serbian culture. Here we can witness at work an agency (of the field researcher and of the clientele) in affective relations, a process that, as Gary Tomlinson has put it, "encompasses affect within the semiotic process, involving it always in agency and meaning" (2016, 152).

In an area where only music that is "really ours" (i.e., of the Croatian territory) could be unproblematically expressive, the deterritorialized milieu of the City Basement was quickly reterritorialized. Yet the exoticness and affect engendered by the band's playing also serve as sites of encounter and commonality among divided Slavic populations with shared histories of patronizing Romani musicians. Thus agency's reach here is not restricted to the semiotic overcodings at work in the tautological exclusion of Roma or Serbs sometimes witnessed in Eastern Croatia. Agency may also extend to copresent forms of feeling whose affect is not brought into meaning but blocked (and, through this blocking, concretizes alternative meanings). Connection, as much as contestation, remains the tambura's legacy in Slavonia and the distributed geographical networks that connect to it through musical performance. In the material, embodied relations of its performance lies the potential for both challenging and solidifying barriers of understanding among these three intimately if often fraughtly connected racio-ethnic assemblages as they continuously emerge and remake themselves.

FOUR

Young Men, Rituals
of Power, and Conscription into
Intimacy's Assemblages

May 2010: On the eve of the STD "Pajo Kolarić's" International Festival of Croatian Tambura Music, the society's president, Antun, held a dinner. Hailing from several regions, the guests represented a number of institutions that propagate the tambura as Croatia's national instrument: members of the amateur tambura orchestra "Ivan Vuković" from the Austrian Burgenland Croatian community of Parndorf, the well-known Croatian tambura singer Vera Svoboda, and her husband Julie Njikoš, the festival's founder. As entertainment during the meal, held at the Erdut winery, Antun had hired the semiprofessional tambura band Šokci. The band played for fifteen minutes, joined us for a quick dinner, and then performed a longer set while we finished eating. During this second set, several men from the tables stood and began engaging the musicians more actively. Antun was one of the first to interact with the band, and Šokci sang a *bećarac* (reveler's verse) in his honor: "Hey Antun, you are an old carouser. However you say, that's how it must be" (my translation; see figure 4.1).

Set with harmonic accompaniment tonicizing G major and then D major and half-cadencing on scale degree 2, as is typical of many tonal settings of folk melodies in the former Yugoslavia, the bećarac melody is decidedly traditional to Croatia, Serbia, and Bosnia. Unlike newly composed tambura songs, which are mostly straightforwardly tonal, the harmonized bećarac descends from a singing practice that Jerko Bezić refers to as "predominantly unison singing of

FIGURE 4.1 Bećarac verse for Antun

a wider pitch range" and that is characterized by hexachords such as the Dorian-like E-F#-G-A-B-C#, which abounds in this melody, despite the prominence of D (1981, 35; my translation).[1] This verse can easily be adapted to any first name, and Šokci's incorporation of "Antun" at the start of a round of bećarac verses situated the song within one of its traditional uses: patriarchal recognition for Antun's role as host.

With its reference to an "old [male] carouser," the verse also set the tone for an evening of rowdy interaction with the men at the dinner. Antun, standing and facing the crowd, recruited other, younger men to join him in front of the band. They included Zoran, a tambura player in his late forties from Vukovar who has lived in Parndorf since the war and plays in its orchestra, and Christien, the son of the orchestra's conductor and one of many Burgenland Croats born in the 1980s who play in the ensemble but speak little Croatian. The three of them put arms around each other's shoulders, stood facing Šokci and swaying in a short arc that mirrored the band's formation, and left a circular, open space in the middle (see figure 4.2).

I witnessed this formation countless times at private events in Croatia at which tambura bands played for hire. Men, typically between the ages of seventeen and forty-five, but sometimes also including older event patrons such as Antun (then in his late fifties), would leave their tables at some point, usually late in

FIGURE 4.2 Male audience members embracing opposite Šokci

the evening, and embrace one another in a semicircular line opposite the arc of musicians. This is part of *kerenje* ("reveling"), a set of socializing activities that a contemporary Croatian jargon dictionary humorously notes may involve women linking arms in similar fashion but is especially characterized among men by "embracing everyone and anyone and miserably wasting away to music" (*Leksikon* n.d.; my translation). Hiring a tambura band facilitates more than passive enjoyment or associating the patron with the ensemble's celebrity; it helps to precondition the fostering of intimacy by setting expectations for musically mediated interaction with the musicians, patriotic songs, and embracing and dancing with other men. Croatian men kindle this intimacy at parties across differences in nationality, language, and age, cultivating important affective relations of masculinity through their rituals. Such intimate inclusion, however, does not always treat these differences gently, and the recruitment of those differently gendered and/or raced reveals the power and ideologies undergirding the affective block of intimacy even in contexts in which difference is ignored or elided.

In this chapter I turn from racialization between ethnic groups to consider the intersections of race and gender within them and demonstrate the importance of affective blocking for masculine subjectivity's continuing emergence in tambura music. This study opens a final pair of chapters treating dimensions of social life that have long interested scholars of ideology: gender and religion. As I argue, these have as much to do with affective and spatial relations as with systems of thought. More important, however, I show that gender and religion become most salient in the externalization of their attendant feelings beyond the consciousnesses and even the bodies of individual musickers. Extending further the point that affect blocks in aggregation (in this instance as an assemblage of intimate, intercorporeal feelings) even as it blocks in delimitation (subverting literal meanings of ideological discourses on inclusion and exclusion), I also demonstrate how these intensities are repurposed to show the limitations of affective inclusion.

In turning to the mutual impingements of affect with ideology and of race with gender and religion, I narrow further the scale of spatial relations, closing in on the intimate spaces of musical interaction. In this, the first of two chapters focusing on ritual, I examine gendered power and the inclusion of men and women, of musicians and audiences, in ritualized contexts on and near tambura stages. I consider the relationship between ideology and intimate physical assemblages of bodies (such as the men's arc), analyzing how in each case those on the outside come to be conscripted into the space and/or systems of thinking of those in the assemblage. I analyze intimacy as physical, spatial closeness that, while certainly emotional as well, is at times accomplished first through the intensities of the spatial assemblage. Through conscriptive acts—pulling a companion into an embrace, grasping one arm with another, aligning bodies in arcs that receive and hold—these intensities are imbued with particular social meanings and feelings. These are inclusive processes, but ones often imbued with power that manifests in the violation of physical and emotional comfort, marking gender in musical performance as an affective experience of space as much as a performance of ideology. Such intimate assemblages themselves can thus pose dangers to those who are brought within them, and I consider intimacy's threatening side, as well as the dangerous yet potentially empowering deviances of those who do not fit neatly within its structures.

GENDERED SPACE

Gender is the most common demographic basis for demarcating the boundaries of inclusion, and women are often isolated from the spaces previously described. Women who do join the arcs in front of the musicians typically stay only briefly, as the men's attention is on other men, and their actions often gently yet purposefully exclude women. For example, at a football club's party near Osijek at which the tambura band Ravnica was performing, ten male and female guests initially formed an arc in front of the stage, but suddenly each man held out one forearm, sank to the floor, and knelt there embracing his neighbors. The women, left standing, soon withdrew to their tables, and the men reassembled into an entirely male arc.

Spaces for listening in front of tambura bands quickly become decidedly masculine. Men gather there at advanced stages in the evenings' merriment when ample drinking has amplified emotive gestures. They grip each other's shoulders firmly, overlapping arms with those of several others, and make eye contact across the circular open space with others down the curved line or in the band. Women's physical exclusion from privileged spaces of intimate listening is certainly not limited to Croatian tambura music,[2] but as I demonstrate, has come at a time when ideological shifts toward greater inclusion of women are taking hold in various registers within the country. Musical exclusion, and female musicians' sometimes forceful physical *inclusion*, help to illuminate how such exclusive assemblages affectively resist otherwise largely successful campaigns for ideological and structural change.

Tambura bands play diverse repertoire but are particularly successful in cultivating responses from male guests with their own original popular songs. These communicate masculine perspectives on the exploits of *stari lole* ("old carousers"), hard-living tambura players, their romantic successes and failures with women, (ignoring) the latter's objections to their drinking, Slavonia's beautiful landscape, and its defense and reclamation during the war with Yugoslavia. They play their songs fast and hard, linking "aggressive" performance (often consciously) to these territorial and gendered themes. Male audiences usually join the band's singers on each refrain, following musical cues that are clear and nearly identical in a large number of songs: the bass and melody tamburas play louder and articulate rising stepwise melodic passages, modulating from the tonic to the subdominant or relative minor and landing with the vocal on the refrain's first note, the fourth or sixth scale degree (or upper tonic or tenth) (see chapter 1). Such cues facilitate the "emotional exchange between professional musicians and clients" (Hofman 2015, 44) long essential to Yugoslav and post-Yugoslav music scenes' affective economies, leading audiences in songs that are "easily accessible because of their internal sequential repetition, frequent recurrence, and similarity to other songs" (MacMillen 2011a, 112).

Šokci employs just such a third-to-sixth-scale-degree run in its video for the anonymous folk song "Vesela je Šokadija" (The land of the Šokci is merry; see figure 4.3).[3] Following several nearly identical vocal and tambura passages, the tambura (the upper line in measure 5) diverges and leads listeners to scale degree 6 at the refrain's beginning (mm. 6–10). This song is known in Croatia from Krunoslav Slabinac "Kićo" and Slavonski Bećari's 1975 recording, and when at the Erdut winery a man whom I will call Matija praised Šokci's lead singer for the band's fast, "uneducated" style, he responded that he and his brother had learned the tambura by listening to Slabinac's cassettes and copying the band's playing. Matija noted preferring Šokci's performance to that of Ravnica, the festival's other hired band, even though the latter were "professionals," for Šokci's members played more "from the heart." Their musical labor's value rested in the affective investment that Matija read into their rough, aggressive style. He and other male audience members seemed to judge this more important than professional experience or skill, likely in part because it reinforced the familiarity that the amateur musicians in attendance were working to forge with the semiprofessionals whom Antun had hired to perform.

Šokci's singer protested, however, that all of the members had received formal tambura training except him and his brother. He added that they aspired to

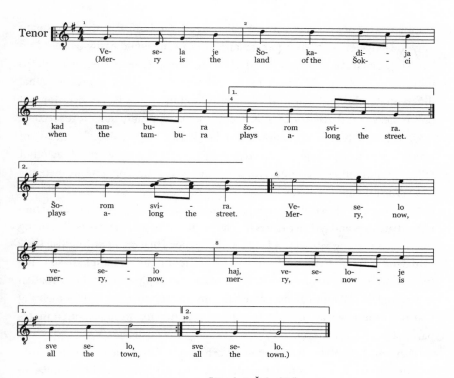

FIGURE 4.3 "Vesela je Šokadija"

perform at the level of Ravnica's musicians, who had earned the honor of accompanying Vera Svoboda in concert and had many original songs and recordings to their credit. Most tambura bands strive to be able to concentrate their efforts on concerts and composition/recording projects rather than on playing at parties. The intimate assemblages in which partygoers (particularly men) attempt to engage tamburaši are not always enjoyed or solicited by the performers, despite the financial incentives (tipping) for working to foster such revelry.

Yet for much of its income Ravnica, too, relies on gigs such as the football club's party previously detailed. Many of this group's and other famous bands' original songs—which less-established bands also play—promote the rowdy male behavior commonly visible at Slavonian gatherings. One can hear even more of the "aggressive" plectrum technique, masculine carouser-themed lyrics, and accented refrain cues in Ravnica originals such as "Svud po selu priče kruže" (All through the village stories are going around, 2006). The song's narrator notes that people rightly call him a "carouser" and then asks the "village grannies" why they bother themselves about "rakes and ruffians" since one ought only to "judge oneself." This particular Ravnica song could easily be based on "Vesela je Šokadija," so nearly identical are the songs' verses' rising, arpeggiated tonic chord melodies and their refrains' descents from scale degree 6.[4] What differentiates this and many other postwar tambura songs is the inclusion not only of heavily male-centric perspectives (which do appear in other 1970s recordings, such as Slabinac's hit "Seoska sam lola" [I'm a village carouser]), but also of overt dismissals of women's concerns, ranging from this song's brushing off of village grandmothers' responses to men's actions to other songs' more blatantly misogynist themes.[5]

Songwriters walk a thin line between reproducing familiar harmonic and melodic structures and lyrical themes that facilitate participation (especially among men) and pursuing musical and textual innovations that could distinguish their own bands from the scores of others active in Croatia. Several emphasized to me the importance of *pionirati*, a loanword meaning "to pioneer" that in Croatian technological and musical discourse has come to refer to innovating something that points a new way forward for other practitioners. In music, it connotes particularly male achievement.

That which tambura bands pioneer can vary greatly. The ensemble Gazde became known in the 1990s for its drum-centered rhythm section (similar to those of rock bands). The members of Ringišpil frequently dress in colorful, casual, nonuniform street clothes rather than the matching, custom-embroidered attire sported by most groups. Members of the women's band Garavuše told me that it wasn't necessary for them to pioneer anything musically because their gender distinguished them. A band need not pioneer something first (e.g., a 1990s all-women band preceded Garavuše); what is important is that a band establish itself as the group that can offer a particular element most successfully in live performances.

Semiprofessional tamburaši in Croatia carry on a tradition of innovation extending back to the socialist period. For Zlatni Dukati in the late 1980s, recording and writing Croatian patriotic music was innovative because musicians had rarely touched such themes following World War II. For ensembles in the post–Yugoslav conflict era, however, the search to pioneer something proves much more challenging, as patriotism is expected in Croatian popular music today. Contemporary music pioneering involves less songs capable of bolstering national unity than the development of "individual style," which as Nigel Thrift notes has become paramount within "practices of aesthetics" given that "the objects and environments that capitalism produces have to demonstrate the calculated sincerity of allure if people are to be attracted to them: they need to manifest a particular style that generates enchantment without supernatural-ism" (2010, 290).

INTIMATE ASSEMBLAGES

"Svud po selu priče kruže" and similar tambura ballads identify in their lyrics a particularly masculine enjoyment that matches well the actions of men who revel in front of the band as they turn their backs on female friends and family members. Beyond mere camaraderie (which is couched in positive terms as *biti dobar*: "being good" with one another), their interactions attain a level of intimacy that is clear from the physical closeness with which they hold one another and the affective exchanges that occur among them and with the musicians. Intimacy, though, is not solely these men's privilege. Other intimacies register in gatherings behind the arcs of listening men: among men and women at tables, over drinks and eating, in poses for pictures, in embraces of greeting and departure. These guests also typically pick up on the familiar or at least easily graspable parts of songs, joining on the choruses to sing to one another. In this respect, they and the men in front of the band alike constitute "assemblages" as Deleuze and Guattari conceptualized them: collectivities of affect, sound, and bodies that, in their machine-like interlockings, generate refrains and, through them, becomings ([1980] 1987, 312).

Intimacy, as a complexly positive characteristic of such collectives, may, like other qualities, function "as a line of deterritorialization of an assemblage, or in going from one assemblage to another" (Deleuze and Guattari [1980] 1987, 306). Men and women who enjoy intimacies beyond the men's arc typically keep their interactions small and somewhat private, content in quiet expressions of familiarity that overlap and disseminate with other groupings. Yet as Deleuze and Guattari also note, ultimately "the role of the refrain [. . .] is territorial, a territorial assemblage. [. . .] [T]he bird sings to mark its territory" (312). Men who stand listening to tambura bands, in juxtaposition with those behind them, create not a deterritorialized milieu but a definite space for intimate exchanges. They call for the other guests' attention, demanding recognition of the intimate inclusions in which they participate and thus also of the physical distinction that necessarily defines their group as, singing, they turn from the other guests. In this respect, one may note that the intimate assemblage is, at the social level, structurally analogous to the affective block of the individual; it, too, involves aggregation as well as delimitation, and that which it excludes (blocks) it also helps to form (to block). As we shall see, however, the interrelations between affective block and intimate assemblage extend beyond structural homology to patterns of social feeling that block (and block) collective feelings beyond systems of conscious thought.

It is not complete distinction from the other guests but the ways in which they include others outside of the arc that characterizes these configurations' intimacy. Not only do the men arrest the other guests' attention; they also take control of the space before the stage by specific acts of inclusion. These acts transpire in moments of individual ascendancy within the group; one or another of the men steps out of his comrades' embrace in order to interact in close proximity with those beyond the arc and thus reterritorializes the masculine space before the stage.

Most often this interaction involves the band. At the dinner at the Erdut winery, Antun called out to Šokci, responding to the bećarac dedicated to him, urging the musicians on, and engaging in lighthearted zafrkavanje, or joking. Several songs later, Antun's friend Zoran suddenly stepped forward to tip Tomo, the band's lead singer. Before Šokci had finished the song that earned the band this tip, Zoran shoved another bill in Tomo's pocket, cut him off after the next verse, and requested "Rastao sam pored Dunava" (I grew up along the Danube). As the band quickly began to play it, Zoran kept his position by Tomo, embraced him with one arm, turned his own body out toward the men's arc, and sang along with the musicians (see figure 4.4). In instances such as this, men in the arc of listeners cross through the otherwise open space in the middle and forge physical connections with the arc of musicians. These two arcs do not otherwise meet (small apertures remain between their ends). When male listeners cross through the space in between to tip the band and request a song, they and the musicians draw one another into their respective proximities. By stepping out in order to include the musicians in the embrace started in the arc of listeners, men such as Zoran can purchase their own inclusion in the musicians' arc and achieve a sense of closeness, familiarity, and similar affective purpose with the band.

Stepping out of the arc of male listeners also enables a very different sort of inclusion: the incorporation of those altogether outside of the circle. In some instances, most often involving women, the inclusion is done from a distance. Next after Zoran, Antun placed a song request with Tomo. He stepped out of

FIGURE 4.4 Zoran singing with Tomo of Šokci

the embrace of his friends, whispered in Tomo's ear, and then announced to the room: "For Gordana, my dearest" (my translation). For his wife, Antun had requested "Jedan život malo je" (One life is but little), a recent hit by the male Croatian pop band Prva Liga, and Šokci played it immediately. Antun remained with the band, facing out toward the other men, the tables, and Gordana as he sang along with Tomo on the refrain. Antun's inclusion of his wife drew her and other audience members into the general arena of musical interaction while simultaneously preserving the masculine performance space configured by the band and the arc of men before it. Within this space, men enjoyed songs for and about women, but always as performances of male love, desire, and fantasy projected out toward those for whom they had great affection yet who remained physically outside of the intimate circle. Among those who *are* physically integrated, such inclusion blocks (aggregates) positive feelings for those beyond the arc, but it also blocks (delimits) these through systems of gendered understanding to which they are often ultimately subordinated. Thus it helps to assemble them as a group (just as it excludes them) beyond the intimate unit assembled with and around the band. The intimate assemblage remains a space for constituting masculinity, blocking (and blocked from) anything else.

In other instances, however, inclusion involves someone from outside the arc (almost always a man). The men who stand embracing before tambura bands at such events perform what I call *conscriptions* of other men into intimacy's assemblages (here, the intimate circle). In moments of individual ascendancy, one or another of the men breaks from the arc and conscripts another guest into its constituency or extends the embrace to one or more of the musicians, who already belong to the circle. While the formations are very often exclusive along strict gender lines, I argue that acts of exclusion are relatively subtle and nonaggressive and that conscription, an act of inclusion, supersedes and at times supplants exclusion as a means of effecting cohesion through the assertion of gendered power.

Researchers have extensively treated conscription, like gender more broadly,[6] from the perspectives of power and ideology. I aim here to redirect this treatment toward a consideration of the affects and physical movements that are sometimes overlooked in studies even of military recruitment. In recent scholarship, theorists have applied "conscription" to processes through which forces of existence, particularly discourses, draw societies into constructed, hegemonic realities. David Scott's *Conscripts of Modernity* (2004) considers conscription as the process by which modernity conditioned the possibilities of choice for New World slaves and for postcolonial narratives of resistance. Scott advances Talal Asad's treatment of colonialism's need to reshape not just colonial subjects' practices but also the discourses and desires that guide them and takes his notion of "conscripts" directly from Asad's (1992) essay "Conscripts of Western Civilization." Scott also engages significantly with the constitutive and productive relationship between power and knowledge as analyzed in writings on discipline and discourse by Michel Foucault (who, after all, had an interest in and sympathy for the plight of conscripted soldiers).

Foucault is by no means the only theorist of gender and sexuality to take a critical stance on conscription's relationship to power and ideology. Judith Butler employs the term similarly in the most recent version of *Frames of War* ([2009] 2010), but her selection of the visual "frame" as the antagonist of the conscriptive process expands beyond discourse to consider a broader range of media, senses, and technologies involved in the constitution of reality. In this sense, her book (which references the work of Louis Althusser, although in passing) continues work that she has been pursuing for more than a decade on ideology, the subject, and an agency and conscience to resist the lure of the law, its apparatuses, and their constitution of the individual (see Butler 1997, 130). Whereas Althusser saw ideology as having *always-already* interpellated individuals as subjects, Butler has called for a consideration of the actions that subjects perform *temporally* and that are simultaneously resistant to, implicated in, and enabled by the relations of power in ideology and the law. Thus it is telling that in her recent work Butler refers not to "interpellation" but to "conscription" and the near synonym "recruitment." Even Althusser occasionally substituted these terms for "interpellation" when describing ideological discourse's necessary capacity not only to interpellate individuals as subjects but also to conscript them into certain *functions* within state structure (for which description he makes a deliberate comparison to the military). Butler writes: "Although the frame initiates (as part of weaponry) or finishes off (as part of reporting) a whole set of murderous deeds, [. . .] its success depends upon a successful conscription of the public. Our responsibility to resist war depends in part on how well we resist that daily effort at conscription" (Butler 2010, xiv). Conscription, for Butler, is an everyday occurrence that happens not always-already but repeatedly (and dynamically) in time. Thus ideology and its rituals make efforts whose success not only conditions but also, in turn, depends on the subjects' agency.

Male guests' and tambura musicians' conscription into intimate assemblages of men before the stage occurs on a more immediately material and spatial plane than do the conscriptions of which Althusser, Butler, and Scott have written. I extend these theorists' concern for material processes in order to illuminate the connection between bodies' physical movement into the male arc and attendant relations through ideology, discourse, and power, considering ultimately how these relations may be affectively blocked in the dual sense of delimitation and aggregation. Conscription is a ritual, performative, but also physical action that is more specific and temporal than Althusser's concept of interpellation or "hailing." Conscription draws the subject into the material structure and affective assemblage—an arc of embracing men, an army, a discipline of knowledge, the media frame of war, and so forth—in which numerous subjects may acquire specific functions within and in the name of an ideology (whether it is an ideology interpellating these subjects into a powerful state apparatus or one emerging among them from the bottom up).

It is in this latter understanding of the organization and emergence of systems of thought that we can see ideology (of gender, nationalism, the state, etc.) in relation to interpersonal closeness, to social intimacy. If we take ideology as a principle of organizing thought and through it behavior within power dynamics, we can begin to expand beyond the top-down rule of law and even the linguistic forms of communication and thinking emphasized in the treatment of ideology by philosophers such as Althusser. At the basic level, ideology is about information and the control of actions based thereon. As Gary Tomlinson argues in his study of musicking's evolutionary emergence, early hominins' processing of information involved an "embodied cognition [that] was extended into *embodied social memory*," generating group experiences of the world in social time that elaborated taskscapes of action and interaction (2015, 75; emphasis in original). Thus early systems of thinking, though not free from power structures (hierarchies are common in most social mammals), formed through patterns of response and mimesis that generated means of external memory storage. This "did not need to await the invention of something like modern graphism or symbolism [but] took shape first as *memory archived* in the form of patterned gesture, transmitted from one body to another" (75).

Musicking emerged out of such embodied archiving and transmission. It presents a particularly important context for social information sharing and processing through gestures and non- or paralinguistic soundings, for "in its modern guises [it] structures acoustical information in complex ways without necessary reference beyond itself" (Tomlinson 2015, 141). Musicking comprises "a highly elaborated mode of entrained sociality, and in this must convey (in a mimetic species with advanced mindreading)[7] deictic, copresent messages of the sort we know"; its meanings, however, "burgeon only in the overlaying of other communicative and semiotic modes onto the embodied production of and reactions to music" (141–142). As such, the mimesis of gestures found in musical action (e.g., the patterned linking of multiple bodies in an arc) affords a certain primacy to affective, nonrepresentational forms of information sharing that amount to an emergent social intimacy. As Steven Shaviro has argued, externalizing memory affords systems of sensing and resensing external stimuli, even to lower-order organisms; the prominence of sentience "all the way down and up" the spectra of species points to important capacities for "cognition as propelled by feeling" that variously converge with, parallel, bypass, and supplant sapience in humans (2015). Onto such feeling- and gesture-based cognition, humans overlay values (e.g., "being good" with someone). In their mutual recognition among participants, values come in turn to bear additional referents ("being good" with other subjects in a union consolidated via the powerful play of an overarching term of ethnicity, gender, etc.) and to constitute systems of thought from the bottom up.

Ideologies involve these far more complicated forms of meaning and referentiality (impossible among early hominins), but musicking represents a site of their potential convergence with affective forms of understanding processes and power. Intimate assemblages afford space for (or emerge with) systems of thought and, as evinced by male listeners' powerful command of other audience members and tambura players, may even constitute repressive apparatuses, though they remain separate from or only partially overlap those of the state. Conscription into the men's circle is a specific instance of spatial and temporal movement into the embrace of power. It is within these movements that musicians and audience members negotiate gendered and financial power as well as their agencies to wield or resist it and ultimately to block certain ideological and affective capacities of the social writ large. Guests who attend private events in Croatia featuring tambura bands typically do so expecting musically mediated intimacy. In realizing these expectations through shared participation, they cogenerate with the musicians both the intensities and the ideas about those intensities that ultimately become important hierarchically for their power to block in aggregate or delimitation. The circle that men form by assembling in an arc before the musicians is one particularly important material, spatial manifestation of such expectations and is a site into whose intensities and into whose systems of memory archiving and meaning making other guests may be conscripted.

Although exclusion of women is part of the process by which men constitute their intimate formation, those involved usually do not achieve this through direct repression or physical violence, nor do they seek seclusion from the other guests. In moments of individual ascendancy (none dominates hegemonically), one or another steps out of the embrace to request a song and by so doing turns to recognize and even to hail the other guests. These performances take place as practices at organized *events* (parties for sports teams, musical societies, weddings, etc.), which happen at what Althusser termed *ideological state apparatuses*, including sports clubs, cultural societies, churches, and so forth. All of these have enjoyed a renewed sense of nationalist purpose since Croatia's separation as an autonomous state, and the ideological tenets regarding shared gender and ethnicity that guide assembling into intimate arcs of listeners thus typically merge top-down and bottom-up ideas of the social. It is important, however, that the expectations that guests tend to hold upon arrival (for intimacy, commonality of gender, ethnicity, state citizenship, etc.) do not amount to the always-already interpellating ideology that concerns Althusser (invitations are not as powerful as interpellations, nor are expectations on the same level as the systems of thought that constitute ideologies). Intimacy, then, is an affective space in which physical movement may parallel but also depart from ideological maneuvering. Within this space ideologies, as systems aggregating from personal agencies at the bottom and building to new forms of power over individuals and crowds at the top, are capable of blocking and being blocked by affective potentials. Conscription into the specific spatial assemblage of the men's arc, then, is a ritualized practice within these apparatuses' material existence (their "events") by which men generate the affective potentials of explicitly and exclusively gendered inclusion typical of such male intimacy and of the event's broader intimacy and physical and ideological spaces.

INTIMACIES, IDEOLOGIES, AND INSCRIPTIONS

Lauren Berlant writes that intimacy "involves an aspiration for a narrative about something shared, a story about both oneself and others that will turn out in a particular way" (1998, 281). This aspiration clearly is guided by (potential) affective attachments, but it also involves systems of belief. Berlant also notes that intimacy "does generate an aesthetic, an aesthetic of attachment, but no inevitable forms or feelings are attached to it. This is where normative ideologies come in, when certain 'expressive' relations are promoted across public and private domains—love, community, patriotism" (285). The specific narratives and forms of their fulfillment are not given or "inevitable" in intimacy but rather come about through processes that tap into ideological relations to specific cultural and historical milieus.

Conscription, then, takes away another level of immediacy. If intimacy generates a general aesthetic of attachment but also becomes ideological through the expression of certain narratives and the expectation of their fulfillment within the appropriate domains, conscription into intimacy's assemblages temporalizes the subject's handling of these expectations of closeness and commonality within specific structures and practices. By attaching the affects appropriate to their deterritorializing and reterritorializing, these structures and practices become capable of fulfilling the narratives in play, such as guests' expectations of intimate patriotic relations at events featuring tambura bands (based on assumptions of granted, shared belonging in a group, event, apparatus, etc., in which they are hailed as subjects).

For tambura music events, the interconnectedness of intimate assemblages and ideologies of gender and nation becomes clear when we consider the importance of circular groupings in the region's folklore and contemporary folk-derived traditions. Kolo dancing in particular provides a compelling parallel to the circle that the men's arc completes with the band (see figure 4.5). In Slavonia, this closed circular line dance moves clockwise to instrumental accompaniment of the tambura band and halts for interjections of *deseterac* ("decasyllabic verse") for *pjevanje u kolu* ("singing in kolo") by one or another of the dancers. Often these interjections respond to or comment upon another participant (although distinct from accompanied *bećarac* singing, the two genres belong to the same overarching tradition, and singers often repurpose *bećarac* verses for *pjevanje u kolu*). Men and women who join in this dance interweave their arms in a front basket hold, each making physical contact with two dancers on the right and two on the left. Interjecting a verse allows an individual to take the spotlight momentarily, but it also requires the close attention and coordination of the other dancers and tambura musicians: the dancers switch from stepping quickly to swaying rhythmically and sometimes join the singing of the couplet's second line or consider with which verse to respond, and the musicians must typically break off in the middle of the instrumental and, if they decide to accompany, match the singer's key. Circular bodily arrangements, moments of individual ascendancy within group performance, and close physical contact facilitate the engendering of social intimacy in this less exclusive practice, too, and the performance (and not only the affects) of roles within specific systems of ethnic and gendered meaning is just as salient here.

FIGURE 4.5 Kolo dancing and singing to the band Zora
at a wedding near Slavonski Brod

Dubravka Ugrešić argues that Yugoslavia's key symbol was "the kolo, which was performed for years at all ceremonial state occasions" ([1995] 1998, 50). She explicitly connects such folklore to ideology in independent Croatia: "The new states, which promptly proclaimed democracy on the ruins of the old, make use of the same strategic device. First they assured their peoples that their national identity was repressed under the Yugo-communist regime [. . .] and then in return gave them (again!) the freedom of folklore, always an effective opiate" (133). While Ugrešić's critique generalizes a complex array of uses, it does sum up pointedly how, within at least the most controlled instances of top-down state appropriation of folklore in independent Croatia, the kolo fulfilled ideology's common political paradox: it served a resistance to an allegedly repressive state ideology by structuring the material existence of a new ideology. The kolo's purported all-inclusiveness at current occasions is similar to that of the past, forming a space for open yet territorialized musical participation by attaching feelings of the nation to its formation. The level of territorial belonging and representation varies widely across the lived practice of diverse kolo traditions, and particular tradition bearers' performance approaches may change between local and national contexts (see Katarinčić, Niemčić, and Zebec 2009). Importantly, though, practitioners have commonly seen in the kolo the perseverance of tradition and identity in the face of threats to national consciousness. Such threats range from "millennia-long Roman and Italian omnipresence" (Cukrov 2015, 151; my translation) and Austro-Hungarian musical and choreographic domination (Niemčić 2005) to the post–World War II ascent of communism and quashing of republic-level nationalism in Yugoslavia (Škugor 2016).

In the circular space that the men's arc forms with the band at private events, inclusiveness is similarly oppositional and nonuniversal in that it visibly excludes women as well as many male guests (though the band, whom the arc opposes in a literal, physical sense, is not resisted but embraced, both metaphorically and physically). Conscription marks intimacy's power and gendered distinction, though not seclusion, from the rest of the event. Talal Asad's work illuminates conscription's specific processes and function within ideology. Writing about the history of Western civilization's colonial project, he indicates that his use of "'conscripts,' as opposed to 'volunteers,' does not suggest merely the recruits' initial attitude, but also the nature of the army and the war it has been fighting. To instill the desire for progress in the non-European world, it was necessary to inscribe modern Western categories into the administrative and legal discourses of that world" (1992, 340). As with the discursive colonial conscriptions of which

Asad writes, inscription is key to men's physical conscription into the intimate spaces of listening at events with tambura bands. Individual men step out of the arc to conscript other men into it, thus inscribing them in the constituency, or they step across the open circular space to speak with, embrace, and/or request a song from the tambura musicians, and thus they inscribe themselves in the arc of the musicians. These inscriptions are so naturalized within the ritual as to attract little attention; their capacity for conscription and the violation and even violence that they may require usually are not obvious. In the remainder of this chapter, however, I consider situations in which the power of inscriptive strategies and of conscription into intimate assemblages becomes overt: in male tamburaši's own efforts to control intimate circles and their peers' and patrons' movement within them and in the men's arc's conscripting of gendered and racialized Others (which reveals tamburaši's limited capacities to assert this control over demands on their affective labor).

INTIMATE MUSICAL CAMARADERIE

Male tamburaši also commonly participate in intimate circular formations constituted solely of musicians, experiencing such assemblages' affective and physical relations outside of patron-laborer power relations. These formations range from circles in which band members stand while rehearsing, to social, nonplaying contexts that bring together musicians (often from multiple ensembles) around tables at bars and cafés, to large jam sessions at gatherings specifically for tamburaši. Client-free settings are not devoid of gender or power relations, however. I consider strategies for manipulating relations through physical space that tamburaši identify and rehearse in these contexts. These prove empowering in dealing with difficult clientele elsewhere, and I turn subsequently to tamburaši's interactions with young men at publicly open paying gigs (without invited guests), where power is arguably more broadly distributed.

Getting Drinks with Brodski Tamburaški Orkestar Members

During my fieldwork in Slavonski Brod from April through June 2010, I typically spent Tuesday evenings at two successive tambura rehearsals. I was renting a room in the *pansion* ("pension") run by Antun Tonkić, the čelo tambura player for the professional group Berde Band, and his wife Ljiljana Tonkić, a schoolteacher, local elected official, and lyricist of several of the band's hit songs. Late on Tuesday afternoons I would ride with Antun in his large pickup truck to Berde Band's rehearsal and, following two hours of hard work on new musical arrangements for upcoming engagements, three of the band's seven members (Budo, Mika, and Mato) would depart for the Brodski Tamburaški Orkestar (Slavonski Brod's city tambura orchestra) rehearsal. Damir Butković "Budo" conducted the orchestra, and he and I usually left together, eventually arriving at the orchestra's rehearsal following an hour of free time spent with Mika or other players from his ensembles. He would sometimes discuss band matters with Mika or talk to me or the orchestra members about upcoming ensemble plans, but this was also a social time. While the orchestra worked through repertoire efficiently, rehearsals similarly afforded members opportunities to socialize, both while playing and during cigarette breaks.

After the rehearsal, at about 8:00 p.m. a small group of musicians would head to Caffe Bar Kaktus across town for drinks. We would order beer, sit around a table outside, and discuss diverse topics, often having nothing to do with tambura ensembles or even music more generally. When tambura music did enter the conversation, it usually was with reference to discussions on the website forum. tambura.com.hr and its largely male tamburaši network. Mladen, the berda player for the band Širok Šor, often pulled up forum postings of *berde* (tambura basses) on his laptop. Like the rest of our time at the bar, this concerned masculinity as much as musicality; he would often show us a berda with a stallion's head carved in place of a scroll above the tuning pegs, speculate about buying it, and make reference to other tamburas with emblems of virility, such as Budo's berda, which had a fully maned lion's head carved above the tuning pegs. A nearly fetishistic attachment to visibly male instruments and to hypermasculinity motivated and characterized intimacy in these settings.

Orchestra rehearsals provided opportunities for musicians to reshuffle into several such small units: their instrument sections during rehearsal, groups of friends during smoking breaks, and frequently still other groups for socializing afterward. These differed from those in which they otherwise spent their time, such as the semiprofessional tambura bands of which most orchestra musicians were also members. Their revelry throughout the night thus included hopping not only from one venue or rehearsal to another but from one cluster of friends to another. The men at the Caffe Bar Kaktus were close friends, most of whom had met long before the orchestra's founding in 2007 but who had not all played together previously or had such a reason to gather and drink. They included Mika, Bernard (a prim player who grew up close to Antun Tonkić), and Bruno (a *brač* player in the orchestra and the band Graničari who lived near the Tonkić *pansion* and gave me rides). Other orchestra members gathered afterward in their own small groups, and the only partial overlap between these and their bands distributed their connections across a broader network. What marked successful social grouping was zafrkavanje ("joking," "ribbing"), a process through which they built affective ties sitting around tables and trading good-natured insults and unrestrained cackles back and forth.

Budo and the rest of the group welcomed me graciously into their nights at Caffe Bar Kaktus. This graciousness, however, marked me as an outsider from their banter, and I found it difficult to shake this separation, which was salient from the start and rooted in mutual expectations about my role as the orchestra's "guest." As a foreigner, I bore this status throughout my research in the former Yugoslavia almost without exception. Although young women would occasionally allow me to pay for drinks when I was interviewing them at a café, I very seldom managed to foot the bill for meetings with men or older women, despite my numerous objections and attempts to corner a waiter and pay furtively. At Kaktus, because I was their "guest," I tried to act as respectfully and obligingly as I could. Although our gatherings were comfortable, it seemed evident to all of us that I remained somewhat outside of their closely bonded circle due to both my own hesitancy to join in the often-raucous behavior and their expectation that they should treat me socially and financially as their guest.[8]

What cemented my inclusion in the group involved social friction as much as the comfort of familiarity: my first successful joke. Zafrkavanje is a vital element of the (male) tambura player's *bećar* lifestyle, and something of which musicians in Croatia (both native born and travelers from Croatia's intimates such as Jerry Grcevich) spoke fondly and which they would immediately begin upon seeing one another. Budo, Mladen, and anyone else who joined them would frequently rib each other about things that they had done or said. After more than a month of my attending rehearsals and drinking sessions, they slowly began to respond to my comments with good-natured sarcasm, and I, too, began to feel comfortable enough to join in their jokes. The delighted surprise and congratulatory handshakes and claps with which they rewarded my first successfully landed sarcastic quip (made in response to one of Mladen's) made it clear just how foreign my politeness had seemed.[9] It was at this point that I first felt that I had moved beyond being *dobar s njima* ("good with them," meaning on friendly terms) to an intimacy in which such positive coding was not only unnecessary, but also wholly inadequate; it was not so much that I had become capable of joking with them without offending as that our comments at one another's expense brought us closer. This exemplified the affective block of tamburanje: our bonds blocked (in aggregate) an affective intensity that in turn blocked (in delimitation) otherwise standard interpretations of discourse based on literal signification (in which a put-down is an insult).

My purchase of a prim tambura from a member of Bruno's band further cemented my participation in the male camaraderie attached to playing and collecting tamburas. This presented an appropriate occasion for me, finally, to stand a round of drinks in celebration. In Croatia and much of Southeast Europe, one treats friends when one has something to celebrate, such as a birthday or a new car. Purchasing a fellow musician's instrument required that I distribute my good fortune, confirming my membership in the social economy of giving and being indebted for both material goods and affective gestures: tamburas, insults, bottles of beer, laughter, and so on. This and the joke began to move me out of the feminized role of one who (like the rare female tamburaši who participated in these interactions) was spared from/could not participate in buying drinks and receiving insults.

For inclusion in the male circle of friends at Kaktus, it was not necessary for me to purchase a hypermasculinized instrument such as a stallion-headed berda; buying and celebrating the small, feminized prim tambura, also known as a "little pearl" (*bisernica*) or "little tambura" (*tamburica*), sufficed (in fact, they questioned me before I bought it to make sure that I would guard and cherish it). As Marilyn Strathern notes, within "the reciprocities and debts created by the exchange," which "are seen to comprise a form of sociality and a mode of societal integration," "the basis for [gendered] classification does not inhere in the objects themselves but in how they are transacted and to what ends. The action is the gendered activity" (1988, xi). The relation to both male and female elements, to the actions of giving and receiving gifts as well as accruing and availing of debts, helps singular persons transform into *dividuals* with multiple, social elements comprising their selves and groups (15), and this is ultimately what the intimate male circles are about.

Buying drinks and engaging in zafrkavanje in these settings bear significantly on interactions within orchestras and, even more so, on playing in contexts where other tamburaši are the only audience. At jam sessions, a small group of players (sometimes from a single professional band) initiates the playing while others gather around. The give-and-take dynamic between those playing and the listeners around them differs greatly from the assemblages of men at paid private performances, for they encircle the band, rather than all gathering in front. The middle remains a space clearly privileged for tambura performance rather than for men to parade about and draw onlookers' attention. Participation consists of voluntarily moving into the middle in order to relieve a musician, though at times a player in the middle conscripts a friend to take over for him. The group fosters closeness through exchanges and musical participation based on shared (rather than physically opposed) talents, knowledge, desires, and gender.

These exchanges, however, are by no means egalitarian. Men in the middle mostly do not volunteer to give up their positions but grant them to others who ask. Here a hierarchy typically emerges based on skill and celebrity among a group of men with otherwise relatively common interests, ethnicity, backgrounds, and ambitions for the evening. The most dangerous players typically have the right to inscribe themselves in the circle of players, relieving a less-established player and conscripting his instrument. The affective bonds built through zafrkavanje (an important intimacy centered on playful insults), however, may also allow one to take over an instrument from a friend who is technically more adept but of equal social standing. Playing dangerously is also to a certain extent about the affective risk and rewards of inflicting insults, and the dynamic hierarchies that emerge across spectra of musical and social skill (and sometimes of age and gender) cultivate flexibilities in negotiating distributions of power that prove essential in dealing with complex patron relations.

On the Dalmatian Coast with Hrvatski Sokol

Skilled performers also learn to apply spatial organization and control in calculated maneuvers among young male patrons. These men are a great potential source of additional income, but for this very reason—especially if they are purchasing food and drinks and are thus of increased value to the proprietors—often gain power over the social and spatial relations at the performance. In July 2013 I accompanied the Osijek band Hrvatski Sokol to a series of paid evening engagements at the bar and restaurant Eko Dalmacija in Vodice on the Dalmatian Coast, where the musicians took charge of their young patrons' physical arrangement from the very start. Around 10:00 p.m. the band would set up by the mostly open-air tavern's entrance and play out toward the crowds strolling along the seafront boulevard. After about twenty minutes of instrumental medleys, participatory bećarac verses, and classic 1990s tambura songs, the band would stop, thank the audience that had accumulated, and invite them inside as the musicians headed toward the tables near the back bar. They usually succeeded in attracting groups of men in their late teens and early twenties, many of whom were regularly in attendance over the course of Hrvatski Sokol's weeklong engagement.

Once the crowd was gathered, however, subtler forms of spatial manipulation often most effectively kept the atmosphere (and tipping) lively. One evening, at about 11:30, I returned from a walk along the boulevard with Matko, the band's hired driver from Osijek, to find a group of young men assembled around Hrvatski Sokol. I had seen them the night before, and Filip, the tambura bassist, commented that practically the same people were returning every night. The band had moved to the far end of the bar and was covering popular patriotic songs such as "Lijepa li si" (Be thou beautiful). Fitting for the Croatian tourists present from all over the country and abroad, including a band member's in-law from Canada, this ballad by Dalmatian rocker Marko Perković "Thompson" celebrates lyrically (and through several folk music references) each of Greater Croatia's regions in turn: Zagora, Slavonia, Dalmatia, Lika, Istria, Zagorje, and Herceg-Bosna (in Bosnia and Herzegovina). The young regulars nearest the band, however, knew one another from their hometown in Slavonia, and they gathered in a closed circle with their backs turned on both the other clientele and the band, whom they drowned out with their raucous singing. The band responded by striking up a set of bećarac verses, a tradition especially popular in Slavonia (more so there and in parts of Bosnia and Serbia than in Dalmatia). This coaxed the men in front of them to open their circle into an arc facing the band as they picked up the humorous verses, repeating each second line in the traditional manner. Though a few of them turned back toward each other after the verses, Hrvatski Sokol managed to keep several of them engaged as the band subsequently began to play popular Slavonian tambura songs.[10] The switch worked; those who stayed began to inscribe themselves within a circle formed with the band as they went up one at a time to place requests.

Soon, however, Hrvatski Sokol undertook more directly physical and spatial forms of intervention. As the band struck up Grcevich and Škoro's "Moja Juliška," two men and a woman began to dance a kolo, and Tihomir, the lead singer, pointed his finger away from the rest of the crowd. With this gesture he managed to direct those who wished to participate in the Slavonian dance step to a large, open, uncovered space in the back where they would not interfere with the arc and atmosphere that the band members were working hard to cultivate directly in front of themselves. Musicians and audience members alike employ the word *atmosfera* ("atmosphere") to connote a range of affective and sonic dimensions of energized space and interpersonal relations at a performance. The ambiguous grounding of a good "atmosphere" or "party" in a tambura concert's physical and technical production makes these difficult to sustain. As Ben Anderson has noted, furthermore, "it is the very ambiguity of affective atmospheres [. . .] that enable[s] us to reflect on affective experience as occurring beyond, around, and alongside the formation of subjectivity" (2009, 77). Musicians' attempts to shore up particular intersubjective relations defined through spatial proximity, sound/audition, and monetary exchange often produce unexpected and sometimes undesirable affective and otherwise physical responses from listeners. (Bands naturally had more and better options for this among friends; at a private party that the band played in Vodice that week, one of the *brač* players called me up to replace him so that he could socialize with Slavonian friends who had engaged the group, and as he circulated among the tables he connected with both them—telling jokes and keeping spirits high—and us—keeping ours high as well by winking and posing humorously with friends.)

Despite the musicians' efforts to sustain this particular atmosphere between them and their most proximate audience members, many of the men before them departed as well, and the dancers formed a large, closed circle in the back of the restaurant. Hrvatski Sokol obliged them with an instrumental dance medley more directly suited to this dancing than "Moja Juliška" (a song associated with *czardas*; see chapter 2), but after the medley the musicians declared it was time for their break and headed up the stairs to an open patio reserved for them. Accompanying them, I commented to Darko, their prim tambura player, that this seemed like a well-advised and strategic move, since people stopped tipping once they were dancing to medleys. He confirmed that "it was a good party" and that they would continue as long as the atmosphere and tipping were good but take a break when the audience stopped interacting as directly with them. In the case of a closed circle dance such as the *Slavonsko kolo* or *taraban* that Slavonian patrons typically know, bands, too, could find themselves excluded from guests' intimate circular formations. The mirrored arcs that represent the best potential for cultivating positive atmospheres and generous tipping are spaces that musicians assert their musical prowess and control to create.

This is especially important when the patrons are not guests of an event for which the band has been hired (by a particular, primary host) but rather clients of restaurants or bars, where their financial relationships with the venue and band remain continuously in flux. Bands must strategically cater to the affective, musical, and financial interests of multiple parties, often mediating among competing powers over their labor. After breaking from about 12:30 to 1:00 a.m., Hrvatski Sokol came back downstairs where, as Matko noted to me, the young male regulars of the past several nights were once again awaiting the musicians. So was Tihomir's in-law (his wife's cousin), who, I then learned, had given the band $200 Canadian during its earlier set. He thus had both familial and financial claims on the musicians' time and labor that he was congenially but actively asserting following the break. The young Slavonian men, however, were much louder and more adamant than the graying Croatian Canadian; as they formed a circle with the band around a table (later expanding to encompass two tables), they continued to crowd him out along with Eko Dalmacija's other older clients. They shouted a request for "Zorica," a hit single released earlier that year by the pop-tambura band Mejaši that celebrates all-night partying and that they had been requesting at Eko Dalmacija every night. As usual, they wanted to hear it multiple times in succession, which was tedious for the musicians (this piece, which was in the dance music style of tambura songs then popular, the band's driver described as *bez veze*: "meaningless").[11] It was also financially risky, since the young men offered no further tips for the repetitions, and potentially of less interest to Tihomir's in-law, who was more familiar with music played in Yugoslavia before his emigration more than forty years earlier.

Hrvatski Sokol took notice and called out a kolo, using it advantageously. Several lines of young dancers formed open circles around the perimeter, drawing men from the male arc and breaking their monopoly over the performance. This allowed Tihomir's in-law to reenter the previously blocked space before the musicians, who succeeded in taking his requests and keeping him prominently in front of or among the remaining young men for the rest of the set. This might not have been necessary with a more assertive individual; many domestic male tourists would quickly take younger men to task, asserting their privilege within the space of listening and interaction. The Croatian Canadian man, however, appeared to defer to them as locals, yielding his potential power as an elder to considerations of proximity and citizenship. In part, this marked an identification with them via the sharing of young, masculine affect; as he told me, he still "feels" that which he "remembers" from his teenage experience of music in Croatia and takes pleasure in seeing the "younger generation" doing it. The band, however, made sure that such deference did not lead to exclusion. Its means of honoring his monetary, familial, and generational status within the event points to the distributed nature of power figured through intersections of affluence, masculinity, and seniority.

Distributed Intimacies

Berlant's observation that intimacy involves "tacit fantasies, tacit rules, and tacit obligations to remain unproblematic" is apt here (1998, 287). Though operating at different levels of familiarity, the intimacies of closely bonded men playing in the band, of musicians with young men whom they get to know over several nights of performing, and of the broader tambura network that facilitates the incorporation in public concerts of men and women from Croatia's intimates rely on similar fantasies, rules, and obligations. These guide the maintaining of intimacy at all three levels; the younger men were not so problematic as to refuse suggestions from the band (whose services the restaurant and the Croatian Canadian man had compensated more than they). Similarly, Hrvatski Sokol's members knew at key moments to use subtle, nonverbal cues to influence rather than control their audience, just as the Croatian Canadian man seemingly understood that a large tip alone did not privilege him with dominance over locals attending this publicly open performance. As in the instances of musicians testing their ability to insult and supplant one another outside of contexts with paying (non-tamburaš) audiences, the process of becoming or remaining "good" with one another in the context of musical socializing and performance required an unspecified but recognized decorum of interaction, one from which no one diverged so far as to create problems, and in which control and status were continuously (if not equilaterally) redistributed. Control in these situations is ultimately about inclusion, but in an appropriate hierarchy that is constantly emerging, despite being based on fairly consistent ideological tenets regarding gendered, ethnic, national, generational, and financial status.

Anahid Kassabian (2013, xxiv) situates such distribution of power and subjectivity in affective responses to what she terms "ubiquitous musics": those that "fill our days, are listened to without the kind of primary *attention* assumed by most scholarship to date" (xi). Here, however, she describes a transformation in subjectivity that seems particular to the modernity of post-Enlightenment Western Europe. A wealth of anthropological literature has documented the societal prevalence of the *dividual*, or multiple person, and of networks distributing its affects, finances, thoughts, gifts, and words intersubjectively in contemporary societies around the world (see Strathern 1988). It need not be only ubiquitous musics, then, or even music at all, that should distribute subjectivity in societies with different conceptions of the in/dividual, family, state, and so forth (though Kassabian argues convincingly for the pioneering work of ubiquitous musics and their technologies in cultivating the European and North American subjectivities needed for the networks of distributing and processing information that developed into ubiquitous computing; 2013, xxv–xxvi). In Croatian tamburaši's downtime drinking and talking about instruments, in their music making outside of rehearsal and official performance contexts, and in their interactions with men at hired gigs, we can recognize such distribution of power and subjectivity through *attentive* forms of listening (to tamburas, jokes about instruments and musicians, and other musical activities).

Kassabian does offer important insights on the dynamic, unbalanced play of power and affect. "Distributed subjectivity," she writes, "is, then, a nonindividual subjectivity, a field, but a field over which power is distributed unevenly and unpredictably, over which differences are not only possible but required, and across which information flows, leading to affective responses" (2013, xxv). Through these flows and responses, but also, importantly, through blockages, through cuts in the networks that distribute them (Strathern 1996), new affective and power relations—which are nearly the same thing here, the power to affect—continuously emerge, though some prove more stable than others. Intimacies, too, are dynamic and emerge over time; as musicians become more familiar with their audiences as in/dividuals, as affective assemblages, and as social entities (categorized by gender, age, etc.), they privilege emergent hierarchical organizations. Such hierarchies are not only difficult for musicians and audiences to manage in their diachronic shifts, but also complex in their synchronous natures and exigencies. Thus an older man who has tipped generously but given up ownership of the contemporary music scene by emigrating competes with younger, less wealthy, but multiple and confidently local men for the band's labor. Among patrons of heterogeneous intentions and demographics, the issue is more the prevalence of ubiquitous listeners (to many of whom the band cannot attend at once) than of ubiquitous musics. Musician and nonmusician listeners alike often respond with forceful cuts, or inscriptions, in the physical assemblages of bodies and the spatial organization of the soundings at these events. It is to the more volatile cuts (and their affective blocks) that I turn in this chapter's final ethnographic section.

GENDERED AND RACIALIZED OTHERS

Not every band is poised to control the flux of power within such circular spaces, nor is everyone in the arc of listeners equally or even minimally empowered. The power dynamics are more complex than the most salient interactions between

FIGURE 4.6 Garavuše performing at Zlatne Grive festival in Otok

the band and arc would suggest, drawing within their emergent and unstable hierarchies even those of much slighter capacities to affect intimacy's grip. I turn now to two counterexamples—the first involving female tambura musicians and the second involving me, a young male audience member but distinct outsider—to demonstrate inscription's violating role in the process of conscription into intimacy's assemblages.

May 30, 2010: I attended the Zlatne Grive horse and sports festival in Otok at the invitation of Garavuše, one of three semiprofessional female Croatian tambura bands then active. Garavuše has been playing semiprofessionally since 2003, when the band began to compete at festivals for *autorske pjesme* ("original songs"), and when I met the musicians they were all in their early twenties. The six women in the group have maintained a busy performance schedule for several years and have made a name for themselves at festivals and private engagements while simultaneously studying at first the high school in Kutjevo, Croatia, and later the university in Osijek.[12] They were engaged to play for Otok's weekend parties, and I accompanied them to their Sunday afternoon performance (see figure 4.6).

Conscription into Intimacy's Assemblages **189**

The band had recently released its first album and included on it the song "Ja sam mala garava" (I'm a dark little [woman]), composed and arranged by male colleagues Robert Vojvodić and Krunoslav Dražić. The song's title makes an obvious allusion to the well-known Yugoslavian Romani song "Ciganka sam mala" (I'm a little Gypsy girl), which shares the Garavuše song's titular first line: "Ja sam mala garava." Vojvodić's composition recasts the song's narrator as a Croat girl whose soul is just as *bećar* as her *lola* (carouser) boyfriend. The allusion to the Ciganka as a highly desired (gendered and racialized) musical Other suggests, however, other dimensions of desirability and novelty with which male tamburaši receive them. For their part, the band members have handled this role's benefits and challenges admirably, and in 2012 Garavuše managed to get the bid for the CFU's annual North American tour (its first female ensemble). Unlike the Romani tambura bands discussed in the previous chapter and the female Romani singers celebrated in songs such as "Ciganka sam mala," they have achieved noteworthy social and financial status in Croatia and beyond via musical and gendered innovations. As we shall see, however, their inclusion in the scene relative to that of Roma performers has exacted certain tolls.

Theirs was also the first female tambura appearance at Otok's annual Zlatne Grive festival. Most guests responded quite visibly and audibly, but with diametrically opposed, heavily gendered expressions of enthusiasm or skepticism, to Garavuše's playing. Initially, four enthusiastic teenage to middle-aged women and one older man entered the space before the low stage and linked arms in a small, closed circle reminiscent of kolo dancing. Soon, however, several men stepped in front of the women, facing the stage in an arc. Two of them, in alternation, stepped into the circle to perform actions with the musicians that paralleled moments of individual ascendancy that I have already ascribed to male guests interacting with male musicians. These guests, however, modified their actions such that they transgressed propriety, creating problems and thereby revealing the power at stake in their assertions of access. One of them walked up near the band and stood smirking and gesturing at a male friend in the audience. Later, both he and the second man shouted jokes and song requests in the middle of verses, rather than waiting for a break between songs (typically a more respectful and effective approach). None of these actions was foreign to the context of tambura performance, but the timing, volume, and attitude with which the men carried them out lent them a sinister aspect (not lost on the musicians or audience), a force contradicting their typical significations.

The first man's friend in the audience suddenly came forward and placed his arms around the shoulders of the two men, coaxing them into singing and moving away from the stage. By making his own individual foray into the middle of the circle, this friend managed to conscript the two men back into the larger arc of swaying, singing men facing the stage. More men stood and left their tables to join them. Thus the friend also helped to augment the bodily barrier delimiting the intimate, circular space of the men and the musicians. This had the usual effect of excluding other guests, and in fact they crowded out the standing female fans.

The integrity of the open, circular space did not remain unchallenged for long, however. The first man broke free of the arc again, placed his leg on the stage, leaned forward to talk to lead singer Ivana Ketović, and inserted a 100 kuna bill (worth approximately 14 euros at the time) into one of her tambura bass's F holes. It is nearly impossible to retrieve money from inside of a bass. His placing it there rather than behind the bass's tuning pegs—a more appropriate area and one decidedly masculinized in the instance of a lion- or stallion-headed berda such as that of Berde Band's bassist Budo—negated its expected monetary transfer and feminized the instrument as an object of consumption. By thus altering a typical act of musical patronage, he made the power dynamic explicit: as a male guest with hard currency, he could demand a song from the hired band, whether or not his tip bore the musicians any profits, and could gain access to typically restricted areas of their instruments. In this respect, his actions paralleled those of a strip-club patron inserting a bill into a dancer's garments in areas of the body not typically accessible to strangers. As Garavuše performed the requested song, he kept his foot on the stage, staying to enjoy in proximity the purchased performance.

The second man stabilized this proximity a few minutes later when he pulled a chair into the middle of the circle and sat down, placing his right foot on the edge of the stage (see figure 4.7). The first man walked over and sat on his lap, placing his boots fully on stage. The two of them formed a physical bridge between the musicians and the male arc behind them, inserting their own, exaggerated form of male intimacy—a gesture, perhaps, toward a strip-club lap dance—into the formerly open space in the middle. Their actions parodied typical forms of interaction and conscription and left enduring inscriptions on the musicians and their space; the tip remained inextricably inside the berda, and the men kept their bodies in the circle and their feet on stage beyond the moment of explicit communication. They thus challenged Garavuše's desire and resolve to take part in a practice that typically facilitates ritualized male intimacy, demonstrating the physical and psychological toll that inclusion would exact.

June 26–27, 2010: My last example comes from a wedding near Slavonski Brod (see again figure 4.5). The tambura band Zora played several times throughout the day, finishing with a party after the ceremony. At several points during the party, young men assembled in the typical arc to listen and sing along. The *kum* was from a Bosnian Croat family, and many of the young men had immigrated from Bosnia or been born to refugees. Guests of different backgrounds combined at the day's various events, in kolo dancing, in *pjevanje u kolu* and bećarac singing, and in men's arcs.

I was particularly marked as an outsider, and most of my initial interactions were facilitated by personal contacts in the band. Just after midnight, however, a friend of the *kum* with whom I had spoken earlier broke briefly from the arc, caught my gaze, and motioned for me to join their embrace. I left my seat, entered beside him, and stood swaying and singing in the middle of the six men. Soon another man down the line broke loose and walked back and forth across the

FIGURE 4.7 Garavuše performing while a seated male audience member keeps his foot on the stage

circular space, raising his hands in the air and turning slowly to address first the band and then us. He then entered the arc next to me and put his arms around my shoulders and those of the man to his left. Suddenly he placed his right cheek against my face and pressed hard, hurting my cheekbone. He rotated his head and planted his lips on my cheek, giving me a hard kiss. As he turned his face forward again, I could still feel a tingling sensation in my skin and the dull ache of the gently bruised bone.

Although kissing is a fairly common exchange of affection between two male friends, the young man's kiss surprised me. I had never met him and had only ever received a kiss from one Croatian man: Antun, the president of the STD "Pajo Kolarić." Antun had kissed me once on each cheek, as I did him, in the customary Catholic Croatian manner as he bade me farewell upon my leaving Osijek, where he had been my host for several months. The kiss at the wedding was different: it was hard; its placement on just a single cheek from an angle that precluded the possibility of my reciprocating negated the action's potential to be read as part of Catholic tradition; and it forced upon me a closeness that I felt we had not developed, that I had not earned. Yet it seemed that that was precisely the point: this kiss exacted of me the closeness required for joining. The pain that lingered after he turned away inscribed this closeness on me and conscripted me more fully into the men's arc around me.

Pain is a close attendant experience to intimacy. Those who share in intimacy—even those who do so almost automatically by right of gender, race, ethnicity, citizenship, and so forth—are often assumed to have endured common pain and to be willing to endure it for the sake of the group. Those whose belonging is uncertain—who like Garavuše and I are included yet do not hold the masculine, Croat identity otherwise commonly enjoyed by the men in circular spaces of listening, who are slightly out of place—must earn their belonging through physical discomfort and insult. Pain lingers; it bears the inscription through which those who are already intimates of the arc conscript others into its constituency.

The pain of inscription is greatest (and must be) for those who inflict discomfort in their own right. Intimacy bears the risk of powerful confrontation for those who visibly and sonically create problems for the proponents of tacit fantasies of commonality. As Jane Sugarman observed, "The form of 'violence' shown in each encounter [is] appropriate to the way in which each [is] seen to violate some aspect of the social and moral order" (2011). The men make clear the tacit rules and obligations by adapting (not completely breaking with) the performance setting's codes of behavior. Indeed, as the postrehearsal drinking sessions at Kaktus demonstrated, insults are important to such socializing, though typically as a matter of zafrkavanje, of intimate joking rather than injury. Garavuše and I, on the other hand, were inserting ourselves into intimate contexts where we did not fit and were doing so voluntarily (Garavuše even received payment). The men who stood listening in each case changed the terms of our involvement by converting voluntarity into conscription, suggesting that while we initially had chosen to enter, they had the power to keep us there and to exact and inscribe a toll.

We were, in our respective situations, physically trapped by the men: the women of Garavuše had their backs to the tent and the men were in front; I was held from both sides by several men. We could not easily leave during these moments of inscription, and in staying we became parts of these assemblages, which were intimate, if painfully so. Garavuše eventually did leave, earlier in the evening than many audience members would have liked, and justifiably so due to a later breach of the evening's written and social (intimacy) contracts.[13] The women's departure was not easy, requiring them to carry equipment out through the ranks of standing and seated audience members, but they did break through the men pressing in around their stage and thus extracted themselves decisively from the assemblage.

As in the more common instances of local men listening to local male tamburaši, conscription in these cases did not exclude but include. Most of the men in Otok did not leave when Garavuše began to play (or, alternatively, try to drive the band off); they drew close to the musicians and forcibly made them a part of their group. The men at the wedding celebration did not ignore me or block my participation; they drew me into their midst. Of course this happens already to a certain extent even with male, Croatian musicians and guests whose right of inclusion goes largely unchallenged. Inviting a male guest inscribes him in the list of the included and hails him to attend, just as hiring a musician inscribes him in a contract. In Althusser's words, the employee's ability to perform his function at multiple events is ensured "by giving labor power the material means with which to reproduce itself: by wages"; these in turn limit his power to resist conscription and, while implying an initial voluntariness, make certain voluntary actions such as leaving impractical, if not impossible (Althusser 1971, 130). The intimate assemblages at tambura performances function through apparatuses in which inclusion necessarily excludes (the uninvited); with such events, other internal exclusions manifest as well. But men do not assert power in order to exclude. Those drives, both affective and ideological, that become salient at these occasions involve inclusion; male listeners assert their power in order to conscript toward an effected cohesion.

MASCULINE BLOCKS

Garavuše broke onto the tambura scene just as efforts for change at both ideological and infrastructural levels within the country were bringing women more into the professional foreground. Garavuše's invitation to perform at Otok's town festival testified to the symbolic weight given to rethinking gender roles in the early 2010s. Just before the band's Otok performance, in the 2009–2010 Croatia presidential election female candidate Vesna Pusić ran a relatively successful campaign centered on European integration and women's and LGBT rights. With the endorsement of women's human rights groups such as Be Active, Be Emancipated (B.a.B.e.), Pusić came in fifth out of twelve candidates (Lumpkins 2013, 71).[14] This marked a significant change from the wartime and early postwar periods, when those women's rights groups that could work directly within national politics consisted of "patriotic feminists" who sacrificed certain women's rights issues in the name of patriarchal nationalism (Bijelić 2007, 292). More squarely feminist groups, such as B.a.B.e., that sought to address gender issues as such spent the 1990s working largely in private (Lumpkins 2012, 71). Some who spoke publicly against gendered violence as a domestic and not only a Serbian or war-crimes issue were vilified by the Croatian press, as happened to the radical feminists branded "the five witches" (the majority of them, including Dubravka Ugrešić, subsequently took up residence abroad) (Pavlović 1999, 136). Garavuše and other female professionals have enjoyed far greater professional freedoms in the first decades of the twenty-first century, and significant ideological shifts toward expectations for women's inclusion professionally and in discourses of civil society have precipitated their active involvement in new social and professional roles. While Garavuše by no means proclaim themselves feminists, their adoption and fulfillment of the *bećar* image as they bend gender roles in playing out late at night is decidedly a move of gendered empowerment.

Yet many men and women still often find themselves subsumed under a patriarchal hierarchy, especially at the events where tamburaši typically perform. There, relatively progressive systems of thought regarding gender roles and relations still come up against more conservative structures of understanding masculine and feminine positionalities. These structures, however, are not purely conscious or ideological, but involve also the assemblages of bodies and the understandings and affects archived in participants' external gestures and distributed subjectivities. More than analogues to the affective block, intimate assemblages are indeed sites for the blocking of affect in aggregation and, simultaneously, the blocking in delimitation of ideological tenets that might otherwise counter earlier existing systems of thought (whose resilience lies in being translated into habitus). At the confluence of information sharing and extended group archiving of affects, these are prime sites for homosociality, which is linked to modern music-listening practices the world over. As Will Straw has shown for rock culture, "the bonds which produce [it] and which have rendered it primarily 'homosocial' in nature, are organized around the sharing and circulating of knowledges. Record-collecting, historical contextualism and the connoisseurist creation and ongoing revision of a canon are [. . .] the activities in which that culture's masculinism is most clearly located" (quoted in Whiteley 1997, xviii; cf. Straw 1997). Croatia's more patriarchal traditions, in which homosexuality is so unthinkable as to escape mention almost entirely,[15] afford ample space for such homosocial negotiations of knowledge regarding music repertoires and the gestures and interactions essential to gendered power. Within this space the sharing and circulating of affects serves even further to structure and delimit the ideas and sensibilities possible within the social.

Chapter 3 showed how counterdiscourses were similarly blocked (delimited) through affective experiences. Here I address conscious notions of gendered hierarchies that do not necessarily need to be expressed into discourse to be countered by progressive ideas and yet overcome them, residing persistently in embodied habitus. What is particularly important is the form of collective embodiment that enables this. Affective traces accrue between bodies and come back in musical performance as a nonmemorialized past to inflect ideas in the present, whether this is received positively or, in Karl Marx's formulation of the ghostly lingering of past traditions, "weighs like a nightmare on the brain of the living" ([1852] 2005, 7).

In her critique of the musicological notion of "pieces of music [. . .] hailing us as bourgeois subjects," Anahid Kassabian argues for affect as a circuit in which stimuli register prior to their conscious apprehension, writing that, "once apprehended, the responses pass into thoughts and feelings, though they always leave behind a residue. This residue accretes in our bodies, becoming the stuff of future affective responses" (2013, xiii). What seems most important from the standpoint of rethinking ideology and hailing, however, is that this accretion is social, transpiring not only within but also between and among bodies. Intimacy itself is affect's shared accretion; the group that fosters intimate relations shares among its various members the archived, externalized stuffs for future affective response. (This is precisely what was happening when men in the arc in front of Garavuše responded, in a gut-level, presymbolic fashion, to one another's gestures, which corresponded to past traditions of musician-audience and exotic dancer–client relations in ways that may eventually have been apprehended at higher-level, conscious forms of meaning making but that were much more directly sinister for the first- and second-order meanings of their forceful proximities.) The distributed subjectivities that attend closely to such musical performances thus continue to reify a collective subjectivity, a masculinity blocked in aggregate that enters into the proximity of women but never of a becoming-woman.[16]

For the most part, musicians recognize the tacit rules and obligations that attend expectations and fantasies of intimate masculine subjectivity, especially those formulated and projected within the proximate bodily formations in which their music resonates most immediately. Particularly when their incomes depend on successfully following these rules and meeting these obligations, they work hard to be unproblematic and, moreover, to foster successfully the intimate "atmosphere" and relations in which so many guests eagerly join in order to "be good" with the musicians. This almost always requires negotiating gendered power relations, though in many cases without the need for deliberate alteration of behavior, repertoire, and so forth, given most male bands' experience with and integration in the scene.

Yet in-group relations, too, are characterized by power negotiations, even in the engendering of solidarity, and sometimes explicitly so. The first two entries on the Garavuše thread on forum.tambura.com.hr (2008), which praised the band for "really knowing how to create an atmosphere" with its "excellent matching of repertoire" and even for surpassing an established women's tambura band, drew a reply from the latter ensemble that there are so few women players that it is "smarter for us to support and help one another than to quarrel" (my translation). Individuals of diverse gender or racial backgrounds often face more palpably volatile relations, however. When musicians or audience members perceivably violate expectations for their behavior based on groups with which they are identified (women, foreigners, etc.), the assertion of power between audiences and bands that is almost unnoticeable at most events suddenly mobilizes to enforce a physical, violating, yet ultimately restabilizing closeness. This closeness both corrects for and inscribes the problem caused by the musicians or audience members who are out of place.

Yet it is a closeness whose code robs outsiders of that which they desire in aspiring for freedom: what Sara Ahmed has called "happy objects" (2010, 46). It is worth considering in conclusion what one might call an *affective politics of pain*. As Ahmed writes:

> The experience of being alienated from the affective promise of happy objects gets us somewhere. Affect aliens can do things, for sure, by refusing to put bad feelings to one side in the hope that we can "just get along." [. . .] [W]e might want to reread melancholic subjects, the ones who refuse to let go of suffering, who are even prepared to kill some forms of joy, as an alternative model of the social good." (50)

Intimacy's affective promise is, so to speak, a happy object for musicians and audiences alike. Yet risk and discomfort offer valuable contributions of their own, in their social as much as in their musical dimensions, where the concept of "playing dangerously" is already much idealized by tambura players for its affective mix of excitement and fear. Some pains, such as the insults between bonding men, are enjoyable or can become so through exposure and the building of intimacy, but some must remain sources of displeasure in order for meaningful change to come. Pain, after all, is contextually contingent and mediated, at least at the level of the emotional attachments that form through experiences such as those described in this chapter. Expanding Butler's ([2009] 2010) call to resist the frame of war's conscription, we can recognize in those who register pain and discomfort in their own gestures (and do not simply yield to them as inscriptive tolls) an agency to resist the residual structures of feeling that stiffen up against and block novel ideas. Garavuše eventually left the performance at Otok, breaking through the crowd of men before the stage; as painful as this may then have been, it also certainly summoned fortitude and agency. This deviance, this resilience in the face of a complete conscription, bears an important affective danger in its own right. As much as those who are alienated in their inclusion become conscripts of intimacy's assemblages and ideology, their disruptions of established structures and expectations hold the capacity for ideological and affective work on the hierarchies that would fix them.

FIVE

Metaphysics, Musical Space, and the Outside

At our first tambura lesson at my house in Pittsburgh, Jerry Grcevich began without explanation to play an ascending chromatic scale with tremolo. He stopped on a pitch—it might have been B♭, memory escapes me now—and asked, "Can you hear it?" Not certain what I should be listening for besides his tremolo, I smiled and shook my head. "It's the room's pitch," he explained, "every room has its frequency. Can't you hear it?" Such was my introduction as a graduate student researcher and aspiring tambura player to an elite form of spatial listening situated deeply within a metaphysics of sound, bodies, and substance.

I refer throughout this book to "space" as though it exists a priori, as indeed, for many of my interlocutors, it seemingly does (see chapters 2 and 4). Recent literature on the topic, furthermore, resists notions of space's subjection to human agency; anthropologist Alexei Yurchak rejects the idea that unofficial music aficionados in the Soviet Union "carved out" authentic space (2005, 156), and Adam Krims rechampioned space over place as a counter to naïvely heroic anti-capitalist narratives of protecting certain venues from the abysses of mercantile space in which music purportedly circulates (2007). Yet human sensorial and sound-making capacities can also create space as a perceptual field (Ingold 2000; Hahn 2007). Here I am interested in how sounding and listening create space—perhaps even open space beyond the constraints of specific physically and ideologically defined places such as a home practice room—and, simultaneously and through space's dimensions, engender relations of power, affect, and thought.

For certain, exceptionally attentive tamburaši, sound generates space. Tremoloing (*trzanje*) a note with a plectrum (*trzalica*) and listening to it resound attunes musicians to a room's dimensions, its solid and gaseous contents, and, most important, its optimal frequency. While physical properties of chambers or even expanses in which musicians perform determine in part the quality of sounds as perceived, I argue here for a phenomenological ontology of space rooted in sonic perception (alongside but predominating over other senses). Sound's substantive property of reaching and reverberating from the walls of performance spaces, domiciles, churches, classrooms, or luthiers' workshops engenders in hearing (more directly than does seeing in light) these musicians' perceptions of presence, absence, and relationality: of space (*prostor*).

Yet sonic, substantive knowledge of spaces that tambura musicians activate in playing has developed into a broader metaphysics (*metafizika*) that recognizes an ordered world of forces beyond or at the limits of human perception. Through this metaphysics of sounding chambers, musicians push beyond everyday perceptual phenomena, attuning themselves to changes in rooms but also in humans' physical, resounding bodies, in their instruments, and, above these, in the atmosphere and cosmos. They exercise a musical magic that, like the voice in opera, "connects its bearers and hearers to ordinarily supersensible realities" (Tomlinson 1999, 4). These realities are not only spatial but also temporal; they conjure histories, lifting them out of narrativization into pasts that transcend the quotidian and political and remain situated in material rather than imagined, ideological realms. This metaphysical supersensation is affective, making it potentially dangerous to those who would uphold national and religious teleologies. The boundary between feeling and heightened rational perception is the locus of affective block. It is here that affect—how music affects one—can variously block or be blocked by ideologies of race, nation, and the divine. It generates in either case an emergent block (aggregation) of felt strangeness, a becoming-Other that is the by-product of affective-ideological confrontation. Thus within this locus lies a powerful maneuverability between sensorial and significative understandings of intimacy, inclusion, and conscription.

Musicians wield their power across several scales of spatiotemporal relation. In everyday experiences of the world, haptic sensation typically requires the closest proximity (touching), while hearing can grant access to distant phenomena and vision, unless obstructed, to those still farther away (e.g., people out of hearing range; as I show here, outdoor, unobstructed spaces afford tamburaši important points of reference). Moving behind an object or closing a door sometimes hinders vision's reach more than hearing's, but metaphysical sensation of realities beyond ordinary perception enacts—at least temporarily—a far greater reversal of perceptual scale. Musicians transcend mere visual (or audial) spatial understanding through supplementary sensing of the (spatial and temporal) beyond; their somatic responses to force and vibration bleed into hearing and, through attention, into emotion.

A CHALLENGE TO CATHOLIC RITES?

Somatic listening at different spatial, temporal, and sensorial scales enables a metaphysical relationality in which the physical, affective work of reverberation—which exists in its own right but also happens to and through the listener—can supersede national, racial, and gendered relations that otherwise often overdetermine tamburist-listener interactions. Yet tambura music has long been touted as Croatia's national music; in Croatian Catholic churches it engages a different metaphysical relation to spaces scaled through hierarchies of national and spiritual (and implicitly, racialized and gendered) authority. Spatialized rituals of tambura performance at Croatian Masses reveal how different musical subjectivities—those of priests, congregants, musical metaphysicians, and others—pull listeners toward competing notions of sonic boundedness, highlighting a limited but crucial affective block to national, hegemonic ideologies of listening. I revisit ideology's situation within the materiality of rituals, and materiality's claims to passion and love, as debated in the works of Althusser, Dolar, and Butler. I argue ultimately for an affective slippage (and conversely, blockage) that facilitates certain musicians' positioning outside the subjectivities most successfully hailed by organized religion.

I reject, however, the notion that Catholic churches are sites only of hegemonic conscription. Churches and other powerful music institutions have continued to appeal strongly to many tambura musicians in Croatia and its intimates long after their wartime period of reemergence and relief efforts. Elite performers and listeners such as Grcevich, who perform their greatest metaphysical feats outside of churches, also attend and perform at church services; their supersensorial reality probing is not a fully alternative or oppositional religious undertaking, nor do they view churches and priests as homogenous or monolithic spiritual presences demanding passive, unqualified allegiance. Many audience members and musicians prefer the sounds, celebrity, and more "pioneering" approach of small professional bands, yet larger institutions such as schools and churches long sustained the organization of tambura ensembles and performances, particularly in the postsocialist period. In Croatia and some of its ex-Yugoslav intimates, this is in part because the Catholic Church and folklore institutions were given new license during the wars in the 1990s to organize public as well as private performances of specifically Croatian material. They thus reemerged within the public sphere in tandem with nationally conscious tambura performance.

Yet in the former Yugoslavia they are also popular for affording public performance opportunities to musicians left out of the rapidly expanded professional scene of private tambura enterprise. For many women tambura players (*tamburašice*) and others reluctant or unable to break into the professional spaces available to Croatian men, institutionalized performing ensembles have kept alive the opportunities of Communist Party–run ensembles and of earlier institutions that Tito's Communists overhauled or replaced. Some minorities (e.g., Hungarians) enjoyed greater footing as nationalities in Yugoslavia, but others (e.g., Roma) were classified merely as ethnic groups and held few rights for organizing. For them, minority cultural institutions and large folklore societies that organize multiethnic events have established performance opportunities either lost since or never enjoyed under socialism. While private professional performance (such as male Croats enjoy) may offer the greater ideological and musical freedoms sought also by musicians of different gender or ethnicity, large institutions' operation outside of or with indirect relation to music markets has allowed them to cater successfully to such musicians.

It would be overly reductive to view performance at religious and folklore institutions as ideologically restrictive and small-scale professional organization as unqualifiedly liberative. Such a view would subscribe too closely to simplistic notions of postsocialism in which religious institutions reemerge as atavisms or remnants (albeit oppositional ones) of authoritarian, socialist, and institutionalist organization. Both zones of performance have their strictures and hierarchies but also their liberties from other powerful societal structures and even the potential for opening up arenas of agency "outside" of oppositional politics (see Yurchak 2005). Yet small professional ensembles remain in some respects a clearer recourse to those already choosing (and privileged with the ability) to work clear of institutional support. Their turn to metaphysics outside of, or paralleling, Catholic practice as a means of relating spiritually to the broader world and cosmos can be seen as a reaction to religion's political commandeering during the Yugoslav conflicts, a process that Srdjan Vrcan describes as the "ontologizing of existing social, political and cultural differences, projecting them on to a metaphysical backdrop" (1994, 374). This, Sabrina Ramet notes, "transform[ed] religion, subtly changing the meaning of its terms of reference and substituting a national ontology for divine ontology" (1998, 179).

Yet rising "religious mysticism" during these wars accompanied "growing ethnicism, which frequently turns into the malignant tumor of nationalism" (Vreg 1993, 664; translated in Vrcan 1994, 367). This turn brought critics of ethnoreligious nationalism forcibly into metaphysical opposition with narratives of the Catholic nation's salvation. Dangerous mystical attributes became linked to negatively gendered and racialized figures, such as in the previously discussed branding and ostracization of feminists as witches and of Serbian soldiers as demons. Even setting aside economic considerations, for musicians in Croatia and its intimates who hold minoritarian gendered and/or ethnic positions, metaphysics in the public sphere is not simply liberative. Although national and religious institutions are often implicated in such oppressive ideological discourses, they sometimes afford surer positions for marginalized performers to participate than do small groups of supersensorially gifted players.

Elite (mostly male Croat) tambura musicians' and luthiers' alternative understandings of spirituality and musical space suggest another way in which affect can block (aggregate and form) space outside hegemonic ideologies. This in turn reinscribes certain less-privileged subject positions. In this chapter, however, I compare elite musicians' philosophies and actions to those of more diverse ethnic and gendered performance spaces created within Croatian Catholic churches and show how ideologically steeped hierarchies emerge within both sets of musico-spatial ontologies and epistemologies. Churches themselves have housed alternative agencies within their walls, not just for those seeking musical opportunities or asylum but also for musicians who metaphysically access the outside from within church architecture. An emergent affective resilience summons sound and audition in the face of powerful forces of confinement to slip outside of racial and national ideologies, but through practices tempered by reliance on hierarchies that are implicitly gendered in requiring access to musical sites, labor, and free time.

LISTENING AND DEPTH

Grcevich's renown stems from not only his compositions and recordings but also his capacity for listening to musical vibrations at or beyond the boundaries of everyday aural perception. Well-respected Croatian and Serbian musicians praised him repeatedly for his abilities, including prowess at detecting and playing to the resonant frequencies even of spaces with little resonance (like my living room); aural openness to the singing, spoken wisdom, and drumming of an American Indian healer whom he consulted for his ailing father; and proficiency at hearing and appropriately accompanying (*pratiti*, literally "to follow") vocalists by leaving enough space in the lead prim solo. In the latter, the space that Grcevich leaves is not metaphorical but the three-dimensional space of sonic reverberation; at key moments he literally leaves performance spaces unsaturated with the vibrations of his myriads of virtuosically improvised plucked notes, allowing the singer's voice to fill the room prominently with sound waves.

That such listening and restraint involve spiritual subjectivity and metaphysical understanding of what lies within and beyond sensorial understanding became clear from other interlocutors' comments. "Jerry really feels it," one told me. "Jerry really is deep, not everyone understands that about him," said another, referring to Jerry's turn to the healer for his father's care. One Croatian American who regularly tours Croatian religious sites with clergy members noted wanting "Jerry and his band to play at my funeral, and he and a couple of the others have already agreed. If I really am going to a better place it should be a joyous time. If I'm going somewhere else, so what!" The last two comments connect performance to religious practice, and this fieldwork acquaintance made explicit the parallel reliance on alternative musical and mystical practices as well as Catholic rites. Tambura performances at funerals, Masses, and other Catholic ceremonies have been common since at least the early 1990s, and playing at weddings (though usually apart from Catholic rites) dates back centuries. Yet part of what is "deep" about Grcevich is his intense affective commitment to sounding and listening well and to engaging his audiences and fellow musicians apart from the particular allegiances and ideologies of any religion, national movement, or ethnic organization. His depth is similar in certain respects to what Clifford Geertz, drawing upon the philosopher Jeremy Bentham, calls "deep play": a form of risk-taking—spiritual rather than financial, yet just as closely tied to honor as the Balinese cock betting that Geertz describes—whose dangers make it central to social hierarchies (1972, 14–17).

Mobilizing sound, Grcevich and other tamburaši navigate a spiritual, metaphysical relation to space that sometimes melds with and sometimes diverges dangerously from the particular subjectivity and metaphysical awareness supported by the Croatian Catholic Church. This constitutes a risky maneuverability, dangerous due to the social and spiritual ostracizing that have plagued not just women and non-Croats but also some Croatian men who have spoken out about nationalism and religion (Crnković 2001, 31–33). Historian Vjekoslav Perica discusses how some church leaders and media "overtly threaten non-Catholics, secularists, and liberals, or atheists who criticize such a Church [for its Croatian nationalist rhetoric], calling upon the state to prosecute them and mobilizing public opinion against anyone who dares to criticize the religious establishment"; he adds that "not even Serbs were the principal villains in the eyes of the Church" (2001, 64, 65). Catholic catechism became all but mandatory in schools, "since in practice non-attendance involved the stigma of 'un-patriotism,'" and "candidates for positions in the state bureaucracy had to provide letters of recommendation from parish priests and bishops, as well as warrants about Holy Communion, confirmation, and children's attendance of religious doctrine" (61). Nor has Catholic responsibility to the nation been easier to overlook in Croatia's intimates, "where Croat clerics [...] raised millions in hard currency for Tudjman's electoral campaign" (58). While the Church's inclination and ability to reinforce nationalism in the political and public spheres have fluctuated with changes in state and religious leadership, the return in 2015 of a Conservative government has reinvigorated nationalist sentiments in the wake of EU accession. The risky maneuverability of musicians in the face of pressure to turn back from international and interethnic networks toward Catholic Croatian nation building can offer insights into affect's potential blocking of overdetermining ideologies of race, nation, and gender.

Understanding sound, and music in particular, as bridging material and ethereal matter connects to the region's medieval and likely even ancient metaphysics. The notion of plucked strings and song affectively mediating liminal space between material and spiritual realms has strong roots in Thrace's Orphic traditions. The beautiful, tragic performance of the figure of Orpheus himself moved earthly and divine presences to grant passage to the underworld as he sought to bring back his fallen wife Eurydice. While some Southeast European musicians look directly to Orphic traditions, others draw influence via several long, continuous lineages of philosophical development. Nancy Van Deusen (2017), for example, argues that Hungarian notions of sound as substance (*szilfa*) descend from discussions of its Latin predecessor, *silva*, in Caldicius's translation of Plato's *Timaeus*, surviving in the region's more formalized theories from the Middle Ages until the early twentieth century.

For much of this time, Croatia was part of Austria-Hungary, where the Enlightenment brought scientific notions of physics to bear on Catholic belief and humanism survived largely in secular form (O'Brien 1969, 39). Yet many

Croatians remained under Catholic Italy's humanist influence and, distancing themselves from northern Enlightenment skepticism, pursued metaphysics' reach toward truths and entities beyond rational sensory experience (Zovko 2015, 249). The Jesuit philosophers Ruđer Bošković and Ioannis Baptist Horvath rejected Kant's "conception of space and time as subjective forms of intuition," seeking to understand them as "real modes of existence" comprehensible through Bošković's "theory of forces" and "concept of matter" (250). These ideas resonated with Horvath's notion that, in hearing, vibrations are received both within and outside of the soul (*anima*); in such dual hearing, one experiences space and matter through forces moving in souls, sounding bodies, media along which sound travels, and sense organs (Horvath [1770] 1817, 227). Croatia split from Austria-Hungary, uniting with Serbia after World War I. Subjugation to Belgrade as the seat of Serbian and then atheistic Yugoslav authority led the Croatian Catholic Church to make a Romantic nationalist and isolationist push to bolster Croatian autonomy (see Lampe 1996, 59). With this, new conceptions of music's spiritual impact broke from broader, long-held doctrines of universal mission.

The modern tambura's physical construction and playing technique also seem to affect contemporary tambura musicians' metaphysics. Developed for outdoor performance, though also part of indoor orchestral and combo practices since the mid-nineteenth century, tamburas have retained double courses on their highest strings to produce high volume when played with tremolo. The tremolos in turn create the effect of pulsations of vibration with little to no decay, dispersing into space with series of separate yet aurally almost indistinguishable sound waves, filling rooms with multitudes of reverberating notes. The "clean," "aggressive" strumming that Croatian tambura musicians prioritize in playing also enables controlling both attack volume and saturation (delivery rate) of relatively undecayed sound waves that fill performance spaces.[1] These sounds' participation in sensory perception of space is potentially true in any music, but I argue that tamburas' particular tremolo technique and construction philosophy make them especially active agents in heightened intercorporeal experiences of sound.

The tambura's capacities in this regard are due not only to elite male tambura musicians but also to luthiers. The practice of the late Andrija Franić, a *majstor* (master instrument maker) based in Županja, Croatia, illuminates the tambura's fostering of spatial awareness for attentive musicians. I first met Franić when visiting his workshop with Duško Topić, the director of HKUD "Osijek 1862."

Franić spoke to me about his "philosophy [*filozofija*] of playing and of building tamburas": a way of theorizing musical priorities that I came to understand was based on deep reflection on listening (2009). A particular tambura philosophy could apply to aesthetic considerations of tone, proper musical arrangement, and composing and could characterize a region or people. Roma, he offered, have a playing philosophy that includes the feeling that what "sounds best" in harmonizing a given note is a major minor seventh chord.[2] He complained that many luthiers work only for money, making numerous instruments without caring about or employing a proper philosophy of the instrument. Franić showed me a tambura *samica* and elaborated how he had spent time getting to know its three-thousand-year history intimately. He next presented drawings that he had made of various tambura types' physical proportions—Pythagorean ratios along the necks and within the instruments' hollow bodies—and of sound waves as emitted from instruments and speakers (e.g., monophonic vs. stereophonic sounds). He called our attention in particular to diagrams of the "best" sounds that tamburas can produce. The relationships between their frequencies were represented with circles encompassing them, and it was to these relations that he applied the term *metafizika*. His concern here was not simply aesthetic appreciation of well-resonating frequencies but a philosophy of their greater potential for interacting in and between the spaces and bodies of performance.

Franić and I frequently ran into one another at concerts the following spring and developed a rapport that sharpened when he invited me to visit his workshop again that summer. He also invited a tambura pick (*trzalica*) craftsman who typically drove him to concerts, as Franić did not drive at night, and the pick maker took me aside early in my visit to explain how rare a person Franić was in paying such careful, philosophical attention to music, listening, and instrument building. His comment's subtext quickly became apparent: we would discuss matters that, while not secret, were thought to be understandable and interesting only to an elite group of tamburaši, whose membership I stood on the cusp of joining, even if in a limited fashion. That such elite knowledge had ancient depths (and long lineages of tutelage), he and Franić stressed throughout my visit. For instance, they took me to visit a hilltop overlooking burial sites from the area's Roman battlefield and later treated me to a ham slow cured by the pick maker whose preparation, he stated, drew upon thousands of years of scientific and artisanal development comparable to those employed by Egypt's pyramid builders. Accessing this knowledge—as opposed to practical involvement in its material labor and consumption, such as carrying pyramid stones or eating ham—required capacities for thinking and sensing but also acceptance into an echelon of affective and aesthetic appreciation. The extension of physical into temporal space (reaching back to ancient sources) amplified this echelon's hierarchical distinctions.

At the workshop, following a rather abstract conversation about sonic, spiritual, and gravitational forces spanning the sensible and supersensible, Franić gave a practical demonstration. This also proved to be a test of my interest and capacity for listening. Picking up a prim tambura, he walked over to a long workbench on which rested a square wooden block. Franić asked me to position the block on the table; again uncertain how to respond to what was clearly another pedagogical test from a master musician and artisan, I simply righted the block to the four 90-degree angles of the bench. Franić smiled good-naturedly, exchanging comments with the pick maker about my somewhat obvious choice to position the block symmetrically in the bench's center. He then asked his colleague to strike an open E string and, as it rang, Franić quickly rotated the block, stopping it suddenly, as though it were sliding into place, with its sides locked at approximately a 30-degree angle with the bench. He explained that at that angle the block amplified the tone's resonance through relation with both the bench and the workshop walls. The pick maker nodded, evidently agreeing that rotating the block to this angle changed the resonance of the room (though whether he, too, could hear it I wasn't certain). Franić's metaphysical listening involved making sensible certain supersensible truths of proportion and force by manipulating the sonic environment.

This manipulation involved much more than sound and listening. Franić also judged my positioning of the block by sight, and subsequently in rotating it employed haptic sensing of texture, weight, pressure, and perhaps vibration. As anthropologist Tim Ingold has written in challenge to long-held assumptions about differences between hearing and seeing, various senses involve experiencing vibrations (sonic, photic, etc.) out in the world rather than a Cartesian dualism of internal mind and external object; the latter theory is complicit with the false notion that light gives us objective knowledge of external things while sounds *are* the objects to be sensed and break through the mind-world barrier (2000, 244–245). Thus "any one sense, in 'homing in' on a particular topic of attention, brings with it the concordant operations of all the others" (262). Citing Maurice Merleau-Ponty, Ingold elaborates that this integration is comparable to the collaboration of duplicate sense organs, such as the eyes' coordination in binocular vision, arguing that the unity of a thing as an "inter-sensory entity" lies not in the mental fusion of images found on different registers of sensation, but in the bodily synergy of the senses in their convergent striving towards a common goal. Thus "my gaze, my touch and all my other senses are together the powers of one and the same body integrated into one and the same action." (Ingold 2000, 262, citing Merleau-Ponty [1945] 1962, 317–318)

Our shift in attention (from vision to audition) as Franić's Pythagorean-proportioned prim tambura sounded involved integrative sensorial combination. Following this, we might also surmise that silence (a type of unfruitful listening in this instance) was initially part of the experience of my attempt at positioning the block, at least for Franić. An apt listener, he likely *heard* (even in the absence of a sounding instrument) the positioned block's potential for flattened resonance expanded into muteness in the same way that Merleau-Ponty describes his ability to "see a sound, I mean that I echo the [lack of] vibration of the sound with my whole sensory being" ([1945] 1962, 234).

Yet Franić evidently employed this shift deliberately to highlight this combination's importance in light of my inability to recognize the space's greater, supersensible truths. This additive shift from his visual experience of my visual and haptic interaction with the block to his combined visual, haptic, and audial perception of positioning the object added the most informative sense last. It thereby reversed temporally the order of senses (hearing, touching, sight) historically credited in European philosophy with lower to greater capacities for making spaces and objects known to perceiving bodies. Tim Ingold invokes John Hull's experience of losing his vision to compare these senses thus:

Visual space is presented to the sighted all at once, but tactile space has to be assembled by the blind, bit by bit. [. . .] Acoustic space is similarly temporal. Unlike the objects of touch, however, [. . .] the manifold inhabitants of acoustic space have an ephemeral nature [. . .]. This is not a world of being— "the silent, still world where things simply are"—but a world of becoming where there is only action, and where every sound marks a locus of action. (Ingold 2000, 271, citing Hull 1997, 72–73)

Franić's additional employment of audition helped the space become optimally resonant based not on the 1:1 correspondence of right angles among walls, bench, and block but on the more dynamically Pythagorean 1:2:3 proportions

(30, 60, and 90 degrees) of these objects' potential spatial (and acoustically real-ized) acute angular intersections.

Franić demonstrated, on a small scale, how sound can communicate not only action but also, through skillful attending, the positional and spatial relations of solid objects. Ingold notes that for the blind, hearing the rain's temporally constant and spatially dispersed percussions comes closest to the visual experi-ence of perceiving a lighted chamber (2000, 271). This point of comparison can perhaps best translate the twofold physical and metaphysical contributions to listening that elite tamburaši bring to sensation; tambura ensembles' intensive tremoloing can replicate raindrops' constancy but not their spatial dispersion. It is there that skilled, attuned listeners engage in the world outside the mind, filling in the rest of the space through the perception of reverberation and phi-losophies of angular and vibrational harmony. Simultaneously, Franić used this perception to figure what *might be*; just as he used Pythagorean proportions to construct harmonious chambers in his instruments, he used sound to find the angles and relations of objects in the workshop that would create harmony there, instrumentalizing the room into another proportioned resonance chamber.

AFFECTIVE ORDERS

Such perception's affective dimension involves the excitation of faculties for feeling linked to emotion. Mario Zbiljski, Slavonske Lole's lead prim tamburaš, told me that "sound is metaphysics" in that "the beauty of sound is not mea-sureable," for it is "something that leaves an impression on someone" (2010b; my translation). His phrase here, *ostavlja dojama na nekoga*, can also refer to leaving a sensation or feeling, and he clarified that this is an intensely personal mystical experience: "It depends on the person who was listening, and not only on the sound's quality [. . .] therefore it *is* enchantment." If one were interested only in reproducing "what is measurable, certain values and amounts," the result "wouldn't be music, but rather [. . .] a hundred-meter sprint" (2010b). His com-parison to sport left no doubt about his valuation of feeling as a supersensory, arational modality of aesthetic appreciation.

Similarly, Grcevich has remarked of electronic amplification that "sometimes the more we're having microphones and different sound systems, the less feeling that comes out of the instrument. [. . .] I feel that there's a better connection when everyone can hear what we're playing. [. . .] [T]hat's why I enjoyed so much playing in [the Gypsy Café] in Pittsburgh because it was so intimate. People could see our fingers moving, how we were holding our picks" (2017). Technologically enhanced sound production detracts from intimate tambura performance's total sensory experience, which involves not only clear sound transmission but also visual and affective perception.

Yet these and other elite performer-listeners' approach to heightening musical beauty relies on calculation as much as on affect and intuition. Zbiljski occupies a somewhat rare role in in being much sought-after as a musician, recording engineer, *and* craftsman who works on instruments, whereas most full *majstori* are not famous performers. When I first met Zbiljski at his home recording studio outside of Osijek through my friend Filip Pešut of Hrvatski Sokol, they told me that Zbiljski has a calculated method of finding a spot in an instrument where by piercing an acupuncture-like hole he can make it "sound five times better." Zbiljski called this a part of his "*metafizika*" and noted that Franić also had an interest in this practice (2010a). There is often a point in the soundboard where the sound resonates weakly and this hole helps to bring it out. He did not reveal his secret for locating it, but he described it as a methodical process of listening and measuring. The result, however, is potentially much greater than the measurable change produced in a particular instrument's volume or timbre, and here such operations join a larger metaphysical project of understanding the relations between sounding chambers (instruments, performance spaces, etc.). If, he explained, two people play together, one with a good instrument and one with a poorer instrument, the good instrument will bring the other up to its level (2010a). Thus by making a calculated change to the soundboard's perforation he can facilitate a rapid, mystical expansion of beauty as felt rather than measured in performance.

Zbiljski, however, only offers this operation to those who can differentiate the sounds before and after. Filip Pešut seemed particularly pleased to share this tidbit with me and to include himself among the favored few who have earned Zbiljski's assistance through their adept, even supersensory listening. Through such aural practices, and the tests that signal metaphysical commonality to these gifted musicians and listeners, emerge new distinctions. They order a hierarchy of affective and spiritual immediacy to musical space based on musical and auditory access and transcendence of mundane concerns over national, religious, and other forms of official, institutionalized belonging. Metaphysical commonality may even transcend music, as I discovered through my own fuller adoption into the fold. Though I struggled to hear changes in the resonant chambers of Franić's workshop and Zbiljski's and Pešut's tamburas, Franić appreciated my interest and training in energy and gravitational principles that we discussed in his workshop. Then on a short visit to Croatia in 2011, while walking through the monthly antique bazaar on the square in Osijek's Tvrđa fortress, I called Franić to inquire about visiting him at home, many kilometers away in Županja, and discovered that he, too, happened to have come to Osijek and was walking around the bazaar. As we sat in a café to catch up and marvel at the coincidence, he raised his hands to both temples, pointed his index fingers out at me, and told a third companion that he and I "have antennae" (*imamo antene*). Our discursive connection over interest in musical space and energy, he affirmed, had translated into metaphysical connection through heightened, insect-like awareness of one another's presence in a shared space, placing me, it seemed, in at least a low position in the order of supersensing tamburaši.

During his residency at Oberlin College, Jerry Grcevich described a similar experience of being tested by Franić, who could "feel vibrations that no one else could feel . . . I don't know how" (2017). Grcevich demonstrated the practice of feeling for vibrations by picking a note on his prim tambura, which he was holding outstretched from his body, and leaving one arm hovering over its strings. "He would say, 'do you feel that?' and I would say, 'Let me see.' And, 'yeah,' I would say, 'kind of.'" Other of Franić's abilities were easier to grasp, however. Walking across the classroom, he remarked that Franić "told me that every couple of steps you take, [. . .] the instrument has a different sound." Grcevich started to play the prim while still crossing the classroom, adding, "I feel it happening" (2017). Franić's testing afforded opportunities to learn to feel resonance noncochlearly (e.g., with one's hands or "antennae") as much as it distinguished those with potential to join the metaphysical fold, and his warm, encouraging approach emphasized such elite status's intimacy rather than exclusion.

As mentioned at this chapter's outset, however, two additional dimensions of this status pertain to the affective work of inclusion and exclusion that this book examines. First, importantly, this hierarchy does not depend on racialized or ethnic distinctions, though most metaphysical tambura elites believe strongly that what exactly a particular person finds beautiful depends, in Mario Zbiljski's words, on a cognitive "sense" (*smisao*) and affective "feeling" (*osjećanje*) for music that are rooted in "genetics" and "region," in addition to listening experience (2010a). Second, however, this hierarchy admits men almost exclusively. This has mostly to do with practicalities of access; few women make a living solely by playing or building tamburas—an economic consideration structured through gendered societal expectations for familial roles within a network of tambura

musicians and consumers much broader than the "elites." Most women performers do not dedicate the majority of their waking hours to tambura music the way
that Grcevich, Franić, Zbiljski, and Pešut typically have.

According to one female tambura director at an Osijek children's folklore society, it is much more difficult to attract girls to the instrument than boys. Those
few who pursue professional tambura performance careers find it, according to
Garavuše lead singer Ivana Ketović, "more difficult for girls," as male concert-
goers and organizers treat them like children (2010). A slightly more common
professional route for women tambura players is to earn a university degree in
music and secure a position directing an ensemble and/or teaching tambura in
schools or societies. This, however, often draws derision and exclusion from some
accomplished male tamburaši (though not the men I am considering here), who
see these women as capitalizing on an education system that prioritizes intellectual credentials over uneducated men's proven technical abilities.

Franić, for his part, spoke frequently of his and his wife's deep intellectual
and emotional connection, which included her active interest in his work. He
also noted the "wondrous" nature of sexual relations between men and women,
in which two human entities meld into one in more than simply an anatomi-
cal sense. Yet outside of romantic connection, I have been privy to no forms of
metaphysical connection involving women tamburaši and either other musicians or physical space. Such connections likely exist and may well form a part
of the intimacy shared by female performers with one another. The orders of
male listenership, however, form bonds that, though eschewing national, racial,
and religious boundaries, depend again on gendered exclusivity and intimate
communality. In the next section I examine how such inclusion and exclusion
are reversed in the metaphysically very different spaces of Catholic tambura
performance.

TAMBURA MASSES

On Christmas Eve, 2016, Jerry Grcevich entered a Zagreb-area church. He had
agreed to play the first Christmas Mass and met there with local youth musicians
to set up to play in the midnight service. In discussing the service, he noted being impressed that the priest gathered the young players next to him at the altar,
granting them physical and spiritual closeness, as well as symbolic import, for
the evening's rituals (2017). For Grcevich, music contains vast spiritual dimensions even in nonreligious settings, and he eschews large-scale, institutionalized

performance contexts for more intimate spaces in bars and restaurants. Yet there was something particularly moving about performing the Proper in coordination with a Catholic priest in a midnight Mass in Croatia (2017). In many parts of Croatia, tambura music has become common in midnight Christmas Masses, marking the ritual as special, since it is reserved for important holidays and events.

These special occasions do not merely follow the Church calendar. They also are set in coordination with gatherings of music institutions around Croatian causes at local, national, and even international levels, solidifying close relations among Church, state, and national culture. As Jerry Grcevich noted, churches across Croatia "usually stor[e] the costumes and a lot of the [. . .] written music," which is "an important part of folk traditions"; "usually where the church is located in the villages and towns, over there next to it will be another building where they have rehearsals and get together" (2017). Collaborations between churches and folklore/tambura ensembles on matters ranging from storage to ritual performance align national and Catholic religious doctrines across Croatia and its intimates. This collaboration's import for national culture and faith became particularly clear at Zagreb's largest gathering of Croatian American musicians.

July 5–7, 2013: Shortly following Croatia's accession on July 1 to the EU, I attended the CFU Junior Cultural Federation's 47th Junior Tamburitza Festival, an event held annually in a North American city but organized this year for the sixth time in Croatia's capital. Apparent throughout was the close coordination of state, diaspora, national music institutions, and the Croatian Catholic Church. The Croatian government sponsored the festival, whose opening and performances in Zagreb's main Vatroslav Lisinski Concert Hall and closing at the Zagreb Cathedral were coordinated through the Croatian Heritage Foundation and attended by clergy and members of parliament alike (Hrvatska Matica Iseljenika 2013). The opening concert featured Croatian Radiotelevision's Tamburitza Orchestra, which variously accompanied and turned the spotlight over completely to other groups. These included Zagreb's Folk Dance Ensemble "Dr. Ivan Ivančan," performing a staged folklore set, "Divine Mercy Sunday in Međimurje,"[3] and the Croatian Navy's a cappella Klapa "Saint George," singing "Mi smo prvaci" (We are the champions), a song by popular Croatian singer Gibonni that finishes with nineteenth-century Croatian separatist Ante Starčević's famous motto "God and Croats."

Following the concert and the CFU's presentation of a $25,000 check to Zagreb Children's Hospital came a party. There, a tamburaš relative of CFU president Bernard Luketich whom I knew from Pittsburgh elaborated on how earlier his family had met with former Croatian president Stjepan Mesić to discuss his humanitarian causes and EU accession. The following day, he announced, they would meet privately with current president Ivo Josipović.

It was on the festival's second and third days, however, that tambura music integrated the national and the sacred in a deeply ritualized manner. The following morning, fifteen North American junior tamburitzan ensembles that would perform that afternoon took the stage and led the audience in singing the national anthems of Croatia, the United States, and Canada. This common CFU practice as usual had the many of us attending from North America singing along loudly, as we would throughout the day. It reached a particular climax, however, with the amplification of Croatian voices on their country's hymn "Lijepa naša domovino" (Our beautiful homeland). Immediately thereafter, Monsignor Mile Bogović, bishop of the Gospić-Senj Diocese, walked onstage and delivered a sermon and blessing for the festival's participants. Monsignor Mijo Gorski, the assistant bishop of Zagreb, would, the organizers announced, lead the Sunday tambura Mass the following day. Thus the Church both blessed the festival and called upon the participants and attendees to move to the Zagreb Cathedral's sacred space the next morning. Following three folk songs performed jointly by all fifteen tamburitzan ensembles under the baton of festival guest conductor Katarina Lukačević, the director of the Office for Relations with Croats Outside of Croatia (Darija Krstičević) echoed this call to faith with one of ethnic belonging. She announced "in the name of the president of Croatia": "To all those who live outside of *Lijepa naša* we have extended our sincere message" (my translation). Switching to English, she proclaimed being "really happy to see with what love you guard and protect your Croatian identity," a statement that the audience nearly drowned out with applause.

That moving to the sacred space and the Mass at the Zagreb Cathedral for the festival's conclusion the next morning was intended to answer both calls simultaneously was apparent in the service's textual, musical, and spatial organization. Those of us from the United States and Canada attending but not performing at the 10:00 a.m. Mass gathered alongside local congregants in the churchyard before the Cathedral of the Assumption of the Blessed Virgin Mary. We entered, filing into the pews between the doors and the transept-like spacing dividing us from the foremost pews and altar. We could see several tambura musicians, including some directors, parents, and select older youth performers from the Rankin Junior Tamburitzans (with which I had previously conducted fieldwork in East Pittsburgh), standing in their positions in the chancel before the sanctuary. They were facing one another across an empty central aisle running from our seats in the central nave up to the altar just beyond the musicians (see figure 5.1). We stood with the altar in front of us, while the men, women, and youths assembled in the chancel began to play, still facing the aisle. Their instrumental processional welcomed and accompanied Assistant Bishop Mijo Gorski, three other elder priests, and a teenager whom I took for an altar boy. Draped in bright green robes, they emerged from the wings and stood facing us from the pulpit with the altar to their right. The younger musicians were mostly reading from sheet music propped on short stands, but the adults were largely playing from memory. As they began to play and sing "Gospodine, smiluj se" (Kyrie eleison) following the priest's performance of the penitential rite, they looked around, making eye contact with one another across the aisle and with those of us seated farther back in the north, central, and south naves. Due to physical demands of resonance and the priority that the national instrument's sounds reach those farther back in the building, the musicians' role in musically accompanying a Mass celebrating diasporic return to the country's main cathedral afforded them a different spatial orientation than the rest of the congregation. As with the clergy, it allowed them to see and be seen by (and hear/be heard by) most of the congregation.

Their privileged physical position at this Mass paralleled their liturgical role: they performed mostly settings of texts from the Mass's Ordinary. This contrasted with other tambura services that I attended. Musicians otherwise largely played and sang Proper and supplementary texts selected in accordance with the Church calendar and thus remained distinct from the priests and regular church choir who performed the basic liturgical elements (see chapter 1). Following the North American tamburaši's performance of "Gospodine, smiluj se" (the Ordinary's first text), in fact, the Cathedral's organist and choir boys accompanied and led us in singing "Lijepa si, lijepa" (Beautiful art thou, beautiful). This Marian song honoring the Cathedral's dedication to the Assumption of the Virgin departed musically and textually from the tambura performance of the Ordinary.

As is typical in many functional (rather than through-composed, concert-oriented) musical settings of the Ordinary, the celebrant intoned the Gloria and Credo ("Slava Bogu na visini" and "Nicejsko-Carigradsko vjerovanje") on his

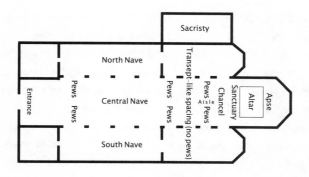

FIGURE 5.1 Zagreb Cathedral floor plan

own, then the tamburaši rejoined the assistant bishop for the Sanctus ("Svet"). In lieu of accompanying Agnus Dei, the Ordinary's final text, the tamburaši next performed another "Gospodine, smiluj se" (Kyrie eleison). Then followed an instrumental that again occasioned long looks by the musicians around the Cathedral's chambers and congregants as the assistant bishop presided over the transubstantiation of bread and wine into Christ's body and blood—a vital realization of divine substance in sacred space that is understood metaphysically (see later in this section). The tamburaši sang only one setting of a Proper text: "Čuj nas, Majko" (Hear us, mother), another Marian song with which they accompanied Holy Communion (see discussion and figure 5.2 later in this section). The North Americans around me stood and walked forward to the altar to receive the Eucharist; except for reciting the Lord's Prayer in English (or exceptionally in Croatian) at the appropriate time, it seemed to me that until this moment they had remained as passive as I, a non-Christian, during the long Croatian service (which impression made their move to the front more noticeable than it might have been in other circumstances). The musicians, alternatingly breaking to receive Communion, finished with a recessional for the clergy and congregation. In between these last two performances, the assistant bishop, while not specifically naming the tambura, marked the connection between national and religious belief and authority in addressing special greetings to Bernard Luketich and other CFU leaders. He also called the Cathedral a "symbol of faith and the Croatian people" and stated that with such ceremonies and performances "we guard our national, cultural identity" (my translation).

To what extent was the incorporation of musicians and other worshippers into the assemblages and structures of belief at this service a form of conscription? And did the musicians' physical inscription into the Mass's typical spatial assemblage involve at all the sort of power analyzed in chapter 4? Certainly the service's alignment of religious and national ideologies and the fact that both Croatian and North American festival participants had been hearing calls throughout the festival weekend to come attend to their spiritual and folkloric practices at the Cathedral mark their inclusion as a very literal form of hailing. Yet the musicians' positioning near the priests and altar—which musicians consider an honor—also points to a powerful, even liberative agency on their part that must be acknowledged. Situated so that they could see and hear one another across the aisle, as well as the priests and much of the congregation to either side of them (peripherally or on the many occasions that the service had them turn one way or the other), they were afforded a position more like the clergy's than were other congregants. The Ordinary texts that they had arranged to perform at this particular Mass are not necessarily more important than the Proper, but performing the Kyrie eleison and Sanctus aligned them more with the priest's privileged role in stating the Credo and other regular parts of every service that are powerful for their centrality to the metaphysical aims of realizing God's spiritual power in material works.

Playing a role in this power's materialization does not preclude the possibility of the musicians' conscription (even rulers are hailed by the law). Rather, it points to power's hierarchical, spatial, and distributive nature; dispersing even limited amounts of religious authority in this way is itself a powerful act in conscripting subjects fully into both the recognition and the propagation of authority. This simultaneously allows for emergent subjectivities, perceptions, and systems of thought and feeling to accrue at the ground level of religious congregants who bring diverse desires, attachments, and attentions for the spiritual space within (and beyond) the Cathedral. The committing anew (from the bottom up) of these affective forces to the Church and the Divine manifests most poignantly in the surge of participation in the transubstantiation and taking of the Eucharist. At that moment, the Holy Spirit's presence in the Cathedral's space is most palpable for many Catholics.

The diversity not just in affect but also in subject positions of those perform-ing or simply present at the Mass is significant, as the hailing to national and religious works and particularly to receiving the Eucharist affects different people in different ways. As Vjekoslav Perica writes, transubstantiation has even come to connote material power and hierarchy within ethnoreligious Croatian politics (rather than Christ's sacrifice's potential extension to all humans); President

Franjo Tuđman, inspired by theological training while in office, "inaugurated in daily political jargon the concept of the *pretvorba* (literally meaning "transformation" but also used by the Church as liturgical term for the Eucharistic *Transubstantiation*) to designate the post-communist privatization" (2001, 62). Receiving the transubstantiated Eucharist during Holy Communion similarly highlighted the ritual transformation of a congregation largely unfamiliar to the presiding clergy (and therefore of unrecognized status and belonging within the Church) into visible tiers of membership and redemption. All of the performing musicians were of age to receive Communion. This may have had as much to do with musical as with spiritual authority and training but still reinforced the congregation's division into subjects fully initiated into the service's rituals and those too young to participate in this way. Certainly those of us non-Catholics who were present remained at a still greater distance—both physically and hierarchically—from the faculties and reach of religious power. Language also played a prominent role in differentiating experiences, as many North American Croats around me and in the ensemble spoke little Croatian. Their ability to follow the service's structure and respond in English, and the culminating rush forward for Communion, nonetheless demonstrated an intimate inscription of foreign-language worshippers within Catholic practice in Zagreb's Cathedral.

Perhaps most significant to ritual space and time's hierarchization, though, was gender. Women have more limited roles in the Catholic Church than men, and at this Mass the only nuns present were, as far as I observed, no more actively involved in the service than the Catholic congregants. Performing in choirs also involves women in delivering the Ordinary and Proper in many churches; but the particular combination of singing these texts and performing on tamburas, especially at services of heightened significance such as this, affords a central, even authoritative spiritual and musical role, realms in which women typically enjoy far less power. Men, on the other hand, typically have more opportunities to perform tambura music in public and to hold greater religious authority as deacons or, depending on their life paths, as priests than do women (even as nuns). This distinction likely accounts in part for men's comparatively strong interest and engagement in musical spirituality outside of or paralleling the Church; noninstitutional access to higher metaphysical realities through dedicated pursuit of supersensorial musical attention may outweigh their musico-spiritual opportunities in the Church in ways that are not true for women, few of whom are privileged to dedicate so much time to performance outside of family, folklore institution, or church.

Yet for both male and female performers at tambura Masses—even services as clearly charged with religious *and* national devotion as that which closed the festival in Zagreb—other potential forms of power come from tambura music itself. One side of this is the syncretism of religious practices that have absorbed tambura performance: As Zrinka Stimac notes, Yugoslavia's extrusion of religion from public into private spheres encouraged Christian practices' blending and reemergence within new national holidays and old pagan traditions (which were more acceptable than Christian rites within socialist folkloric practice) (2008, 217). This fostered a continuing, fluid, and creative agency in the interpretation of music's spiritual capacities (see Rountree 2016, 74).

Writing about music in Santería, Juan Mesa Díaz argues that one should not "fail to consider syncretism as a tool of resistance and as one of the variables of reinterpretation within a process of affirmation, continuity, and expansion that empowered an organized regrouping" of oppressed but musically active believers (2007, 56). Attempts by Croatia's Catholic Church to reassert its doctrinal authority in independent Croatia led to many of its members embracing "popular religion" in order to put secularization behind them while retaining a critical distance from powerful Catholic ideologues (Stimac 2008). Tambura traditions present clear recourses to pagan practices absorbed into Catholic rituals (e.g., men receive rosemary sprigs as guarantors of fertility as they walk past tambura bands into church weddings).

On the other hand, tambura musicians embrace their music's capacity to transcend physical confines. The same basic musical style (though not song genre), the same techniques and sounds, even the same instruments that they play in churches they also regularly employ in performances well outside of religious and sometimes even Croatian national contexts. The memories, affects, and spiritual forces that accrue in certain tamburaši and tamburas potentially bring residual metaphysical attentions into Catholic worship's distinct spaces and musical aesthetics. Yet transcending physical space transpires not merely through association but also via metaphysical extensions of sensation. To invoke again an analogue in Santería, there is, as Katherine Hagedorn notes, a liminal space that forms in and around the body in which the sacred and the folkloric may come to "inhabit the same sphere of sacred intent" (2001, 77). Musical techniques that are not sacred, or at least not strictly Catholic, may become sacred through intent, yet may also bring the body into awareness of spirit moving beyond the physical spaces of Church rituals and architecture.

As Antoine Hennion argues, it is important "to move away from an opposition between [vastly different musical styles] based on rigid aesthetic criteria, towards a focus on the observable difference in the ways in which they affect the body"; he calls attention, for example, to how rock music's encouragement of embodied and emotive listening "brings the audience up onto the stage, turning each individual into the alter ego of the rock star," while opera's "ascetic discipline" is "a powerful way of projecting the mind onto the stage, far from the body" ([1993] 2015, 263). Tambura Masses, then, represent a potentially destabilizing, even liberative melding of the two ways of embodying performance and thinking in space; if "the rock concert is an empty stage whereas the opera is an altar" (264), at church performances the consecrated altar typically demands this operatic distantiation (even with singing from the pews) from the bodies and performance around the sanctuary. The exception is during Communion, when the Eucharist elements become Christ's body and blood and the congregation's bodies in turn ingest these. Yet tambura music also has its rowdy, rock-and-roll side. There remains the potential for congregants (in relation to the musicians) and even for musicians (in relation to the priests, who stand atop the platform supporting the altar) to mobilize the accrued affects of a tambura practice that was recently and could again become the music of the tavern, disco, or luthier shop. In this, they may seek a way of reaching outside, not so much through conscious escapism as via a metaphysical extension of space beyond the walls of a church, beyond its physical emplacement and metaphysical direction/circumscription of its congregants.

"Čuj nas, Majko" is particularly significant here. A traditional (anonymous) Marian song harmonized in major tonality, it differs strikingly from popular tambura repertoire in its tonal stasis, repeatedly elaborating through limited motion a linear descent between scale degrees 5 and 3 (see figure 5.2). It closely resembles (and likely influenced) Branko Mihajlević and Miroslav Slavko Mađer's 1967 Šokac-themed tambura festival song "I kad umrem pjevat će Slavonija" (And when I die, Slavonia will sing), whose refrain begins with an identical descending (whole tone-semitone) appeal to a "mother." This popular tambura song, however, starts the phrase on the upper tonic and uses the whole-tone descent to modulate to the subdominant, harkening back to modulations in traditional dances and anticipating the dominant archetypal melodic and harmonic structures of the 1990s (see chapter 1). Thus, while the Marian song might not "pull" anywhere (to borrow Zvonko Bogdan's phrase), over the past half century it has remained in close association with a tambura song that does move tonally. Both songs have their affective capacities for eliciting participatory, intercorporeal feel-

FIGURE 5.2 "Čuj nas, Majko"

ing, and these can bleed multidirectionally between song practices and contexts. Yet the force that gathers with such performances tends toward a destabilizing of stasis and ultimately facilitates a musical, affective, and metaphysical pull toward that which lies beyond the shelter of stable architecture, ritual, and belief.

This is the sense in which affect holds the potential for blocking (in delimitation) religious ideologies of place's spiritual, moral, and national dimensions. I turn in the next section to affective breaks in the spatial and spiritual boundedness of religious buildings that music facilitates there and in the secular buildings that Jerry Grcevich noted are so often associated with churches. I also consider the possibility of the opposite move: the shift from distanced, cognitive perception of a spiritual stage to proximate, embodied joining of a stageless milieu, and from affect blocking ideology to affect being blocked in delimitation by permeating ideological power. As I do so, I take up the debate on ideology, interpellation, and materiality that Judith Butler led with the works of Louis Althusser and Mladen Dolar and reassess the place of love and passion at the limits of structures of thought, feeling, and sensation.

CHURCH PERFORMANCES AND PROXIMATE SPACE

Tambura Masses vary in both the ensemble's liturgical role and the extent to which the church architecture's ritual use excludes or opens to mundane experiences and spaces outside. In chapter 1 I detailed a tambura Mass in Parndorf, Austria, in which the town's tambura society "Ivan Vuković" performed many of the important texts of the service's Proper. "Pajo Kolarić" similarly performs at Masses that bring its members together with Croatian intimate communities in Holy Communion. Yet one Mass that I attended also suggested division within the church interior and that associated spaces of rehearsal, costume storage, and socializing extend sacred space physically and metaphysically, sometimes fostering intimacies not achieved within churches themselves.

December 22, 2009: The "Pajo Kolarić" children's orchestra and girls' choir departed by bus from Osijek to perform at a Croatian church in Mohács, Hungary. I made the trip north with the groups, and as we passed through the intervening Croatian region of Baranja, the directors described its occupation up until some eleven years earlier. It was one of them who had been evacuated and expressed fear about traveling abroad (see chapter 1). Yet as we arrived in Mohács, it became clear that this town in Hungary's own Baranya province was very much an intimate of Eastern Croatia. "It's as though we are in Osijek here," one of the group's administrators told me. He explained that until the end of Eastern Slavonia and Baranja's Yugoslav/UN occupation, prices were much lower in southern Hungary, and they regularly visited there to shop and see friends (new immigrants from occupied Croatia and members of Mohács's long-established Croatian Hungarian community).[4] A local Croatian friend of one of "Pajo Kolarić's" administrators, who worked at Mohács's Tourist Center, met and led us to the Town Hall's upstairs room for a reception with other locals.

Following a brief walk around the town, we boarded the bus again and traveled to a Catholic church on the town's edge. We spoke briefly with the priest in Croatian (he had learned the language to serve the Croatian population, many of whom spoke Hungarian as a second language) and learned that he would deliver the Mass in Hungarian. Of the Osijek crew, only the administrator who felt "at home" in Mohács and I attended, while in the storage and dressing room beyond the church's right aisle the children changed into performance wear and the directors socialized. Neither my companion nor I spoke more than a few Hungarian words, but the administrator took part nonetheless, reciting Croatian responses to the priest's service and finally standing to take Communion. The only person remaining seated among a small group of mostly local, Hungarian-speaking Croats, I felt particularly exposed and wondered whether I should have remained with the children and directors. Soon, however, our host from the

Tourist Center stood and welcomed "Pajo Kolarić" and a six-piece tambura and vocal group from Mohács, whom she praised for keeping the music and language strong. The Mohács group hosted the Osijek musicians, opening the afternoon's Christmas-themed performance with two holiday songs. The "Pajo Kolarić" ensembles then performed Croatian-language Christmas songs, international holidays hits (e.g., "Jingle Bells" ["Zvončići"]), and less season-specific Croatian folk songs such as "Ej Pletenice" (see chapter 1). After several requested encores and curtain calls, the congregation crowded around the performers in the small space before the altar. Locals told the children and directors how it had "gone to their hearts" to hear them perform certain traditional Croatian songs. One woman made a pounding motion with her hand moving outward from her chest and back to emphasize the physicality of the feeling and autonomic response that the music elicited in her.

As in Parndorf, local Croat musicians and congregants later received the Osijek guests for a meal in intimate settings (an interior room of Mohács's town hall). Such church performances are typically free of charge and ostensibly advertised and open to the general public. In practice, however, linguistic and religious boundaries tend to select for ethnically homogeneous congregations and audiences. The movement from the town hall's private room to the church and back solidified the somewhat exclusive nature of the relationship cultivated between Osijek and Mohács Croats. Yet the combination of a Hungarian service and Croatian singing further narrowed the public that could readily engage in the overall event, and most of the Osijek musicians elected not to attend the Mass. What effectively compensated for this (via sociomusical rather than religious communion) was the use of the town hall for the reception and dinner. If in this instance the storage/dressing room to the side of the church aisle afforded a space that became alternative to the extreme, in that the ensemble's leaders and members remained there rather than joining in the Mass, the town hall's interior room remained just as significant an external space of reference, association, and metaphysical connection. This space's metaphysical copresence became clear through the woman who beat her chest when praising the musicians for playing to her heart; she moved with us to the town hall and continued to extol the ensembles for how much their performance had meant to her. She had participated in the Mass, and it was clear from her interaction with Osijek's musicians inside the nave that despite many of the songs being secular, it was in part religious meaning that had moved her heart (which remains a locus and visual symbol of spiritual devotion related to the Sacred Heart of Jesus; see

Morgan 2008), but the songs also meant intimacy and commonality, and these sentiments became more fully realized as we moved to the town hall.

The perhaps obvious points that one enters churches from (and departs into) other spaces and that one can attend to extrareligious associations, attachments, and even ideologies inside a church take on new relevance in this context. The physical and even metaphysical connections to exterior spaces enacted by intensely affective experiences (such as the Croatian Hungarian woman's heartfelt response) are prepared through spatial distributions of feeling, belief, and ritual/temporal practice. My own unease at being an intrusive inscription into the church space and at possibly being conscripted in some manner, as sometimes happened in nonreligious intimate listening contexts (see chapter 4), proved unfounded. Those with intimate insider experience of this church simply realized in advance what I came to discover: without the language skills to engage fully in the texted, ideological meanings of the service, our most meaningful participation would come through the performance of Croatian tambura music and song texts and from interactions that these facilitated outside the church. That space, and these interactions, extended from the religious into the secular, cultural domains and (symbolically and metaphysically) opened other ideological and affective commitments.

MASSES, MUSIC, AND INSCRIBED WORLDS

The Mohács Mass was unusual in several respects and highlighted these possibilities. Yet release into mundane spaces and temporalities from the ritual inscriptions that maintain churchgoers' communion in the faith also transpires through tambura performance integrated within the service itself. This can happen even — perhaps especially — absent such linguistic or religious boundaries, as I detail in two short case studies.

October 28, 2012: The Tamburitza Association of America's annual Tamburitza Extravaganza, held this year in Columbus, Ohio, finished with a pair of church services: a Roman Catholic Mass administered by an invited priest in one of the Extravangaza hotel's conference rooms and an Orthodox Liturgy held on its regular schedule in a local Serbian church to which Orthodox participants were invited. As Richard March notes, the two services demonstrate the event's interethnic and interfaith nature (2013, 166). Yet the custom of scheduling the Catholic Mass in the hotel is based on an important difference between the two religions: Catholic services admit instrumental performance, while Orthodox services utilize strictly singing, and holding the former in the hotel encourages Extravaganza musicians to play a tambura Mass. In Columbus the musicians sat in rows of chairs next to the priest along the far end of the room facing the many congregants who had come. Although I did not attend the Orthodox service, my experience in Serbian churches told me that the sensorial contrast was great: fluorescent lights flooded the bright, white, and (in comparison to the frescos typical of Orthodox church interiors) visibly nonreligious architectural space, and the scent of burning candles that one often smells in Catholic and Orthodox churches was noticeably absent. The priest seemed cognizant of the service's context, and he kept the mood light throughout. His furthest comedic venture came at the outset, when he jokingly asked forgiveness for having lapsed in his devotion to the tambura, which he noted having played as a youth. His adoption of religious terminology for musical rather than spiritual commitment drew laughter from the congregation, diffusing the solemnity in the room. It also acknowledged that the spaces adjacent to the conference room—the "breakout" rooms where those same musicians had played until the early morning before catching a few hours of sleep and then drowsily shuffling in to play the Mass— had been sites of more intense and rowdily secular concentration throughout the weekend.

April 2009: An elderly congregant at a Croatian Catholic Church near Pittsburgh had recently passed away. As she had liked tambura music and her closest friend played in the church's tambura choir, of which I was a member, the clergy arranged for us to play at the funeral liturgy for the deceased. We met before the service at the church's stairs and, ascending slowly, took our positions at the back choir loft as the deceased's friends and family filed into the nave and sat in the pews. The deceased woman's close friend did not perform with us, but sat weeping quietly close to the pulpit, from which the priest called special attention during the service to the two women's friendship and mutual love of tambura music. Meanwhile, up in the choir, the mood was considerably lighter as we played and sang secular and religious Croatian songs that seemed only loosely functional within the liturgy. At the beginning, one member even turned and noted his pleasant surprise that I was there after joining only a few weeks beforehand. While expressing gratitude for my contribution to a ritual that was clearly important to the ensemble and to the Croatian community, his comment also spoke to the musicians' attention to their craft, which was evidently an object of relaxed enjoyment as much as a duty or rite. This seemed particularly true when, having finished a popular tambura ballad, the musicians reclined against the back wall or slowly ambled around the choir space. They visibly allowed their attention to wander to other matters as they glanced casually at watches, cell phones, and sheet music for upcoming concerts. No one seemed to mean or interpret this as a sign of disrespect; rather, it affirmed the music's role in a variety of contexts that extended well beyond the space of the church and the time of the funerary ritual.

Jerry Grcevich spoke about the benefit of such sociomusical detachment from the grief provoked by funerals, describing "tambura players playing right at the gravesite" and noting that he had "played a lot of funerals [by] myself in Croatia and this country [. . .]. It's too hard, sometimes, to play for a funeral by yourself" (2017). In contrast, he mentioned Pittsburgh's large Hungarian Roma violin bands that once marched in funeral processions — "those were really times that were spirited" — and suggested that they shared spirit and possibly influence with New Orleans brass band funeral processions (2017). These three traditions differ greatly in the emotions and purposes of their musical performances, but the social aspect was of common significance in differentiating mood. It was playing on his own that made performing at funerals so difficult, whereas at churches or graveyards musicians build off one another both musically and affectively, performing the celebratory music that the Croatian American noted having persuaded Grcevich's band to provide at his eventual burial. It is in this respect that many musicians and audiences consider Grcevich "deep"; his intense feeling permeates his playing and the space around him. Unless emoted with qualities that are conducive to the situation — for example, crossing from sorrow into bittersweet celebration through musical and social interaction with his peers — it risks transgressing or breaking down the musical, social, and religious roles that he has agreed to fill. This is another of musical affect's dangers.

Another still is affect's lines of flight from the structures of proper religious and social etiquette upheld in the religious rituals described here. The priest's joke about seeking forgiveness for his lapsed tambura practice capitulated to the levity of the Tamburitza Extravaganza's broader space and time, whereas within actual Croatian Catholic churches' walls and temporal cycles, conventions help to focus and at times rein in congregants' affects and attentions.[5] Tambura musicians should not, and do not, play dangerously in churches. The danger remains, however, of spiritual depth becoming a form of deep play and transgressing the sanctity, comportment, and, metaphysically, the spatial confines that the Church expects services to uphold. It is here that a reevaluation of ideological theory can illuminate the limitations of this upholding.

Judith Butler's critique of Louis Althusser's interpellative theory, introduced in the previous chapter, engaged a pertinent intermediary voice: Mladen Dolar's suggestion that love might be beyond interpellation (1993). In response, Butler pursues Althusser's classic question of why, upon being hailed, the subject turns toward the police (or other apparatus); acknowledging that Althusser "would have benefitted" from considering love, she nonetheless counters that the fact that "the subject turns round or rushes toward the law suggests that the subject lives in passionate expectation of the law. Such love is not beyond interpellation; rather, it forms the passionate circle in which the subject becomes ensnared by its own state" (1997, 129).

Before addressing love, however, it seems necessary to examine the faculties of perception implied in this discussion. In this hypothetical, hailing takes the form of vocalization ("Hey, you there!") and hearing. The subject responds by turning, with the implied result of engaging faculties other than audition. As Won Choi (2012, 33) argues, Butler's reassessment of this example interprets the subject's response in light of "the risk of 'death'" and the evaluation "I would rather exist in subordination than not exist," which her book's introduction discusses (1997, 7). Thus recognizing physical danger and anticipating and perhaps preventing the state apparatus's tactile contact and violation (the long arm of the law) is bound up in this process of being interpellated, suggesting a move from auditory to haptic sensation. Intermediary to these, however (if included only implicitly in the presumably complete sensory faculties of the able-bodied hypothetical subject), is the act of seeing: one visually verifies, in time to receive or avoid haptic contact, that the voice heard belongs to a state apparatus with the repressive power to subject those it hails to its ideological and material structures (and is not a passerby's voice, whose hailing might produce a sort of subjectivity but not the same ideological reinforcement). Here, audition as an inceptional interpellative faculty sets off a relationality between two faculties (sight and touch) that, for those with normative sensory abilities, lie on opposite ends of the spectrum of sensory proximity. Much in the same way, for supersensing tambura elites, audition reverses this very spectrum between touching what is at hand and seeing what is far away. What is out of sight in spaces beyond walls becomes sensible haptically by metaphysically receiving sound vibrations on the skin (or through physical extensions of the brain à la Franić's "antennae"). Eliciting an intermediary act of seeing an apparatus of power from an initial act of hearing a voice suggests that there may be more to the motivation to turn around than simply an engaged passion for the law. Given Dolar's work on the voice and gaze, a reconsideration of the relationship of love to interpellation seems warranted.

Dolar has more recently reevaluated the Aristotelian distinction between the voice (vocal sound; cry) and logos (speech; oral judgment). He theorizes the former not as "some remnant of a previous precultural state, or of some happy primordial fusion when we were not yet plagued by language and its calamities [but as] the product of logos itself, sustaining and troubling it at the same time" (2006, 106–107). This explains the fact that in the three "religions of the Book," "prayers and sacred formulas [. . .] carefully stored on paper and in memory, can acquire performative strength only if they are relegated to the voice" (107). Thus the interpellating voice divides into two processes: hailing the subject into an ideology and troubling the hegemon's very centrality to this call by the "pure excess of the voice," which amounts to "a dislocation of the imposing voices of domination" (122). "[I]n the first case one turns into a subject precisely by assuming the form of the autonomous 'I,' disavowing its heteronomic origin, so that ideological domination and autonomous subjectivity work hand in hand," as theorized by Althusser (i.e., the subject who passionately longs to be recognized by the state), yet "if one wants to become a subject, recognition and obedience are never quite enough; in addition to and apart from these, one has to respond to the 'mere voice' which is just an opening, a pure enunciation compelling a response" (122). Into this division (between the voice that draws passionate recognition of subjectivity and the voice that troublingly exceeds the legal or divine code's reach) intercedes the intermediary, hypothetically visual verifying of the state apparatus from the previous example. As Dolar notes, "the distance between the two voices opens the space of the political" (123). Within this space, new agencies can take hold. Among the greater tambura milieu's elite metaphysicians, this takes the form of reordering capacities of perceiving and affecting. While the "pure enunciation compelling a response" is "something one would perhaps rather escape by obeying the sonorous voice of statements and commands" (122), I argue that these musicians respond with a different sort of want: a love that voices itself.

I demonstrated previously how congregants in Croatian Catholic churches typically meet the calls of the clergy with visual and aural attention, and how tambura players sometimes receive spatially and sensorially privileged positions in which they both see the priest(s) and gaze upon the congregation, hearing the officiant while sounding the Ordinary texts to those farther back. It is tempting to interpret their visual and sonic acts within the teleology of interpellation: as meeting the interpellative voice with the gaze, which objectifies in its own right, but almost instantaneously subjects itself to the voice and becomes its guarantor (in lieu of the voice tied to logos fulfilling this function and sufficing in its texted truths). Yet one should not overstate the role of vision here, particularly given tambura metaphysicians' nonvisual abilities. The point is not that interpellation requires vision, but that human faculties (and agencies) are manifold. Often coordinated in everyday perception, within demanding contexts of manifesting passion and interpellation by powerful apparatuses they may become more diffuse and disjointed. While seeing the Church, hearing it, even adopting its logos, tambura players are able to verify other realities, which through the sensorial spectrum's reordering become supersensorially more proximate than that which they see around them. It would be hard to defend absolutely the position that love is beyond interpellation. Yet the split simultaneities of voice/logos, passion/preference ("I would rather exist in subordination . . ."), affect/rationality, and audition/vision/touch allow for various alignments in divided subjectivities, attentions, and desires. This is not to say that this is purely secular, for this is indeed close to how many theologians describe Divine love. What is special about certain elite tambura players is that the tambura makes objects of the world in the manner of the voice and gaze and does so in parallel to the divisional processes of the vocalized sacred texts' logos. Tambura music of course functions in systems of national and religious meaning in these contexts, but also as something like an additional voice. This approaches the "unsung voice" that Carolyn Abbate has identified in nineteenth-century operatic repertoire, which "is defined not by *what* it narrates, but rather by its audible flight from the continuum that embeds it" (1991, 29).

This is affective block at its most basic relationship to meaning: a delimiting of the reach of logos on the becoming subject and an aggregation of force of being into voice. The musicking that facilitates this is not of necessity dangerous. Its danger lies in resisting the *logoi* of structures of power. As we have seen, Croatia's Catholic Church has sometimes propagated ideologies of national and religious superiority, which many congregants do not uphold, and targeted recalcitrance even more than ethnic and religious difference as threatening national, sacred power ("God and Croats"). Since, however, certain exceptionally metaphysical tambura players' and listeners' affective block (their transcendent love) runs deeply beyond performances of ideology, those who do not wish to recognize themselves in the Church's or nation's hailing need not resist directly.

Yet therein also lies this love's potential blocking in delimitation: it remains susceptible to the affective work of rituals, which is not in any one individual's hands but moves collectively. While the priest's joke about lapsing in tambura performance capitulated to the meaning and general mood of the Tamburitza Extravaganza, it also diffused that larger event's intensities, bringing attentions around to the significatory work of texts, both sacred and secular, canonized and impromptu. In such contexts, musical and affective work to transcend specific meanings—systems of belief, discourses, even entire narratives—by extending beyond ritual space's physical confines and above its temporal dimensions to longer, ancient realities becomes, again, entirely political.

EPILOGUE

Musical Affect and the Political Beyond

Physical movement into and between Croatian lands, and extending through ethnic networks to areas beyond Croatia's borders, remains a political act for tamburaši of diverse backgrounds. The threats to sovereignty and physical safety of the 1990s conflicts no longer motivate territorial agendas or remain extant to any comparable extent. Yet musical travel to certain towns, performance venues, and sites of remembrance continuously reterritorializes these lands and routes and indeed allows us to speak of Croatia and its intimates as a geography of performance. I have argued that affective, metaphysical extension to spaces outside the physical and ideological structures of state apparatuses still admits the political through residual feelings that intensify during musical performance. More quotidian instances of material motion and conveyance, while similarly capable of transporting musicians and audiences beyond specific places (even beyond territorializing emplacement itself), must then become political all the more frequently.

These dual potentialities, and their embodiment in affect blocked and blocked, registered frequently when tambura musicians brought me from Osijek to Vukovar, the Croatian city most famed for wartime destruction. As a non-Croatian from the United States, the territorializing responses that my research prompted in the events detailed in chapter 3 weighted the distribution of such potentialities in my interactions in Vukovar heavily, though not singularly, toward the political. On my first visit to Osijek in 2008, "Pajo Kolarić's" president Antun took me to Vukovar to see its iconic shelled water tower and other evidence of the city's bombardment, including a memorial center just beyond Vukovar commemorating Croatian medical staff and patients killed in the Ovčara prisoner camp in 1991. Later trips confirmed such travel's political significance.

Late June, 2010: During the last week of my longest fieldwork stint, Antun, his wife Gordana, and I retraced this trip en route to a small village south of Vukovar in Eastern Slavonia called Nijemci. Antun's family had once lived there, and he and Gordana, along with his siblings' families, took care of and frequented a weekend cottage. Antun wanted to take me there once before I left, and so I returned to Osijek, ostensibly so that they could show me Nijemci and send me off with a special final lunch. The trip proved also to have another purpose. As we drove in their car from Osijek to Vukovar and on south toward the village, Antun began to relate his family's hundred-year history there. This included their move from the Austrian Burgenland, a great aunt's emigration to the United States (where she made a fortune running moonshine during Prohibition), and her descendants' loss of the money to Communist seizures in the late 1940s. He and Gordana pointed out various sites of significance to their families, and I learned more about their lives before the Yugoslav conflicts when Slavonian villages had been "very rich."

Soon, however, we began passing ruins of buildings shelled in 1991, and they related a different, more recent history. One small village had only a few surviving older buildings among a long line of demolished structures, some of which had been extensively repaired or rebuilt. The older buildings, they told me, were local Krajina Serbs' homes, which the Yugoslav army had spared while destroying Croats' houses. The following village, they added, had been completely razed and looted by local Serbs. They spoke calmly but bitterly about the decimation and clearly felt that I should understand this part of their experience before leaving Croatia (and in forming an opinion of Nijemci in its current state). I knew from conversations that the war had damaged their own cottage and prevented them from returning for several years. When we arrived, before lunching or beginning new yard and repair work, they surveyed the house's rebuilt sections and remaining damage, comparing it to photographs they produced of the rubble awaiting them upon their return in the late 1990s.

Residents of these areas continue to live with the war's destruction. Ružina Ulica, the street on which I lived as Antun and Gordana's guest and neighbor, suffered light shelling during the war, enough to damage several structures. The house where I roomed had a hairline fracture running across the front wall that my landlady informed me was from the war. On a few separate occasions I found her standing on the sidewalk, staring up at it, and she commented that each year it grew a little and became a bigger cause of concern.

No longer the nexus of wealthy agricultural villages and industrial towns it once was, Slavonia retains much of its wartime material damage, which penetrates its buildings as well as industries, psyches, former and continuing relationships, and musical practices, while also fostering new strategies of affective resilience. The connections between residents' physical and social worlds operate at a deeper level than metaphor or even structural homology; the fractures run from one realm into another and branch fractally throughout. One loss remembered or rupture sensed triggers the memory and sensation of another. These compound one another quickly, as I discovered in conversations during fieldwork that quickly escalated into nostalgic, saddened, or even angry outpourings about the difficulties of being a working tambura musician or of life more generally in Croatia since the war.

Yet beyond conscious acts of remembrance, architecture and urban environs more broadly function as their own sort of archive, which can in turn trigger conscious memories but which works more immediately in structuring an "archive of affect" (Wald 2015, 8). Such an archive scaffolds "structures of feeling" (Williams 1977, 128) beyond individual and even collective human experience, pairing signs that remain readily interpretable as loss with the material conditions of feelings both new and residual. Fractures, then, are but one of several reasons that architectural interiors in Croatia are never fully deterritorialized but connect to memory and to presence beyond the temporal and spatial confines of their use. Tamburaši avail themselves of metaphysical recourses to the outside when playing in nationally, gendered, and/or religiously delimited contexts. Yet so also are would-be spaces of escape (from dominant ideologies, narratives, and discourses) subject to the political and to the confrontation and propagation of structures of both meaning and feeling. This is music's danger: while musical performance always has the potential to signify power and reterritorialize its milieus, residual affects hold the capacity to reintensify and to reignite the oscillation of feeling toward meaning even when the latter has been strategically (and seemingly effectively) blocked. The alterity of representation can easily veer back to a representation of alterity.

February 1, 2010: The St. Trifun's Day celebration at the Serbian Cultural Society "Prosvjeta" brought me out to Vukovar for an evening party with music by my kontra tambura instructor Mirko Delibašić's tambura band Vučedolski Zvuci in one of the society's buildings. The patron saint of viticulturists in the Orthodox tradition, St. Trifun is typically celebrated on this day with the drinking of new wine, and "Prosvjeta" was throwing a proper party with bottles from local vineyards, food, guests, and live music. Although the Serbian Orthodox Church utilizes only human voices and certain bells in its liturgy, saint day celebrations in secular buildings often bring together instrumental performers with Orthodox rituals. Two priests opened the evening by chanting a blessing and prayer, during which they also purified the space with incense and bells. I was sitting in with Vučedolski Zvuci, and we set up to accompany two semiprofessional singers specializing in estrada, newly composed folk music, and old city songs. This repertoire, although in keeping with the spirit of St. Trifun's Day celebrations, had decidedly nonreligious texts. As we played tamburas, often joined by other musicians on accordion and/or keyboard, people drank and sang along rowdily but happily.

A Croat tambura musician who had made his career in Vojvodina but moved to Croatia during the war and founded one of this period's leading tambura bands was there to see and hear Mirko, his longtime friend and onetime protégé. Noting that we were playing the Vojvodina repertoire well, he added that since the 1990s he has found most Croatian tambura music "too aggressive." He prefers the "melismatic" music of Bosnia and Vojvodina, in which there is a basic melody that each musician elaborates in his or her own way. The solution, he said, would be for more Croatian musicians to learn to use the plectrum properly, alleviating the need for striking downward twice quickly in succession and compensating for the resulting rhythmic difficulties with extra physical and affective force. Thus the counter to aggression was not a different channeling of affect but rather its mitigation, or blocking, through cerebral and kinetic knowledge.

Evenings and spaces such as this suggest the continuing importance to diverse tamburaši of milieus on the outside: away from the delivery/realization of dominant narratives, out of the spaces of hegemonic performance, even beyond affect's politicization. An Orthodox celebration in an intact Serbian building on the outskirts of Vukovar at which instrumental secular performance was clearly differentiated from vocal religious practice occasioned a marginal, minoritarian appreciation of the milder affects of playing. It transported musicians and audience members of various backgrounds to the soundscapes of Vojvodina without territorializing it as Serbia or as part of Greater Croatia (an intimate). As Mirko's former mentor would tell me later as he drove me around his favorite towns in

Western Vojvodina (which for him were richly diverse tambura performance milieus and not territorialized Croatian enclaves), what drives Croats to associate only with one another is "human stupidity" (*ljudska glupost*). Being "close" with those who share your musicianship and musicality makes more sense—an argument in favor of understanding and knowledge as a counter to ignorance augmented with aggressive feeling. This argument, however, brings the marginal back into a central politics of affective transgression and restraint.

Alexei Yurchak warns of the fallacy of viewing the outside "as spaces of authenticity and freedom that were clandestinely 'carved out' from the spatial and temporal regimes imposed by the state," when actually they "were paradigmatic manifestations of how these regimes functioned" (2005, 156). Yet this is not so only because such regimes come to incorporate and rely upon citizens existing outside the political; it is also so because such deterritorialization on the outside prompts a corresponding reterritorialization (perhaps unbidden or unacknowledged) upon the polis. They are "not opposed to one another but linked as processes of formation and change in assemblages" (Tomlinson 2016, 165). Affective block is such a de- and reterritorializing assemblage, a shoring up of feeling through both blocking and being blocked (in delimitation) by discourse. Within this assemblage emerge tendencies and, at times, strategies for mobilizing affect and signification to maneuver between these dual potentialities. Musical extension into spaces beyond—ranging from musical travel narrated as territorial reclamation to supersensorial listening understood actively as metaphysical access—remains central to this maneuvering. The dangerous intimacies of the familiar and the strange that accrue to the pluralities of aggressive, nomadic, and gentle *meloi* deterritorialize and ultimately reterritorialize Croatia and its intimates. This reterritorialization extends beyond a core territory whose limits do not map firmly onto the boundaries reaffirmed by the 1998 UN-administered transition of sovereignty. Rather, they ebb with the blocking and blocking of affect attached to clean rhythm, dangerous playing, foreign becomings, and emergent and disintegrating domestic structures that have been reclaimed politically, ideologically, but still not fully materially.

NOTES

Introduction

1. "Tambura player" (pl. *tamburaši*). Its common translation, "tamburitzan" (from the diminutive *tamburica*), is largely associated with the Tamburitzans (a Southeastern European dance and music ensemble, formerly based at Duquesne University in Pittsburgh, Pennsylvania) and its affiliated junior Croatian and Serbian American ensembles. Croatian tamburaši use *tamburica* as a term of endearment but consider outsider use belittling. I employ "tambura player," "tamburaš," and "tamburaši" rather than "tamburitzan" (or the English equivalent "tamburist").

2. Musicians in the former Yugoslavia who perform other styles of music, particularly rock, use this expression as well. It is within tambura music circles that the phrase *opasno svira* ("plays dangerously") often refers to Romani playing style.

3. Bešlić notes that with the album on which this song was released, *Prvi Poljubac*, he broke back into Croatian radio airplay for the first time since the Yugoslav wars (Bešlić 2009).

4. The Roma (sing. Rom, adj. Romani) are a people of South Asian origin thought to have arrived in Southeast Europe eight hundred to one thousand years ago. The region's non-Roma commonly call them Cigani (masculine singular Cigan, feminine singular Ciganka), a term that Roma variously embrace, revile, or treat ambivalently. "Cigani" is etymologically distinct from "Gypsies," and I often use the former when quoting interlocutors. I refer to individuals, groups, and their culture by the more widely accepted "Rom," "Roma," and "Romani."

5. Another common sobriquet humorously referencing dangerous Others was Jerryonimo, a play on Geronimo (the nineteenth-century Apache warrior chief).

6. The Croatian verb *svirati*, meaning "to play [music]," does not have the English verb's flexibility to signify games or other activities. The translation's implicit relationship to its opposite—"playing it safe"—serves only in English to embrace the more diverse referents that this title conjures.

7. Similarly, regarding European football, my interlocutors used the adjective humorously to describe a player's strategic threat to an opponent but would apply the adverb *opasno* earnestly to characterize physically dangerous maneuvers (e.g., high kicking).

8. Yugoslavia translates literally as "South Slavia."

9. According to Hofman and Marković, "there are different claims about their ethnic origin": that "the Bunjevci are Croats," "an independent group," or "Catholic Serbs" (2006, 316). They migrated several centuries ago from the Buna region of Bosnia and Herzegovina, fleeing Ottoman forces (Baerlein 1922, 86).

10. Multiple families of tamburas have existed, though the Srem/Srijem system from Western Serbia and Eastern Croatia described here dominates.

11. Tambura ensembles were particularly common in the KUDs of Croatia, Serbia, Bosnia and Herzegovina, and the province of Vojvodina, although I have also heard of ethnic Albanian societies adopting tamburas in Kosovo in the 1970s (Sugarman 2010).

12. In Yugoslavia, *nations* such as Serbs and Croats had their own nominal territories; *nationalities* such as Albanians and Hungarians had large populations in Yugoslavia and nation-states abroad; and *ethnic groups* such as Roma had no nation-states anywhere.

13. Croatian language was officially subsumed under the broad Yugoslavian heading of Serbo-Croatian, alongside Serbian, with which it and Bosnian are fully mutually intelligible. Certain grammatical and lexical differences set them apart, the amplification and standardization of which were promoted by Croatian national activists from the late 1960s until their successful realization following Croatia's independence.

14. I use "nationalism" anthropologically to encapsulate constructing the nation and socially propagating supporting sentiments. In Croatian, this term may also connote affinities with National Socialism, a meaning not intended here.

15. Many Duquesne Tamburitzans felt that their pan-Yugoslav repertoire was not welcomed by the CFU.

16. Šovagović's *muziciranje*, the gerund of the verb *muzicirati* ("to musick"), could also translate as "tambura musicianship."

17. She gifted me Šovagović's book *Bridges through the Strings of the Tamburica*, which for her commemorated intercontinental bridges established with her distant cousins.

18. For example, tamburas and his mother.

19. Gary Tomlinson eloquently states this process's significance for music: "Indexicality and musicking alike are caught up in the parahuman, semiotic play of transversals that *re*territorialize as they *de*territorialize. These transversals constitute new territorial outcomes, in the interassemblage, of machinic operations" (2016, 168).

20. It dates to the Septuagint, the Greek translation of the Hebrew Bible.

21. Popular Dalmatian Klapa (men's a cappella) ensembles, Croatian rock and pop bands, viticulture, and association football motivate additional networks among Croatia and its intimates.

22. In Nigeria, repatriated slaves "introduced distinctive syncretic styles of worship, food, dress, dance, and music developed under slavery" that became seminal to Yorùbá identity (Waterman 1990, 370). Zimbabwe's nationalist leadership emerged among its cosmopolitan middle class, infusing transnational musical dissemination with a distinctly national purpose (Turino 2000, 13).

23. Although tambura ensembles remain popular in Vojvodina, the *frula* end-blown flute common in nationally popular Serbian folk orchestras "works singularly as the sound sign of Serbia" (Rasmussen 2002, 29, 110). Some Serbs locate Serbia's "core" territory abroad in newly independent Kosovo and import its Monastic Orthodox chant and *kaval* (another folk flute) traditions (Atanasovski 2011, 2015).

24. This also involves the nation: "Intimate distance places indigenous expressions, particularly musical ones, at the core of national pride; but shared national pride in indigenous expressions hardly budges the entrenched racial hierarchies" (Bigenho 2012, 138).

25. For most, paid performances constitute at best a secondary profession.

ONE *Tamburaši and "Sacral Buildings"*

1. Croatian musicians abandoned the once popular Farkaš system for Srijemski or Janković tamburas in the mid-twentieth century (Janković tamburas remain popular, though less so than the Srijemski system). Farkaš instruments were carried to Bulgaria in the late nineteenth century by Czechs and Croats through pan-Slavist networks following liberation from Ottoman rule (see Dimov 2008).

2. Earlier versions of this chapter appear in MacMillen (2011b, 2014).

3. Amid significant hostilities, Eritrea seceded from Ethiopia in 1993, Palau from Micronesia in 1994, Timor-Leste from Indonesia in 2002, and South Sudan from Sudan in 2011.

4. "Balkanization" originally connoted such complexities, having emerged in the post–World War I *consolidation* of the Kingdom of Serbs, Croats, and Slovenes (the first Yugoslavia), "whose creation was, technically speaking, the reverse of balkanization" (Todorova 1997, 33).

5. Falcons are common symbols of strength and resistance dating back at least to nineteenth-century pan-Slavism.

6. Award levels are based on overall scores, but no ranking or overall winner is declared. Theoretically, all the ensembles (or none) could receive gold plaques.

7. Croatian songwriter Jura Stublić famously addressed a Belgrade comrade turned enemy as "drug" in his 1992 hit "Ej moj druže beogradski" (Hey, my Belgrade comrade).

8. Forty-two ensembles submitted recordings to compete for twenty-seven (fourteen "pioneer" youth, thirteen "senior") festival spots (STD "Pajo Kolarić" 1989, 8).

9. The bombing partially destroyed Osijek's Croatian National Theater, where many of the festival concerts were held in 1989.

10. Singing and bells are the only acceptable sonic practice in Serbian Orthodox churches, making tambura church concerts a singularly Croatian enterprise.

11. During socialism, the ensemble was named after the antifascist Yugoslav heroine Milica Križan.

12. *Svoi* in Russian similarly means "us" or "ours" (Yurchak 2005, 103).

13. Small numbers bear out Mary Douglas's "classic anthropological argument [. . .] that all moral and social taxonomies find abhorrent the items that blur their boundaries (1966). Minorities [. . .] the religiously deviant, [. . .] and the unwelcome in the space of the nation-state—blur the boundaries between "us" and "them" (Appadurai 2006, 44).

14. Slovenia's group features mixed membership and repertoire, but credits its tambura tradition to an influx from the Croatian plains (KUD "Oton Župančič" 2007).

15. One Croatian tambura luthier chuckled disappointedly to me at the "pointless," "nonsensical" patriotism of the festival's paradoxical billing as simultaneously "international" and "Croatian."

16. For example, Šandor Bosiljevac, born in 1860.

17. Fine notes Šokci's possible Hungarian-language folk etymology (2006, 503), while Baerlein claims it derives from šaka ("palm"), a Serbian reference to Catholics crossing themselves with open palms rather than clasped thumb and fingers (1922, 88).

18. This was a matter more of self-selective inclusion than exclusion, as Zoran's wife and one of his parents were Serbian Orthodox.

19. I was unable to identify any non-Croats, though they might not have wished to identify themselves openly as minorities.

20. Such melodic cadences predate functional harmony; Ivanković's description speaks to current tambura folklore hermeneutics more than to historical musical development.

21. They also sometimes play jazz and international popular music.

22. Nearly ubiquitous since 1992, these archetypes appeared sporadically in Yugoslav hits (e.g., the 1969 Krapinski Festival entry "Suza za Zagorske Brege") and traditional, anonymous songs (e.g., "Zora rudi, dan se bijeli"), which likely originated in nineteenth-century musical plays (by forgotten composers) "set in functional harmonies for a conventional theater ensemble" that "successful[ly] captur[ed] the rural nuance of rhythm and melody" (Forry 1990, 142–145).

23. For a full transcription and analysis, see MacMillen (2011a, 110–112).

24. Figure 1.2 compares them in C major, but examples exist in many major and minor tonalities. Chapters 4 and 5 analyze "Moja Juliška" and "Vesela je Šokadija" in their original keys.

25. Grcevich's "Šumi, šumi javore" also elaborates a progression from the tonic; thus his three initial hits with Škoro span three quintessential progressions.

1. George Simmel famously posited that the stranger's "position as a full-fledged member involves both being outside [the group] and confronting it" (1950, 402–403).

2. One does not become "man" or "white," which Deleuze and Guattari argue are "majoritarian par excellence, whereas becomings are minoritarian; all becoming is a becoming-minoritarian" (1987, 291).

3. This Lacanian barred subject "is not free to merge with its object, but remains trapped in a dynamic that motivates the subject to pursue continually a merger" (Vatalaro 2009, 23). The stricken-though text indicates the subject's simultaneous pursuit of and rejection from a white majoritarian positionality.

4. In Yugoslavia, Russian romances (translated into Serbian) were frequently performed by and popularly associated with Serbia's Romani musicians (see Forry 1990, 145, 196).

5. Bogdan identifies as a Bunjevac (pl. Bunjevci), which he calls an "ethnic group. They are Catholics and belong to the Croatian peoples" (2013). Thus "our people" had to encompass at least Croatian ethnicity in order to include Škoro.

6. South Slavic folklore ensembles have long employed tamburas across diverse national repertoires, and professional tambura bands also hybridize multiple traditions.

7. They admit non-Croat participants, whose tambura practice orients primarily to Croatian traditions; Serbia-oriented groups are the other primary North American ethnic tambura ensemble type.

8. Interpreted differently, it is an Anglicization of the Croatian word *zbrkan* into a word recognizably similar to "broken."

9. The dialogue (from Škoro's autobiography) appears in the middle lines. English equivalents appear above Croatian words, Croatian equivalents below the English. Parts of English and Croatian equivalents utilized in hybridized words are underscored. The "proper" spelling of words written using the other language's orthography appears in square brackets.

10. Several professional tamburaši associates of Jerry joked good-naturedly about his use of *lajkaš* (from the infinitive form *lajkati*, pronounced "like-ah-tee," which Jerry adapted from "like" years before this became common Croatian parlance on Facebook).

11. As one Pittsburgh musician put it, "it wouldn't make sense" to write songs in English.

12. Their original recordings' renown extends beyond Croatia and North America to tamburaši in Bosnia, Serbia, Hungary, and Austria (young Burgenland tamburaši at Vienna's Croatian Center discussed Kosovec's recordings with particular enthusiasm and verbosity).

13. This linguistic emergence parallels other North American linguistic hybridizations such as "Spanglish," which is less a stable entity than a "mode of communication" with

an ongoing "development" that can be theorized through the racio-linguistic concept of *mestizaje* (Stavans 2003, 23–24).

14. More than imitating Škoro's dialogue, Grcevich entered into relation with bits of speech that emitted a molecular Croat: he used the English word "like" ("lajk") the way a Croat would use it ("lajk-aš") if he or she were molecular.

15. Intrigued by Škoro's questioning of the given nature of Grcevich's identity, I had asked whether Grcevich's Croatianness might be more a matter of becoming than birth. Škoro's ready, thoughtful response suggested that this term's introduction had imposed little on his conceptualization of Grcevich's Croatianness.

16. This parallels Antun's comment about a "Pajo Kolarić" orchestra director who, though Jewish, "feels like a Croat" (see chapter 1).

17. His philosophy is informed by "unfair" musicians who recorded his compositions and changed the melody beyond simple embellishment or claimed credit for his copyrighted material (e.g., song arrangements). Curbing adaptation is somewhat at odds with wishing copyright authorities would require that arrangements make greater changes before copyright be transferred, but both desires distinguish between authorial innovations in composing/arranging and interpretive stylization in performance.

18. The result was Bogdan's 1986 "Svaku ženu volim ja" (I love every woman), also known by its first line, "Kada padne prvi sneg" (When the first snow falls), which is closer thematically than Les Paul's legally disputed adaptation "Johnny Is the Boy for Me."

19. "Music" primarily encompasses melody. "Arrangement," however, can range from basic chordal accompaniment and strophic structuring to part writing, representing a compositional gray area in which musicians can innovate and justify a copyright claim for a song with melody and text owned by others (Bogdan's contribution of a new, nontranslated text represents another).

20. Their time at Duquesne University ended in 2016.

21. Batyi was born in Pittsburgh to immigrant families from Slovakia and Hungary, who enjoyed strong relationships with other immigrants from Austria-Hungary.

22. Not everyone views this as a carefree event, however. Following Pittsburgh's 2008 Extravaganza, Croatian Americans from Missouri expressed surprise that Croats were planning to attend the Serb Club's after-party. They attended with obvious trepidation, as Croat-Serb relations elsewhere had led them to expect problems (though to my knowledge, none materialized).

23. Batyi seemingly responded to the racially objectifying notion of his contributing a "Gypsy element." Batyi otherwise employs "Gypsy" in marketing his music and initially found it humorous when non-Roma began saying "Roma" (Batyi 2013).

24. Non-Roma members often emphasize Romani repertoire, too, but highlight their Romani violinist, prioritizing ethnic background and instrumentation over repertoire in this style's marketing.

25. See *Deep Polka* (1998) and *Deeper Polka* (2002), for which March solicited new Jerry Grcevich recordings, including a version of "Moja Juliška," which along with his "Vatrogasna Polka," Charles Keil notes, is one of the compilation's faster pieces (2005, 119). At 128 bpm, however, it is recognizably slower than Škoro and Grcevich's original (136 bpm).

26. The system differs in Croatia, where folklore ensembles tend to have mono-ethnic repertoire and memberships and to divide members into instrumental and singer/dancer roles.

27. In Canada's 2011 Census, 74,020 Ontarians declared Croatian "ethnic origins," 56,760 declared Serbian, and 25,975 declared Yugoslavian (Statistics Canada 2011).

28. Facing anti-German sentiment during World War I, Germans either assimilated into WASP culture or retreated into isolated enclaves (Traumbauer 2005, 66–68). Thus "German" is variously a term of ethnic whiteness or represents an entryway into America's white "melting pot."

29. These relationships also descend from Yugoslav labor relations between publics and *kafana* (tavern) singers, who "describe their work not as a one-sided commodification of the audience's emotion, but as an emotional exchange between professional musicians and clients" (Hofman 2015, 44).

30. Ancient Asian origins seemingly do not factor into Hungarians' racial proximity; they are figured as closer (culturally, racially, and geographically) than both Chinese and Germans.

31. In an essay on whiteness and class among female singers, Laurie Stras similarly argues that "boundaries become better viewed as fluctuating rather than permeable" (2010, 11).

32. This unsolicited comment did suggest some discomfort with their proximity and relief that violence had never ensued.

33. Like many adult tambura ensembles, his tambura choir became active only in the 2000s. I have given Krunoslav and other members fictional names.

34. They granted keys to both me and a South Asian devotee of East European dance.

35. I should note that Carson was not actively participating, and that he seemed uncomfortable with parts of it and clearly recognized my discomfort.

36. While the Hrvatski Dom's members would occasionally gather on the sidewalk outside its threshold, evening performances such as these were decidedly occasions of architectural interiority. When departing, most would find that night had fallen. With the exception of a limited few who lived in the area, they would quickly locate their cars and leave in them for other architecturally enclosed spaces across town. The area's depressed economy supported only infrequent public transportation.

37. This slur of racial distinction escaped the English form, drawing the subject into a zone of proximity with the term Croat (a Croat who becomes-molecular, becomes-different, in the process of simulation).

38. To most at the Hrvatski Dom, I was likely just another typical young, straight, male, "ethnic" listener until my silence drew gendered inquiries about my (but not the young woman's) participation. I was the only ethnic outsider downstairs, and the Canadian band and locals probably justifiably perceived this as a gathering of Croatian (or what I call "Croatia-oriented") participants rather than the more diverse audience upstairs.

THREE *Race in Postwar Croatian Music*

1. The figure is reproduced from Bartók (1978) in exercise of fair use. Bartók's 1931 violin duos originally had this melody in 2/4 meter, with each quarter note dividing into two eighth notes or four sixteenth notes. He later revised his transcriptions based upon "Bulgarian rhythms," which he learned combined groupings of two and three sixteenths, prompting his reinterpretation of Serbian and Romanian songs in asymmetrical meters rather than in simpler meters with rubato (Rice 2000, 201–202).

2. In 2010 the Batorek School's orchestra rehearsed several times a composition that was dragging. Slaven Batorek finally stopped the orchestra, instructing the kontra players to play "almost" before the beat, which helped them to synchronize with the ensemble. Most beginners, however, study even "ta-fa-te-fe" duple division (French time names developed by Aimé Paris and John Curwen and utilized in music education across Croatia, including the Batorek School); only advanced orchestras or bands depart from this.

3. Rhythmic asymmetry's association with dirtiness is also suggested by Prljavo kazalište (Dirty Theater), one of Croatia's most celebrated bands since the 1980s. The band's rhythm guitarist plays ahead of the theoretical midpoint offbeat in typical British ska-punk fashion, often without the bassist providing downbeats (or even playing). This rare Croatian example of positive reinforcement of musical dirtiness is more at home in punk rock than in tambura music.

FOUR *Conscription into Intimacy's Assemblages*

1. I employ G major/E minor key signature in keeping with the notational practice that tambura pedagogues use in Croatia. The alternative hexachord G-A-B-C-D-E in mm. 2–3 may suggest a pretonal basis for this notational orientation to a pitch set.

2. Cf. Freya Jarman-Ivens (2006) on homosocial hip-hop spaces; Kisliuk (2000) on BaAka men's failed commandeering of performances; and Pegley (2000) on female students in technology-in-music programs.

3. This Šokci performance (with singer Stjepan Jeršek Štef) appears at 34:25 in their Slavonian Television collaboration *Bećarac* (episode 1), published January 3, 2014 (https://www.youtube.com/watch?v=eHlEolc37cE, accessed June 3, 2016).

4. The lowered seventh scale degree differentiates "Svud po selu priče kruže" slightly, tonicizing the subdominant more completely than "Vesela je Šokadija" (which avoids scale degree 7).

5. Many lyrics do treat women deferentially, even alongside misogynistic references (in "Svud po selu priče kruže," young women gaze upon romantic prospects and incite gossip, much like the men). However, masculinist perspectives dominate, from maligning women as gold diggers (e.g., Željko Lončarić "Žec" and Slavonski Bećari's "Snaša") to relishing a former girlfriend's spinsterhood (e.g., Zlatni Dukati's "Marija").

6. Conscription is a specific concern under a wider rubric of gender scholarship, and European nations historically have practiced conscription in gender-segregated arenas such as armed conflict.

7. A theory of mind allowing members to recognize one another's sentience.

8. I could, they swore, treat them should they come to the United States.

9. The "joke" went like this: it was late and we were hungry, so I asked whether any bakeries in Slavonski Brod worked all night; Mladen responded sarcastically that such bakeries existed and were called "day and night" bakeries; I responded, "Ah, but I didn't ask about the day!"

10. Their length (much shorter than ten-minute *bećarac* series) and the individual tastes that patrons can express in requesting them make them more effective for eliciting tips.

11. "Zorica" (Aurora, a woman's name) incorporates rhythm instruments (guitar and drums) and short, repetitive, minor-key riffs in the chorus and instrumental sections that recall Serbian dance music. Its chorus also traces a neat (though nonsequential) linear progression between the upper and lower tonics.

12. One member who had elected to give up performing upon getting married was subsequently replaced.

13. The members of Garavuše asked me not to detail the events precipitating their departure. Suffice it to say that it related to the evening's physical conditions and not merely the men's rowdiness, which they tolerated for hours.

14. Subsequently, Pusić became minister of foreign and European affairs, and Kolinda Grabar-Kitarović, the first female minister of foreign and European affairs (2003–2005), became Croatia's first female president in 2015.

15. The only allusion I witnessed was the suggestion that one unmarried folklorist was a *peder* (a slur for gay men derived from *pederast*).

16. This masculine subjectivity, though perhaps generalized as "man," is still particular: heterosexual, Croatian, handsome, heroic, Christian, etc.

1. Roma's allegedly "dirty," "sad," and "heavy" playing also demonstrates this capacity, though with what many non-Roma listeners perceive to be a strikingly different effect (suggesting distinct priorities for sonic saturation).

2. This example demonstrates Franić's basis of musical philosophy in ethnicized listening more than the composing/arranging processes of actual Roma tambura musicians (who are known for diverse, often minor harmonic practices).

3. *Pisana nedjelja* (literally "Written Sunday") is the first Sunday after Easter.

4. During the 2000s the direction of travel reversed due to lower prices in Osijek, but people still traveled north for social/religious visits.

5. For example, at an exceptional Pittsburgh Extravaganza tambura Mass held in a church, a famous tambura/rock band's inconspicuous position in the choir loft, coupled with its greater reliance on popular instruments than tamburas, kept the group within conventions of contemporary American Catholic Church music.

REFERENCES

Discography

Deep Polka: Dance Music from the Midwest. 1998. SF CD 40088. Various artists. Compiled, produced, and annotated by Richard March. Released on the Smithsonian Folkways Recordings label. Compact disc.

Deeper Polka: More Dance Music from the Midwest. 2002. SFW CD 40140. Various artists. Compiled, produced, and annotated by Richard March. Released on the Smithsonian Folkways Recordings label. Compact disc.

Ne Dirajte Mi Ravnicu. 1989. 782.421162 (Dewey classification). Miroslav Škoro and Jerry Grcevich. Released on the Croatia records label. Cassette.

Print Sources

Abbate, Carolyn. 1991. *Unsung Voices: Opera and Musical Narrative in the Nineteenth Century.* Princeton, NJ: Princeton University Press.

Agawu, Kofi. 2003. *Representing African Music: Postcolonial Notes, Queries, Position.* London: Routledge.

Ahmed, Sara. 2004. *The Cultural Politics of Emotion.* London: Routledge.

———. 2010. "Happy Objects." In *The Affect Theory Reader,* edited by Melissa Gregg and Gregory Seigworth, 40–50. Durham, NC: Duke University Press.

———. 2012. *On Being Included: Racism and Diversity in Institutional Life.* Durham, NC: Duke University Press.

Althusser, Louis. 1971. *Lenin and Philosophy and Other Essays.* Translated by Ben Brewster. New York: Monthly Review Press.

Anderson, Ben. 2009. "Affective Atmospheres." *Emotion, Space and Society* 2: 77–81.

Anderson, Benedict. 1983. *Imagined Communities: Reflections on the Origins and Spread of Nationalism.* London: Verso.

———. 1998. *The Spectre of Comparisons: Nationalism, Southeast Asia, and the World.* London: Verso.

Andrić, Josip. 1958. "Razvoj tamburaške glazbe." *Tamburaška Glazba* 3: 15–26.

Appadurai, Arjun. 2006. *Fear of Small Numbers: An Essay on the Geography of Anger.* Durham, NC: Duke University Press.

Arendt, Hannah. (1951) 2004. *The Origins of Totalitarianism.* New York: Schocken.

Asad, Talal. 1992. "Conscripts of Western Civilization." In *Dialectical Anthropology: Essays in Honor of Stanley Diamond,* vol. 1: *Civilization in Crisis: Anthropological Perspectives,* 333–352. Gainesville: University Press of Florida.

Askew, Kelly. 2002. *Performing the Nation: Swahili Music and Cultural Politics in Tanzania.* Chicago: University of Chicago Press.

Atanasovski, Srđan. 2011. "Producing the Serbian Core National Territory through the Soundscape of Kaval." Paper presented at Current Trends in Ethnomusicological Research 3 — An International Doctoral Workshop, University for Music, Drama and Media Hanover and Foundation University of Hildesheim, June 22–25.

———. 2015. "Hybrid Affects of Religious Nationalism: Pilgrimages to Kosovo and the Soundscapes of the Utopian Past." *Southeastern Europe* 39: 237–263.

Baerlein, Henry. 1922. *The Birth of Yugoslavia.* London: L. Parsons.

Baily, John. (2001) 2003. *Can You Stop the Birds Singing? The Censorship of Music in Afghanistan.* Copenhagen, Denmark: Freemuse.

Baker, Catherine. 2010. *Sounds of the Borderland: Popular Music, War and Nationalism in Croatia since 1991.* Farnham, Surrey, UK: Ashgate.

Bartók, Béla. 1978. *Yugoslav Folk Music,* vol. 1. Edited by Benjamin Suchoff. Albany: State University of New York Press.

Batorek, Franjo. 2010. Comments made to the author, Osijek, Croatia, Spring.

Batyi, George. 2013. Discussion with members of the class "Roma and 'Gypsies' in the Musical Imagination," Allen Memorial Art Museum, Oberlin College, October 11.

Beljo, Ante. 1983. *Croatians in the Sudbury Centennial: Canadian-Croatian Folklore Festivals, Sudbury Centennial, 1983.* Sudbury, ON: National Association for the Advancement of Croatian Culture and Folklore.

Bellamy, Alex. 2003. *The Formation of Croatian National Identity: A Centuries-Old Dream?* Manchester, UK: Manchester University Press.

Benić, Marko. 2010. Interview with the author in Ilok, Croatia, May 9.

Berić, Snežana. 1998. "Promotion of the Croatian Party of the Right (HSP) in Vukovar." *Serbia in the World,* no. 78 (March): 92–95. Originally printed in *Politika,* February 16, 1998.

Berlant, Lauren. 1998. "Intimacy: A Special Issue." In *Critical Inquiry* 24, no. 2: 281–288.

———. 2008. *The Female Complaint: The Unfinished Business of Sentimentality in American Culture.* Durham, NC: Duke University Press.

————. 2010. "Cruel Optimism." In *The Affect Theory Reader*, edited by Melissa Gregg and Gregory J. Seigworth, 93–117. Durham, NC: Duke University Press.

Bešlić, Halid. 2009. "Interview: Od bosanske kafane do zagrebačke Arene." *Nacional: Dnevno online izdanje*, no. 725 (October 6). http://arhiva.nacional.hr/clanak/68438/halid-beslic-od-bosanske-kafane-do-zagrebacke-arene, accessed March 23, 2016.

Bezić, Jerko. 1981. "Stilovi folklorne glazbe u Jugoslaviji." *Zvuk* 3: 33–50.

Bhabha, Homi. 1990. "The Third Space: Interview with Homi Bhabha." In *Identity: Community, Culture, Difference*, edited by Jonathan Rutherford, 207–221. London: Lawrence and Wishart.

Bigenho, Michelle. 2012. *Intimate Distance: Andean Music in Japan*. Durham, NC: Duke University Press.

Bijelić, Biljana. 2007. "Women on the Edge of Gender Equality." In *Democratic Transition in Croatia: Value Transformation, Education, and Media*, edited by Sabrina P. Ramet, 276–299. College Station: Texas A&M University Press.

Blažeković, Zdravko. 1998. "The Shadow of Politics on North Croatian Music of the Nineteenth Century." In *Music, Politics, and War: Views from Croatia*, edited by Svanibor Pettan, 65–78. Zagreb, Croatia: Institute of Ethnology and Folklore Research.

Bogdan, Zvonko. 2013. Comments made to the author, Subotica, Serbia, June 11.

————. 2017. Comments made to the author, Subotica, Serbia, June 4.

Bogojeva-Magzan, Maša. 2005. "Music as Ideological Construct: Prevailing Ideology in the Music Curricula in Croatia before and after Its Independence." PhD diss., Kent State University.

Bohlman, Philip. 2004. *The Music of European Nationalism: Cultural Identity and Modern History*. Santa Barbara, CA: ABC-CLIO.

————. 2008. "The Nation in Song." In *Narrating the Nation: Representations in History, Media, and the Arts*, edited by Stefan Berger, Linas Eriksonas, and Andrew Mycock, 246–265. New York: Berghahn Books.

————. 2011. "Translating Herder Translating: Cultural Translation and the Making of Modernity." In *The Oxford Handbook of the New Cultural History of Music*, edited by Jane Fulcher, 501–522. New York: Oxford University Press.

Bohlman, Philip, and Ronald Radano. 2000. "Introduction: Music and Race, Their Past, Their Presence." In *Music and the Racial Imagination*, edited by Philip Bohlman and Ronald Radano, 1–53. Chicago: University of Chicago Press.

Bonifačić, Ruža. 1998. "Regional and National Aspects of *Tamburica* Tradition: The Case of the Zlatni Dukati Neotraditional Ensemble." In *Music, Politics, and War: Views from Croatia*, edited by Svanibor Pettan, 131–149. Zagreb, Croatia: Institute of Ethnology and Folklore Research.

Bourdieu, Pierre. 1977. *Outline of a Theory of Practice*. Translated by Richard Nice. Cambridge: Cambridge University Press.

Boym, Svetlana. 2001. *The Future of Nostalgia*. New York: Basic Books.

Brinner, Benjamin. 2009. *Playing across a Divide: Israeli-Palestinian Musical Encounters*. Oxford: Oxford University Press.

Brodkin, Karen. 2000. "Global Capitalism: What's Race Got to Do with It?" *American Ethnologist* 27, no. 2: 237–256.

Brubaker, Rogers. 1995. "Aftermaths of Empire and the Unmixing of Peoples: Historical and Comparative Perspectives." *Ethnic and Racial Studies* 18, no. 2: 189–215.

Buchanan, Donna. 2006. *Performing Democracy: Bulgarian Music and Musicians in Transition*. Chicago: University of Chicago Press.

Butler, Judith. 1997. *The Psychic Life of Power: Theories in Subjection*. Stanford, CA: Stanford University Press.

———. (2009) 2010. *Frames of War: When Is Life Grievable?* 2nd ed. Brooklyn, NY: Verso.

Čapo Žmegač, Jazna. (2002) 2007. *Strangers Either Way: The Lives of Croatian Refugees in Their New Home*. Translated by Nina H. Antolnak and Mateusz M. Stanojević. New York: Berghahn Books.

Čeribašić, Naila. 1998. "Folklore Festivals in Croatia: Contemporary Controversies." *The World of Music* 40, no. 3: 25–49.

———. 2000. "Defining Women and Men in the Context of War: Images in Croatian Popular Music in the 1990s." In *Music and Gender*, edited by Pirkko Moisala, 219–238. Urbana: University of Illinois Press.

———. 2013. "Prema istraživanju ekonomije tradicijske glazbe u postsocijalističkoj Hrvatskoj." In *Hrvatska svakodnevica: Etnografije vremena i prostora*, edited by Jasna Čapo and Valentina Gulin Zrnić, 139–172. Zagreb, Croatia: Institute za etnologiju i folkloristiku.

Choi, Won. 2012. "Inception of Interpellation? The Slovenian School, Butler, and Althusser." *Rethinking Marxism* 25, no. 1: 23–37.

Čičak, Vedran. 2010. Personal communication with the author, in Sarajevo, Bosnia and Hercegovina, June 21.

Cimini, Amy. 2010. "Gilles Deleuze and the Musical Spinoza." In *Sounding the Virtual: Gilles Deleuze and the Theory and Philosophy of Music*, edited by Brian Hulse and Nick Nesbitt, 129–144. Farnham, Surrey, UK: Ashgate.

Clifford, James. 1997. *Routes: Travel and Translation in the Late Twentieth Century*. Cambridge, MA: Harvard University Press.

Cox, Arnie. 2016. *Music and Embodied Cognition: Listening, Moving, Feeling, and Thinking*. Bloomington: Indiana University Press.

Crnković, Gordana. 2001. "Underground Anti-Nationalism in the Nationalist Era." In *Nationalism, Culture, and Religion in Croatia since 1990*, edited by Vjeran Pavlaković, 31–54. Donald W. Treadgold Papers in Russian, East European, and Central Asian Studies, no. 32. Seattle: Henry M. Jackson School of International Studies, University of Washington.

Croatian Fraternal Union. 2014. "About CFU: History." http://croatianfraternalunion
.org/about-cfu/history/, accessed June 20, 2014.

Cukrov, Ante. 2015. "Istočnojadranska obala—čuvarica glazbene i plesne tradicije Hrvata."
Vjesnik Istarskog arhiva 22: 151–170.

Cushman, Thomas. 1995. Notes from Underground: Rock Music Counterculture in Russia.
Albany: State University of New York Press.

Cusick, Suzanne. 2013. "Towards an Acoustemology of Detention in the 'Global War on
Terror.'" In Music, Sound and Space: Transformations of Public and Private Experience,
edited by Georgina Born, 275–291. Cambridge: Cambridge University Press.

Deleuze, Gilles, and Félix Guattari. (1980) 1987. A Thousand Plateaus: Capitalism and
Schizophrenia. Translated by Brian Massumi. Minneapolis: University of Minnesota
Press.

Delibašić, Mirko. 2010. Comments made to the author, Vukovar, Croatia, January.

———. 2015. Comments made to the author, Vukovar, Croatia, June.

DeNora, Tia. 2000. Music in Everyday Life. Cambridge: Cambridge University Press.

Dimov, Ventsislav. 2008. "Observations on Commercial Gramophone Recordings in
Bulgaria." In The Human World and Musical Diversity: Proceedings from the Fourth
Meeting of the ICTM Study Group "Music and Minorities" in Varna, Bulgaria 2006,
edited by Statelova, Rosemary, Angela Rodel, Lozanka Peycheva, Ivanka Vlaeva, and
Ventsislav Dimov, 43–50. Sofia, Bulgaria: Institut za Izkustvoznanie.

Djilas, Aleksa. 1991. The Contested Country: Yugoslav Unity and Communist Revolution,
1919–1953. Cambridge, MA: Harvard University Press.

Dolar, Mladen. 1993. "Beyond Interpellation." Qui Parle 6, no. 2: 73–96.

———. 2006. A Voice and Nothing More. Cambridge, MA: MIT Press.

Douglas, Mary. (1966) 2005. Purity and Danger: An Analysis of Concepts of Pollution and
Taboo. London: Routledge.

Dragun, Frano. 1999. "Izvorište i Središte Tamburaškog Pokreta." Hrvatska Tamburica:
Glasilo za Promicanje Tamburaške Glazbe 1, no. 1: 17–18.

Dueck, Byron. 2013. Musical Intimacies and Indigenous Imaginaries: Aboriginal Music and
Dance in Public Performance. Oxford: Oxford University Press.

Đurašković, Ljiljana (linguist and professor of Bosnian/Croatian/Serbian). 2007. Personal
communication with the author, University of Pittsburgh, Pittsburgh, PA, June 28.

Ećimović, Rajko. 1999. "Tambura u OŠ Matije Gupca u Zagrebu." Hrvatska Tamburica:
Glasilo za Promicanje Tamburaške Glazbe 1, no. 1: 10–11.

Eisenstein, Zillah. 1996. Hatreds: Racialized and Sexualized Conflicts in the Twenty-First
Century. New York: Routledge.

Erl, Vera, and Julije Njikoš. 2008. "Sadržaj." Zbornik Urbani Šokci 2: 4–5.

Factum. 2017. "GLASNIJE OD ORUŽJA." http://factum.com.hr/hr/filmovi_i_autori
/novi_filmovi/glasnije_od_oruzja, accessed April 19, 2018.

Ferguson, James. 2006. *Global Shadows: Africa in the Neoliberal World Order*. Durham, NC: Duke University Press.

Ferić, Mihael. 2011. *Brevijar Hrvatske Tamburaške Glazbe*. Zagreb, Croatia: Matica Hrvatska.

Fine, John. 2006. *When Ethnicity Did Not Matter in the Balkans: A Study of Identity in Pre-Nationalistic Croatia, Dalmatia, and Slavonia in the Medieval and Early-Modern Periods*. Ann Arbor: University of Michigan Press.

Forry, M. 1990. "The Mediation of 'Tradition' and 'Culture' in the *Tamburica* Music of Vojvodina (Yugoslavia)." PhD diss., University of California at Los Angeles.

Foucault, Michel. 1984. "The Order of Discourse." In *Language and Politics*, edited by Michael Shapiro, 114–116. Oxford: Blackwell.

Franić, Andrija. 2009. Comments made to the author, Županja, Croatia, December 2.

Frankenberg, Ruth. 1997. "Introduction: Local Whitenesses, Localizing Whiteness." In *Displacing Whiteness: Essays in Social and Cultural Criticism*, edited by Ruth Frankenberg, 1–33. Durham, NC: Duke University Press.

Geertz, Clifford. 1972. "Deep Play: Notes on the Balinese Cockfight." In "Myth, Symbol, and Culture," special issue, *Daedalus* 101, no. 1: 1–37.

Gelbart, Petra. 2010. "Learning Music, Race and Nation in the Czech Republic." PhD diss., Harvard University.

Gill, Denise. 2017. *Melancholic Modalities: Affect, Islam, and Turkish Classical Musicians*. Oxford: Oxford University Press.

Gilroy, Paul. 1993. *The Black Atlantic: Modernity and Double-Consciousness*. Cambridge, MA: Harvard University Press.

Gottlieb, Peter. 1991. "Rethinking the Great Migration: A Perspective from Pittsburgh." In *The Great Migration in Historical Perspective: New Dimensions of Race, Class, and Gender*, edited by Joe William Trotter Jr., 68–82. Bloomington: Indiana University Press.

Gow, James. 2003. *The Serbian Project and Its Adversaries: A Strategy of War Crimes*. Montreal: McGill-Queen's University Press.

Gray, Lila Ellen. 2014. *Fado Resounding: Affective Politics and Urban Life*. Durham, NC: Duke University Press.

Grcevich, Jerome. 2009a. Personal communication with the author, Pittsburgh, PA, April 13.

———. 2009b. Personal communication with the author, Pittsburgh, PA, March 10.

———. 2012. Public class presentation at Oberlin (OH) College, April 19.

———. 2017. Class oral history interview at Oberlin (OH) College, April 17.

———. 2018. Personal telephone communication with the author, May 6.

Hadžihusejnović-Valašek, Miroslava. 1998. "The Osijek War-Time Music Scene 1991–1992." In *Music, Politics and War: Views from Croatia*, edited by Svanibor Pettan, 165–184. Zagreb, Croatia: Institute of Ethnology and Folklore Research.

Hagedorn, Katherine. 2001. *Divine Utterances: The Performance of Afro-Cuban Santería.* Washington, DC: Smithsonian Institution Press.

Hahn, Tomie. 2007. *Sensational Knowledge: Embodying Culture through Japanese Dance.* Middletown, CT: Wesleyan University Press.

Halilovich, Hariz. 2013. *Places of Pain: Forced Displacement, Popular Memory and Trans-Local Identities in Bosnian War-Torn Communities.* New York: Berghahn Books.

Hardt, Michael, and Antonio Negri. 2004. *Multitude: War and Democracy in the Age of Empire.* New York: Penguin Books.

Hayden, Robert. 2013. *From Yugoslavia to the Western Balkans: Studies of a European Disunion, 1991–2011.* Leiden, Netherlands: Koninklijke Brill NV.

Helbig, Adriana. 2014. *Hip Hop Ukraine: Music, Race, and African Migration.* Bloomington: Indiana University Press.

Hemmasi, Farzaneh. 2011. "Iranian Popular Music in Los Angeles: A Transnational Public beyond the Islamic State." In *Muslim Rap, Halal Soaps, and Revolutionary Theater*, edited by Karin van Nieuwkerk, 85–114. Austin: University of Texas Press.

Hennion, Antoine. (1993) 2015. *The Passion for Music: A Sociology of Mediation.* Translated by Margaret Rigaud and Peter Collier. Farnham, Surrey, UK: Ashgate.

Herzfeld, Michael. 1997. *Cultural Intimacy—Social Poetics in the Nation-State.* New York: Routledge.

HKUD "Osijek 1862." 2014. ". . . Vinila." http://www.osijek1862.com/index.php/component/content/article/48-uncategorised/200-s-vinila, accessed June 13, 2014.

Hobsbawm, Eric. 1983. "Introduction: Inventing Traditions." In *The Invention of Tradition*, edited by Eric Hobsbawm and Terrence Ranger, 1–14. Cambridge: Cambridge University Press.

Hockenos, Paul. 2003. *Homeland Calling: Exile Patriotism and the Balkan Wars.* Ithaca, NY: Cornell University Press.

Hofman, Ana. 2015. "Music (as) Labour: Professional Musicianship, Affective Labour and Gender in Socialist Yugoslavia." *Ethnomusicology Forum* 24, no. 1: 28–50.

Hofman, Ana, and Aleksandra Marković. 2006. "The Role of Cultural-Artistic Societies in Emphasizing the Identity of Bunjevci." In *Shared Musics and Minority Identities: Papers from the Third Meeting of the "Music and Minorities" Study Group of the International Council for Traditional Music (ICTM), Roč, Croatia, 2004*, edited by Naila Ceribašićand Erica Haskell, 315–333. Zagreb, Croatia: Institute of Ethnology and Folklore Research.

Horvath, Ioannis Baptiste. (1770) 1817. *Physica Particularis, Auditorum Usibus Accommodata.* Budapest, Hungary: Ex Typographia Michaelis A. Burgos.

Hrvatska Matica Iseljenika. 2013. "47th CFU Junior Tamburitza Festival Staged." http://www.matis.hr/index.php/en/news/2424-47th-cfu-junior-tamburitza-festival-staged, accessed May 9, 2017.

Hrvatski jezični Portal. 2006. "öpāsan." http://hjp.znanje.hr/index.php?show=o-nama, accessed March 16, 2018.

Hull, John. 1997. *On Sight and Insight: A Journey into the World of Blindness*. Oxford: Oneworld Publications.

Imre, Anikó. 2005. "Whiteness in Post-Socialist Eastern Europe: The Time of the Gypsies, the End of Race." In *Postcolonial Whiteness: A Critical Reader on Race and Empire*, edited by Alfred Lopez, 79–102. Albany: State University of New York Press.

Ingold, Tim. 2000. *Perception of the Environment: Essays on Livelihood, Dwelling and Skill*. London: Routledge.

Ivanković, Josip. 1993. "Razgovor s Josipom Ivankovićem." Interview conducted by Ruža Bonifačić, Zagreb, Croatia, February 5. Cassette housed at the Institut za Etnologiju i Folkloristiku u Zagrebu.

Jackson, John. 2005. *Real Black: Adventures in Racial Sincerity*. Chicago: University of Chicago Press.

Jacobson, Matthew Frye. 1999. *Whiteness of a Different Color: European Immigrants and the Alchemy of Race*. Cambridge, MA: Harvard University Press.

Jambrešić, Renata. 1993. "Banija: An Analysis of Ethnonymic Polarisation." In *Fear, Death and Resistance: An Ethnography of War: Croatia, 1991–1992*, edited by Lada Čale Feldman, Ines Prica, and Reana Senjković, 73–118. Zagreb, Croatia: Institute of Ethnology and Folklore Research — Matrix Croatica — X-Press.

Jarman-Ivens, Freya. 2006. "Queer(ing) Masculinities in Heterosexist Rap Music." In *Queering the Popular Pitch*, edited by Sheila Whiteley and Jennifer Rycenga, 199–220. New York: Routledge.

Jovanović, Đura. 2009. Comments made to the author, Osijek, Croatia, November 21.

Kant, Immanuel. 1783. *Prolegomena zu einer jeden künftigen Metaphysik, die als Wissenschaft wird auftreten können*. Riga, Latvia: Hartnoch.

Kardov, Kruno. 2007. "Remember Vukovar: Memory, Sense of Place, and the National Tradition in Croatia." In *Democratic Transition in Croatia: Value Transformation, Education and Media*, edited by Sabrina Ramet and Davorka Matić, 63–88. College Station: Texas A&M University Press.

Kassabian, Anahid. 2013. *Ubiquitous Listening: Affect, Attention and Distributed Subjectivity*. Berkeley: University of California Press.

Katarinčić, Ivana, Iva Niemčić, and Tvrtko Zebec. 2009. "The Stage as a Place of Challenging Integration." *Narodna umjetnost* 46, no. 1: 77–107.

Keil, Charles. 1994. "Participatory Discrepancies and the Power of Music." In *Music Grooves: Essays and Dialogues*, by Charles Keil and Steven Feld, 96–108. Chicago: University of Chicago Press. Reprinted with additional edits from *Cultural Anthropology* 2, no. 3 (1987): 275–283.

———. 2005. "Review: *Deeper Polka*." *Ethnomusicology Forum* 14, no. 1 (June): 118–120.

Ketović, Ivana. 2010. Interview with the author, June, Osijek, Croatia.

Khannanov, Ildar. 2010. "Line, Surface, Speed: Nomadic Features of Melody." In *Sounding the Virtual: Gilles Deleuze and the Theory and Philosophy of Music*, edited by B. Hulse and N. Nesbitt, 249–267. Farnham, Surrey, UK: Ashgate.

Kielian-Gilbert, Marianne. 2010. "Music and the Difference in Becoming." In *Sounding the Virtual: Gilles Deleuze and the Theory and Philosophy of Music*, edited by Brian Hulse and Nick Nesbitt, 199–226. Farnham, Surrey, UK: Ashgate.

Kiossev, Alexander. 2002. "The Dark Intimacy." In *Balkan as Metaphor: Between Glabalization and Fragmentation*, edited by Dušan Bjelić and Obrad Savić, 165–190. Cambridge, MA: MIT Press.

Kisliuk, Michelle. 2000. "Performance and Modernity among BaAka Pygmies: A Closer Look at the Mystique of Egalitarian Foragers in the Rainforest." In *Music and Gender*, edited by Pirkko Moisala and Beverly Diamond, 25–50. Urbana: University of Illinois Press.

Klemenčić, Mladen, and Clive H. Schofield. 2001. *War and Peace on the Danube: The Evolution of the Croatia-Serbia Boundary*. Durham, UK: University of Durham, International Boundaries Research Unit.

Kolar, Walter. 1986. *Tamburitzans—The First Fifty Years Remembered* [Tamburaši—Prvi Pedeset Godina Upamtjen]. Pittsburgh, PA: Tamburitza Press.

———. 2009. Interview with the author, July 11, Pittsburgh, PA.

Kosovec, Peter. 2008. Interview with the author, Pittsburgh, PA, December 18.

Kotnik, Vlado. 2010. *Opera, Power and Ideology: Anthropological Study of a National Art in Slovenia*. Frankfurt am Main, Germany: Peter Lang GmbH Internationaler Verlag der Wissenschaften.

Krims, Adam. 2007. *Music and Urban Geography*. New York: Routledge.

Kristeva, Julia. 2000. *Crisis of the European Subject*. Translated by Susan Fairfield. New York: Other Press.

KUD "Oton Župančič." 2007. "Heritage." http://www.fs-artice.si/ENG1/Heritage/Heritage .html, accessed August 16, 2017.

Kuhač, Franjo. 1877. "Prilog za povjest glasbe južnoslovjensek: Kulturno-historijska studija." *Rad Jugoslavenske akademosti znanosti i umjetnosti* 39: 65–114.

Kuzmanović, Jasmina. 1992. "Pjesma olovnog vojnika." *Nedjeljina Dalmacija*, April 23.

Lampe, John. 1996. *Yugoslavia as History: Twice There Was a Country*. Cambridge: Cambridge University Press.

Lange, Barbara. 1997. "'What Was That Conquering Magic . . .': The Power of Discontinuity in Hungarian Gypsy *Nóta*." *Ethnomusicology* 41, no. 3 (Autumn): 517–537.

Largey, Michael. 2006. *Vodou Nation: Haitian Art Music and Cultural Nationalism*. Chicago: University of Chicago Press.

Leblon, Bernard. (1994) 2003. *Gypsies and Flamenco: The Emergence of the Art of Flamenco* in *Andalusia*. Translated by Sinéad ní Shuinéa. Hertfordshire, UK: Gypsy Research Centre, University of Hertfordshire Press.

Leksikon. N.d. "Keriti se." http://leksikon.thinking-garment.com/keriti/, accessed May 22, 2018.

Longinović, Tomislav. 2000. "Blood and Song at the End of Yugoslavia." In *Music and the Racial Imagination*, edited by Philip Bohlman and Ronald Radano, 622–643. Chicago: University of Chicago Press.

Lomax, Alan. 1959. "Folk Song Style." *American Anthropologist* 61, no. 6: 27–54.

Lumpkins, Crystal Y. 2013. "B.a.B.e. (Be Active, Be Emancipated)." In *The Multimedia Encyclopedia of Women in Today's World: 2013 Update*, edited by Mary Zeiss Stange, Carol K. Oyster, and Jane E. Sloan, 71–72. Thousand Oaks, CA: Sage.

MacMillen, Ian, with Gavin Steingo and Anna Stirr. 2011. "Gendered Intimacies and Musical Negotiations of Space." Panel Abstract, 56th meeting of the Society for Ethnomusicology, Philadelphia, PA, November.

MacMillen, Ian. 2011a. "From the Center in the Middle: Working Tambura Bands and the Construction of the In-Between in Croatia and Its Intimates." *Current Musicology* 91: 87–122. academiccommons.columbia.edu/download/fedora_content/download/ ac:172718/CONTENT/current.musicology.91.macmillen.87-122.pdf, accessed January 23, 2019.

———. 2011b. "*Tamburaši* of the Balkanized Peninsula: Public Concerts as International and Interethnic Connections in Croatia and Its Intimates." In *Second Symposium of the International Council for Traditional Music Study Group on Music and Dance in Southeastern Europe*, 59–64. Izmir, Turkey: ICTM Study Group on Music and Dance in Southeastern Europe and Ege University State Turkish Music Conservatory.

———. 2013. "Local Color and the Search for the Musical Origin of the Nation in the Early Nineteenth Century, from the German to the Croatian Lands." *Bulgarian Musicology* [Българско Музикознание] 37, no. 1 (Spring): 3–16.

———. 2014. "*Tamburaši* of the Balkanized Peninsula: Musical Relations of the Slavonian Tambura Society 'Pajo Kolarić' in Croatia and Its Intimates." *Balkanistica* 27: 45–79.

———. 2015. "Fascination, Musical Tourism, and the Loss of the Balkan Village (Notes on Bulgaria's Koprivshtitsa Festival)." *Ethnomusicology* 59, no. 2 (Summer): 227–261.

———. Forthcoming. "Affective Block and the Musical Racialisation of Romani Sincerity." *Ethnomusicology Forum*.

Majer-Bobetko, Sanja. 1998. "The Question of National Identity and Nationalism in Music. The Example of Croatian Opera." In *Music, Politics, and War: Views from Croatia*, edited by Svanibor Pettan, 79–90. Zagreb, Croatia: Institute of Ethnology and Folklore Research.

Malvinni, David. 2004. *The Gypsy Caravan: From Real Roma to Imaginary Gypsies in Western Music and Film*. London: Routledge.

March, Richard. 1983. "The Tamburitza Tradition (Yugoslavia)." PhD diss., Indiana University.

———. 2013. *The Tamburitza Tradition: From the Balkans to the American Midwest*. Madison: University of Wisconsin Press.

Marx, Karl. (1852) 2005. *The Eighteenth Brumaire of Louis Bonaparte*. Translated by D. D. L. New York: Mondial.

Massumi, Brian. 1987. "Realer than Real: The Simulacrum according to Deleuze and Guattari." *Copyright*, no. 1: 90–97.

———. 1996. "The Autonomy of Affect." In *Deleuze: A Critical Reader*, edited by Paul Patton, 217–239. Oxford: Blackwell.

———. 2010. "The Future Birth of the Affective Fact: The Political Ontology of Threat." In *The Affect Theory Reader*, edited by Melissa Gregg and Gregory Seigworth, 52–70. Durham, NC: Duke University Press.

———. 2015. "Plenary #7" of the Affect Theory Conference, October, Millersville University, Lancaster, PA.

McDonald, David. 2013. *My Voice Is My Weapon: Music, Nationalism, and the Poetics of Palestinian Resistance*. Durham, NC: Duke University Press.

Menninghaus, Winfried. 2003. *Disgust: The Theory and History of a Strong Sensation*. Translated by Howard Eiland and Joel Golb. Albany: State University of New York Press.

Merleau-Ponty, Maurice. (1945) 1962. *Phenomenology of Perception*. Translated by Colin Smith. New York: Routledge.

Mesa Díaz, Juan. 2007. "The Religious System of Ocha-Ifá." In *Music in Latin America and the Caribbean: An Encyclopedic History*, edited by Malena Kuss, 55–63. Austin: University of Texas Press.

Mills, Charles. 1997. *The Racial Contract*. Ithaca, NY: Cornell University Press.

Morgan, David. 2008. *The Sacred Heart of Jesus: The Visual Evolution of a Devotion*. Amsterdam: Amsterdam University Press.

Nesteruk, Olena, and Loren Marks. 2009. "Grandparents across the Ocean: Eastern European Immigrants' Struggle to Maintain Intergenerational Relationships." *Journal of Comparative Family Studies* 40, no. 1 (Winter): 77–95.

Niemčić, Iva. 2005. "Valcer i salonsko kolo od 19. stoljeća do danas." *Narodna umjetnost* 42, no. 2: 77–92.

Njikoš, Julije. 1995. *Pajo Kolarić—Život i rad*. Osijek, Croatia: Slavonsko Tamburaško Društvo "Pajo Kolarić" and Matica Hrvatska.

O'Brien, Charles. 1969. "Ideas of Religious Toleration at the Time of Joseph II: A Study of the Enlightenment among Catholics in Austria." *Transactions of the American Philosophical Society* 59, pt. 7: 1–80.

Ottaway, Marina. 2003. *Democracy Challenged: The Rise of Semi-Authoritarianism*. Washington, DC: Carnegie Endowment for International Peace.

Pavlović, Tatjana. 1999. "Women in Croatia: Feminists, Nationalists, and Homosexuals." In *Gender Politics in the Western Balkans: Women and Society in Yugoslavia and the Yugoslav Successor States*, edited by Sabrina P. Ramet, 131–152. University Park: Pennsylvania State University Press.

Pegley, Karen. 2000. "Gender, Voice, and Place: Issues of Negotiation in a 'Technology in Music Program.'" In *Music and Gender*, edited by Pirkko Moisala and Beverly Diamond, 306–316. Urbana: University of Illinois Press.

Perica, Vjekoslav. 2001. "The Catholic Church and Croatian Statehood." In *Nationalism, Culture, and Religion in Croatia since 1990*, edited by Vjeran Pavlaković, 55–70. Donald W. Treadgold Papers in Russian, East European, and Central Asian Studies, no. 32. Seattle: Henry M. Jackson School of International Studies, University of Washington.

Pettan, Svanibor. 1998. "Music, Politics, and War in Croatia in the 1990s: An Introduction." In *Music, Politics, and War: Views from Croatia*, edited by Svanibor Pettan, 9–27. Zagreb, Croatia: Institute of Ethnology and Folklore Research.

Pilas, Branko. 1997. *Sjaj hrvatske domovine*. Zagreb, Croatia: Školska knjiga.

Port, Mattijs Van de. 1998. *Gypsies, Wars and Other Instances of the Wild: Civilization and Its Discontents in a Serbian Town*. Chicago: University of Chicago Press.

———. 1999. "The Articulation of Soul: Gypsy Musicians and the Serbian Other." *Popular Music* 18: 291–307.

Povrzanović, Maja. 1993. "Culture and Fear: Everyday Life in Wartime." In *Fear, Death and Resistance: An Ethnography of War, Croatia 1991–1992*, edited by Lada Čale Feldman, Ines Prica, and Reana Senjković, 119–150. Zagreb, Croatia: Institute of Ethnology and Folklore Research, Matrix Croatica X-Press.

Prica, Ines. 1993. "Notes on Ordinary Life in War." In *Fear, Death and Resistance: An Ethnography of War, Croatia 1991–1992*, edited by Lada Čale Feldman, Ines Prica, and Reana Senjković, 44–71. Zagreb, Croatia: Institute of Ethnology and Folklore Research, Matrix Croatica X-Press.

Price, Monroe. 2011. "Strategic Narratives and the Arab Spring." Talk presented at the Communications Colloquium of the Columbia Journalism School, Columbia University, New York, NY, May.

Prosvjeta. 2010. *Naša Riječ* 12/13. Vukovar, Croatia: The Serbian Cultural Society Prosvjeta.

Radano, Ronald. 2000. "Hot Fantasies: American Modernism and the Idea of Black Rhythm." In *Music and the Racial Imagination*, edited by Ronald Radano and Philip Bohlman, 459–480. Chicago: University of Chicago Press.

———. 2003. *Lying up a Nation: Race and Black Music*. Chicago: University of Chicago Press.

Radio Našice. 2011. "Opća opasnost nastupila u Našicama." http://www.radionasice.hr/?p=2566, accessed June 16, 2014.

Ragazzi, Francesco. 2013. "Diaspora, Cosmopolitanism and Post-territorial Citizenship in Contemporary Croatia." In *East European Diasporas, Migration and Cosmopolitanism*, edited by Ulrike Ziemer and Sean P. Roberts, 58–74. New York: Routledge.

Ramet, Sabrina. 1998. *Nihil Obstat: Religion, Politics, and Social Change in East-Central Europe and Russia.* Durham, NC: Duke University Press.

———. 2006. *The Three Yugoslavias: State-Building and Legitimation, 1918–2005.* Bloomington: Indiana University Press.

Rasmussen, Ljerka. 2002. *Newly Composed Folk Music of Yugoslavia.* New York: Routledge.

———. 2007. "Bosnian and Serbian Popular Music in the 1990s: Divergent Paths, Conflicting Meanings, and Shared Sentiments." In *Balkan Popular Culture and the Ottoman Ecumene: Music, Image, and Regional Political Discourse*, edited by Donna Buchanan, 57–94. Lanham, MD: Scarecrow Press.

Rice, Timothy. 2000. "Béla Bartók and Bulgarian Rhythm." In *Bartok Perspectives: Man, Composer, and Ethnomusicologist: Man, Composer*, edited by Elliott Antokoletz, Victoria Fischer, and Benjamin Suchoff, 196–212. Oxford: Oxford University Press.

Ricoeur, Paul. (2004) 2006. *On Translation.* Translated by Eileen Brennan. New York: Routledge.

Roćenović, Lela. 1993. "Rituals Commemorating Deceased Croatian Soldiers." In *Fear, Death and Resistance: An Ethnography of War, Croatia 1991–1992*, edited by Lada Čale Feldman, Ines Prica, and Reana Senjković, 151–162. Zagreb, Croatia: Institute of Ethnology and Folklore Research, Matrix Croatica X-Press.

Roediger, David. 2005. *Working toward Whiteness: How America's Immigrants Became White: The Strange Journey from Ellis Island to the Suburbs.* New York: Basic Books.

Rountree, Kathryn. 2016. *Crafting Contemporary Pagan Identities in a Catholic Society.* New York: Routledge.

Schedl, Christine. 2004. "Phänomen Tamburizza: Zur Genese eines burgenlandkroatischen Identitäatssymbols." In *Musik der Kroaten im Burgenland* (Referate des Internationalen Workshop-Symposions, Grosswarasdorf, November 7–9, 2003), edited by Ursula Hemetek and Gerhard J. Winkler, 37–48. Wissenschaftliche Arbeiten aus dem Burgeland, Band 110. Eisenstadt, Austria: Landesmuseum Eisenstadt.

Schneider, David. 2006. *Bartók, Hungary, and the Renewal of Tradition: Case Studies in the Intersection of Modernity and Nationality.* Berkeley: University of California Press.

Scott, David. 2004. *Conscripts of Modernity: The Tragedy of Colonial Enlightenment.* Durham, NC: Duke University Press.

Sekol, Ivan. 2010. "Iz SAD-a u Osijek došao samo zbog zvuka tamburice." *Glas Slavonije*, June 6. http://www.osijek031.com/osijek.php?topic_id=26148, accessed April 2, 2016.

Shank, Barry. 2014. *The Political Force of Musical Beauty.* Durham, NC: Duke University Press.

Shaviro, Steven. 2015. "Plenary # 7" of the Affect Theory Conference, Millersville University, Lancaster, PA, October.

Shay, Anthony. 2002. *Choreographic Politics: State Folk Dance Companies, Representation and Power*. Middletown, CT: Wesleyan University Press.

Shiloah, Amnon. 1992. *Jewish Musical Traditions*. Detroit: Wayne State University Press.

Silverman, Carol. 2012. *Romani Routes: Cultural Politics and Balkan Music in Diaspora*. Oxford: Oxford University Press.

Simmel, Georg. 1950. *The Sociology of Georg Simmel*. Translated and edited by Kurt H. Wolff. New York: Free Press.

Škoro, Miroslav. 2010. *Stoput Bih Isto Ponovo: Autobiografija*. Zagreb, Croatia: Večernji posebni proizvodi d. o. o.

———. 2011. Personal communication with the author, Zagreb, Croatia, March 28.

———. 2013. Personal communication with the author, Zagreb, Croatia, July 23.

Škugor, Irena. 2016. "Etnografska bilježenja narodnih kola iz Dubrave kod Šibenika." *Ethnologica Dalmatica* 23, no. 1: 153–157.

Small, Christopher. 1998. *Musicking: The Meanings of Performing and Listening*. Middletown, CT: Wesleyan University Press.

Šovagović, Đuro. 1981. *Mostovi Preko Žica Tamburice (Dnevnik s puta po Sjedinjenim Američkim Državama i Kanadi)*. Osijek, Croatia: Matica Iseljenika Zajednice Općina Osijek.

Statistics Canada. 2011. "2011 National Household Survey: Data Tables." http://www12 .statcan.gc.ca/nhs-enm/2011/dp-pd/dt-td/Rp-eng.cfm?TABID=2&LANG=E&APATH =3&DETAIL=0&DIM=0&FL=A&FREE=0&GC=0&GK=0&GRP=1&PID=105396& PRID=0&PTYPE=105277&S=0&SHOWALL=0&SUB=0&Temporal=2013&THEME =95&VID=0&VNAMEE=&VNAMEF=, accessed March 26, 2015.

Stavans, Ilan. 2003. *Spanglish: The Making of a New American Language*. New York: HarperCollins.

Stažić, Igor. 1995. "Predsjednik Tuđman najviše voli 'Suzu za zagorske brege', a premijer Valentić 'Otvor' ženo kapiju.'" *Arena*, April 20.

STD "Pajo Kolarić." 1987. *XIII Festival Tamburaške Glazbe Jugoslavije * Osijek*. Osijek, Croatia: Predsjedništvo XIII. Festivala Tamburaške Glazbe Jugoslavije.

———. 1989. *XIV Festival Tamburaške Glazbe Jugoslavije * Osijek*. Osijek, Croatia: Predsjedništvo XIV. Festivala Tamburaške Glazbe Jugoslavije.

———. 1992. *XV Festival Tamburaške Glazbe Republike Hrvatske u Osijeku*. Osijek, Croatia: Predsjedništvo XV. Festivala Tamburaške Glazbe Republike Hrvatske u Osijeku.

———. 1993. *XVI Festival Hrvatske Tamburaške Glazbe u Osijeku*. Osijek, Croatia: Predsjedništvo XVI. Festivala Hrvatske Tamburaške Glazbe u Osijeku.

———. 1994. *XVII Festival Hrvatske Tamburaške Glazbe u Osijeku*. Osijek, Croatia: Predsjedništvo XVII. Festivala Hrvatske Tamburaške Glazbe u Osijeku.

————. 1995. *XVIII Festival Hrvatske Tamburaške Glazbe u Osijeku*. Osijek, Croatia: Predsjedništvo XVIII. Festivala Hrvatske Tamburaške Glazbe u Osijeku.

————. 1996. *XIX Festival Hrvatske Tamburaške Glazbe u Osijeku*. Osijek, Croatia: Predsjedništvo XIX. Festivala Hrvatske Tamburaške Glazbe u Osijeku.

————. 2001. *XXIV Festival Hrvatske Tamburaške Glazbe u Osijeku*. Osijek, Croatia: Predsjedništvo XXIV. Festivala Hrvatske Tamburaške Glazbe u Osijeku.

————. 2002. *XXV Festival Hrvatske Tamburaške Glazbe u Osijeku*. Osijek, Croatia: Predsjedništvo XXV. Festivala Hrvatske Tamburaške Glazbe u Osijeku.

————. 2003. *XXVI Festival Hrvatske Tamburaške Glazbe u Osijeku*. Osijek, Croatia: Predsjedništvo XXVI. Festivala Hrvatske Tamburaške Glazbe u Osijeku.

————. 2010. *XXXIII Međunarodni Festival Hrvatske Tamburaške Glazbe u Osijeku*. Osijek, Croatia: Predsjedništvo XXXIII. Međunarodnog Festivala Hrvatske Tamburaške Glazbe u Osijeku.

Stephen, Lynn. 2007. *Transborder Lives: Indigenous Oaxacans in Mexico, California, and Oregon*. Durham, NC: Duke University Press.

Stewart, Kathleen. 2007. *Ordinary Affects*. Durham, NC: Duke University Press.

Stimac, Zrinka. 2008. "Catholic Tradition and New Religious Movements: What Is New in the Present Religious Landscape in Croatia?" In *Religion and the Conceptual Boundary in Central and Eastern Europe: Encounters of Faiths*, edited by Thomas Bremer, 215–228. New York: Palgrave Macmillan.

Stokes, Martin. 2010. *The Republic of Love: Cultural Intimacy in Turkish Popular Music*. Chicago: University of Chicago Press.

Stras, Laurie. 2010. "Introduction: She's So Fine, or Why Girl Singers (Still) Matter." In *She's So Fine: Reflections on Whiteness, Femininity, Adolescence, and Class in 1960s Music*, edited by Laurie Stras, 1–32. Farnham, Surrey, UK: Ashgate.

Strathern, Marilyn. 1988. *The Gender of the Gift: Problems with Women and Problems with Society in Melanesia*. Berkeley: University of California Press.

————. 1996. "Cutting the Network." *Journal of the Royal Anthropological Institute* 2, no. 3: 517–535.

Straw, Will. 1997. "Sizing up Record Collections: Gender and Connoisseurship in Rock Music Culture." In *Sexing the Groove: Popular Music and Gender*, edited by Sheila Whiteley, 3–16. New York: Routledge.

Sudnow, David. (1978) 2001. *Ways of the Hand: A Rewritten Account*. Cambridge, MA: MIT Press.

Sugarman, Jane. 1997. *Engendering Song: Singing and Subjectivity at Prespa Albanian Weddings*. Chicago: University of Chicago Press.

————. 1999. "Imagining the Homeland: Poetry, Songs, and the Discourses of Albanian Nationalism." *Ethnomusicology* 43, no. 3 (Autumn): 419–458.

————. 2010. Comments made to the author, Izmir, Turkey, April 6.

———. 2011. "Discussion." Discussion paper presented on the panel Gendered Intimacies and Musical Negotiations of Space at the 56th annual meeting of the Society for Ethnomusicology, Philadelphia, PA, November 16.

Swidler, Ann. 1986. "Culture in Action: Symbols and Strategies." *American Sociological Review* 51: 273–286.

Taruskin, Richard. 2008. "The Danger of Music and the Case for Control." In *The Danger of Music and Other Anti-Utopian Essays*, 168–180. Berkeley: University of California Press. Originally published in the *New York Times*, December 9, 2001.

Tatro, Kelley. 2014. "The Hard Work of Screaming: Physical Exertion and Affective Labor Among Mexico City's Punk Vocalists." *Ethnomusicology* 58, no. 3 (Fall): 431–453.

Thrift, Nigel. 2010. "Understanding the Material Practices of Glamour." In *The Affect Theory Reader*, edited by Melissa Gregg and Gregory Seigworth, 289–308. Durham, NC: Duke University Press.

Todorova, Maria. 1997. *Imagining the Balkans*. New York: Oxford University Press.

Tölöyan, Kachig. 1996. "Rethinking Diaspora(s): Stateless Power in the Transnational Moment." *Diaspora* 5, no. 1: 3–35.

Tomkins, Silvan S. 1995. *Exploring Affect: The Selected Writings of Silvan S. Tomkins*. Cambridge: Cambridge University Press.

Tomlinson, Gary. 1999. *Metaphysical Song: An Essay on Opera*. Princeton, NJ: Princeton University Press.

———. 2015. *A Million Years of Music: The Emergence of Human Modernity*. New York: Zone Books.

———. 2016. "Sign, Affect, and Musicking before the Human." *boundary 2* 43, no. 1: 143–172.

Topić, Jelenko. 1992. "Pjesme iz 'zlatne doline.'" *Večernji list*, September 18.

Traumbauer, Lisa. 2005. *German Immigrants*. New York: Facts on File.

Turino, Thomas. 2000. *Nationalists, Cosmopolitans, and Popular Music in Zimbabwe*. Chicago: University of Chicago Press.

Ugrešić, Dubravka. (1995) 1998. *The Culture of Lies*. Translated by Celia Hawkesworth. University Park: The Pennsylvania State University Press.

US Census Bureau. 2010. "Profile of General Population and Housing Characteristics: 2010 — Geography: Pittsburgh City, Allegheny County, Pennsylvania." https://factfinder.census.gov/bkmk/table/1.0/en/DEC/10_SF1/SF1DP1/0600000US4200361000, accessed January 28, 2012.

Van Deusen, Nancy. 2017. "'Seeing Is Believing,' but Sound Exposes the Material Unseen: The Medieval Concept of Silva and Its Afterlife." Unpublished paper.

Vatalaro, Paul A. 2009. *Shelley's Music: Fantasy, Authority, and the Object Voice*. Farnham, Surrey, UK: Ashgate.

Vrcan, Srdjan. 1994. "The War in Former Yugoslavia and Religion." *Religion, State and Society: The Keston Journal* 22, no. 4: 367–378.

Vreg, France. 1993. "Iluzije o evropskem multikulturalizmu." *Teorija in praksa* 30, nos. 7–8: 659–663.

Wade, Peter. 2000. *Music, Race, and Nation: Música Tropical in Colombia.* Chicago: University of Chicago Press.

Wald, Gayle. 2015. *It's Been Beautiful: "Soul!" and Black Power Television.* Durham, NC: Duke University Press.

Washabaugh, William. 1998. "Famenco Song: Clean and Dirty." In *The Passion of Music and Dance: Body, Gender and Sexuality*, edited by William Washabaugh, 27–38. Oxford: Berg.

Waterman, Christopher. 1990. "'Our Tradition Is a Very Modern Tradition': Popular Music and the Construction of a Pan-Yoruba Identity." *Ethnomusicology* 34, no. 3: 367–379.

———. 2002. "Big Man, Black President, Masked One: Models of the Celebrity Self in Yoruba Popular Music in Nigeria." In *Playing with Identities in Contemporary Music in Africa*, edited by Mai Palmberg and Annemette Kirkegaard, 19–34. Uppsala, Sweden: Nordiska Afrikainstitutet.

Whiteley, Sheila. 1997. "Introduction." In *Sexing the Groove: Popular Music and Gender*, edited by Sheila Whiteley, xiii–xxxvi. New York: Routledge.

Williams, Raymond. 1977. *Marxism and Literature.* Oxford: Oxford University Press.

Yurchak, Alexei. 2005. *Everything Was Forever, Until It Was No More: The Last Soviet Generation.* Princeton, NJ: Princeton University Press.

Zbiljski, Mario. 2010a. Comments made to the author, Antunovac, Croatia, January 27.

———. 2010b. Interview with the author, Osijek, Croatia, May.

Zheng, Su. 2010. *Claiming Diaspora: Music, Transnationalism, and Cultural Politics in Asian/Chinese America.* New York: Oxford University Press.

Žižek, Slavoj. 2015. *Political Correctness Is a More Dangerous Form of Totalitarianism.* https://www.youtube.com/watch?v=5dNbWGaaxWM, accessed May 23, 2016.

Zlatni Dukati. 2014. "Biografija." http://www.najboljihrvatskitamburasi.com/biografija.htm, accessed June 12, 2014.

Zovko, Jure. 2015. "The Reaction to Kant in South-Slavic Countries." In *Detours: Approaches to Immanuel Kant in Vienna, in Austria, and in Eastern Europe*, edited by Violetta Waibel, 249–256. Vienna: Vienna University Press.

INDEX

indigenous peoples, 38, 204, 237n5, 239n24

Indonesia, 239n3

industrial economies: change in, 103, 131, 141, 233–234; and support of folklore in the former Yugoslavia, 62–63; and steel in Pittsburgh, 103. *See also* Rust Belt

Ingold, Timothy, 12, 208–210

inscription, 178–179, 188, 191–194, 218–219, 225

insincerity, 86, 111–112, 114–115, 122–126

insults, 181–183, 187, 193–194, 198

intensity, 111–116, 154–157, 164–165

interiority, 85–86, 99, 119–120, 123, 125–127, 234, 243n36

internalization, 154–156

international competitive festivals, 80–82

International Folklore Festival in Zagreb, 143

internet. *See* online music discussions

interpellation, 173, 175–176, 194, 196–197, 201, 218, 228–230

intimacy, 2; cultural, 13, 38, 64–65; and danger, 30, 36, 183; dark, 37–38; diasporic, 4, 8, 36–38; and distance, 38, 39, 86, 239n24; with ethnic and racial Others, 4, 54, 91–92; and ideology, 173–176; interpersonal, 99, 121, 124, 161–198, 213; and pain, 193–194, 198; and publics, 38–39, 72–74, 113, 224; and technology, 210–211; and unproblematic participation, 36, 187, 197; and violation, 19, 179, 189–194, 197–198

intimates, 35; as alternative to diaspora, 32–33, 35; of Croatia, 32, 33–37, 67–68, 82–84, 223–227, 236, 238n17; of Serbia, 35

Irish Americans, 106–107

Israel, 34

"Istinu svijetu o Baranji reci," 43, 44–45, 59, 78

It Rains in My Village. See Biće skoro propast sveta (film)

Ivanković, Josip, 61, 74, 240n20

"Ivan Vuković" tambura society, 72, 161–163

Ivčić, Tomislav, 64–65

Jackson, John, 100, 112

Jacobson, Matthew, 118

Jambrešić, Renata, 79

Japanese, 110, 116–117

Jarman-Ivens, Freya, 244chap4n2

"Ja sam mala garava," 190

jazz: comparisons of tambura music to, 140, 145; as tambura repertoire, 240n21

"Jedan život malo je," 171

Jeršek, Stjepan. *See* Štef, Stjepan Jeršek

Jewish musicians, 34, 71, 117–118, 242n14

Josipović, Ivo, 65, 215

Jovanović, Đura, 133–134

Jugoton, 25, 28

junior tamburitzans, 27, 92, 106, 119, 214–222

"Kada padne prvi sneg." *See* "Sanie cu zurgălăi"

Kant, Immanuel, 206

Kardov, Kruno, 45

Kassabian, Anahid, 187–188, 196

kaval, 239n23

Keil, Charles, 105, 149–151, 243n25

kerenje, 164

Ketović, Ivana, 191, 213

Khannanov, Ildar, 152–153

"Kićo," Krunoslav Slabinac, 24, 26, 77, 166, 168

Kiossev, Alexander, 37, 83

Kisliuk, Michelle, 244chap4n2

kissing, 109, 193

klapa, 149, 214, 238n21

Klapa "Saint George," 214

Klemenčić, Mladen, 58

Kolar, Walter, 23

Kolarić, Pajo, 20, 76

kolo dances, 120, 149, 176–178, 184–186, 192. *See also* pjevanje u kolu

kontra tambura, 140, 148–152. *See also* tamburas: types of

Kosovec, David, 99, 108

Kosovec, Peter, 1, 26, 31, 79, 94, 99, 108, 241n12

Kosovo, 238n11, 239n23

Krčma kod Ruže, 129, 134

Krims, Adam, 12, 40, 105, 119, 199

Kristeva, Julia, 51, 59–60, 79–80, 85–86

Krstičević, Darija, 215

Kuhač, Franjo, 20

Kulturno-Umjetničko Društvo, 22, 80, 143–144, 238n11. *See also* hkud "Osijek 1862"

kum, 27, 192

and representation, 10; of war in tambura music, 45, 80. *See also* state: official narratives of the
national anthems, 14, 58, 73, 215. *See also* "Lijepa naša domovina"
nationalism, 1, 2, 3, 20–21, 24–25, 238n14; in the dissolution of Yugoslavia, 23; and ethnic homogeneity, 116–117; and nation building, 29–30, 175, 205, 239n22; post-imperial, 36; in Yugoslavia, 178. *See also* nation-state; patriotism
nation-state, 32, 34, 39–40; and core territory, 44; and homogeneity, 29–30; and nationalism, 52. *See also* imagined community
Native Americans. *See* indigenous peoples
Ne Dirajte Mi Ravnicu (album), 85
"Ne dirajte mi ravnicu" (song), 27, 47, 77–78, 112, 129
Negri, Antonio. *See* Hardt, Michael, and Antonio Negri
Nesteruk, Olena, and Loren Marks, 117
newly composed folk music, 23, 49, 149, 235
Nigeria, 34, 239n22
Nijemci, 233
Nikolić, Antun. *See* "Tuca," Antun Nikolić
Njikoš, Julije, 69, 72, 75–77, 161
nomadism, 131–132, 144–145, 152–153
nostalgia, 28
nóta, 151
Novi Sad, 87

objectification, 154–157, 230
O'Brien, Charles, 205
occupied territory: in Baranja, 43–45, 223; in Eastern Slavonia, 28, 45–46, 58, 223; return to, 27–28, 46, 60–63
"Oj Hrvatska Mati," 47
Old Bridge Pub, 135–136
old city songs. *See* starogradske pjesme
online music discussions, 79, 180. *See also* forum.tambura.com.hr
Opća Opasnost, 48
opera, 200, 220–221, 230
original songs, 1, 27, 94, 98, 166–168, 189

Orphic traditions, 205
Orthodox Christianity, 56, 70, 106, 225–226, 234–235, 239n10
"Osam Tamburaša," 134
Osijek, 20, 22, 129, 132–144, 148, 151–152, 212–213; Cathedral in, 56–57; participation in the war, 56–57, 61, 233–234, 239n9; as tambura music hub, 66
Otok, 189–192, 194–195, 198
"Oton Župančić" tambura orchestra, 55, 69, 240n14
Otrov, 31
Ottoman Empire, 20, 30, 50, 133, 238n9, 239n1
"Our Beautiful Homeland." *See* "Lijepa naša domovina"
outside, 119, 121, 123, 126–127, 202–203, 221, 222–223, 234–236
Ovčara prisoner camp, 233

pagan traditions, 220
Palau, 239n3
Pan-Slavism, 21, 239n1, 239n5
Paris, Aimé, 244chap3n2
Parndorf, 30–31, 68, 72, 161–163
participatory discrepancies, 149–151, 153, 156–157
patriarchy. *See* gender: and patriarchal roles
patriotism, 116–117, 168, 176
Paul, Les, 242n18
Pécs, 31, 67, 68
Pegley, Karen, 244chap4n2
Peirce, Charles, 16, 19
Perica, Vjekoslav, 25, 205, 218–219
Pešut, Filip, 184, 211, 213
Petrović, Aleksandar, 147–148
Pettan, Svanibor, 46, 142
philosophy of music, 207, 210, 246n2
Pilas, Branko, 50
pioneering musical styles, 168
pisana nedjelja, 214, 246n3
pitch. *See* frequency
Pittsburgh, 1, 6, 25–26, 199; geography of, 101–108; as tambura music hub, 87
"Pjesma rastanka," 141–142
pjevanje u kolu, 176–177, 192

Vrcan, Srdjan, 202–203
Vreg, France, 203
Vučedolski Zvuci, 80–81, 142–143, 147, 234–235
Vukovar, 61, 63, 80–81, 142–143, 232–235

Wald, Gayle, 234
Waldinger Hotel, 132–134, 148, 159
war: between Croatia and Yugoslavia, 1,
    28–31, 55, 61, 101–102; and destruction of
    buildings, 43–44, 55–57, 232–234, 239n9;
    fear as a legacy of, 43–44; resistance to,
    173. *See also* religion: in the Yugoslav wars;
    World War I; World War II
wasp populations, 91, 101, 106, 243n28
Waterman, Christopher, 34
websites. *See* online music discussions
whiteness, 6, 8, 86, 100, 110, 117–121, 124–127,
    145–146, 157–158, 243n28, 243n31
Williams, Raymond, 234
World War I, 25, 67, 91, 206, 243n28
World War II, 23, 28, 50, 62, 110

Yugoslavia, 238n8; ethnic status within, 238n12;
    history of the Socialist Federal Republic of,
    22; Kingdom of Serbs, Croats, and Slovenes

as the first, 239n4; official ensembles of,
    22–23, 54, 62, 91, 202, 238n11
Yurchak, Alexei, 58, 126–127, 159, 199, 236

zafrkavanje. *See* humor: of zafrkavanje (joking)
    in socializing
Zagreb: bombing of, 67; Cathedral in, 214–222;
    performances in, 213–222; tambura
    ensembles of, 22, 68, 69
Zagreb Folk Dance Ensemble "Dr. Ivan
    Ivančan," 214
"Zaplet," 139
Zbiljski, Mario, 210–213
"Žec," Željko Lončarić, 245n5
Zheng, Su, 32
Zimbabwe, 34, 239n22
Žižek, Slavoj, 124–125
Zlatne Grive festival, 189–192, 194
Zlatne Žice Slavonije. *See* Golden Strings of
    Slavonia festival
Zlatni Dukati, 27–29, 47–48, 50–51, 57, 61, 63,
    77–78, 245n5
Zora, 177, 192–193
"Zorica," 186, 245n11
Zovko, Jure, 206
Zvona, 109

ABOUT THE AUTHOR

Ian MacMillen directs the Oberlin Center for Russian, East European and Central Asian Studies. His primary research focuses on the racialized and affective nature of interethnic and transnational connections forged through music — particularly popular and traditional tambura chordophone bands in multiethnic communities of post-conflict Croatia, Serbia, and Bosnia. This work has been funded by an ACLS Dissertation Research Fellowship in East European Studies, a Research Grant from the Association for Recorded Sound Collections, and Oberlin College Powers Travel Grants. He received a BA in music from Pomona College and a PhD in Anthropology of Music from the University of Pennsylvania. He teaches Ethnomusicology and Anthropology courses at Oberlin College.